CLASSIC
AIRCRAFT

Brian Johnson is a television producer and writer and has worked on several television documentaries including 'Horizon', 'Tomorrow's World' and 'Equinox'. He has written various books including *The Secret War*, *Fly Navy* and *Test Pilot*, all of which were tied into BBC series of the same name. He is also the author of the previous book in this series, *Classic Plant Machinery*.

Classic
AIRCRAFT

Brian Johnson

4 BOOKS

Acknowledgements

I would like to offer thanks to the many people who have contributed to this book. David Gibbings, the archivist at Westland Aviation found excellent photographs of both the Lysander and the Lynx helicopter, and also provided data on the Lynx. Wing Commander Ken Wallis shared recollections with me of his wartime experience flying the Westland Lysanders, in addition to providing photographs of 'Little Nellie', his 'James Bond' autogyro. Michael Oakey, the newly installed Editor of *Aeroplane*, kindly permitted the use of the magazines's line drawings and photographs. Thanks also to Michael Proudfoot and his producers and researchers at Uden Associates, the television production company that made the Channel 4 series. My thanks to Katy Carrington, my editor at Channel 4 Books; to Josine Meijer, the picture researcher, whose dedicated work is self evident; and to Robert Updegraff, who skilfully put all together.

Brian Johnson,
CATTISTOCK, DORSET

First published in hardback 1998 by Channel 4 Books,
This edition published 2000 by Channel 4 Books an imprint of Macmillan Publishers Ltd, 25 Eccleston Place, London SW1W 9NF Basingstoke and Oxford.

www.macmillan.co.uk

Associated companies throughout the world.

ISBN 0 7522 1759 3

Text © 1998 Brian Johnson,

The right of Brian Johnson to be identified as the author of this work has been asserted by him in accordance with the Copyright, Designs and Patents Act 1988.

1 3 5 7 9 8 6 4 2

A CIP catalogue record for this book is available from the British Library.

Cover and inside design by Robert Updergraff
Colour reproduction by Speedscan Ltd, Essex
Printed by New Interlitho, Italy

This book accompanies the television series 'Classic Aircraft' made by Uden Associates for Channel 4.
Executive producer: Michael Proudfoot.
Producer/Directors: Russell Barnes, Sid Bennett, Graham Kelly, Amanda Murphy.

CONTENTS

CHAPTER ONE

BOMBERS

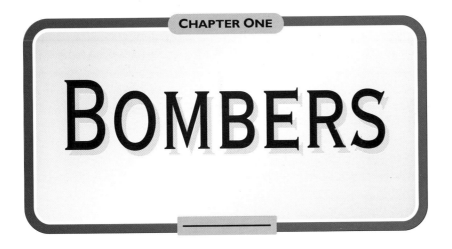

Now I become Death, the destroyer of worlds . . .
The *Bhagavad-Gita*, c. 200 BC

THOSE LINES FROM the *Bhagavad-Gita* were quoted by the American physicist Robert Oppenheimer when, appalled, he was informed of the successful detonation of the first atomic bomb – for which he had been largely responsible – over the Japanese city of Hiroshima. The date 6 August 1945. At eight-fifteen that summer morning, over 78,000 of the inhabitants and 80 per cent of the city were vaporized. That first sortie of the nuclear age was to be the ultimate in bombing from the air; it remains a terrible benchmark in mass destruction. The destructive power of the Hiroshima uranium-based atomic bomb, code-named 'Little Boy', was the equivalent of no fewer than 20,000 tons of the conventional chemical explosive TNT. In 1911, the first bomb dropped on an enemy target from an aircraft weighed under 5lb; from 5lb to 20,000 tons in just thirty-four years represents progress without parallel, not only in the destructive power of bombs but also in the design, construction and operation of the aircraft from which the bombs were dropped.

From the moment in 1903 when the Wright brothers had demonstrated that powered flight was a practical proposition, it was inevitable (despite the protestations of the pioneers to the contrary) that aircraft would, sooner or later, be deployed in battle. From frail beginnings, aircraft duly became bombers, the most formidable weapon of twentieth-century mechanized warfare, extending the front lines hundreds – ultimately thousands – of miles, from distant battlefields to the civilian populations of the fighting powers in the pitiless strategy of 'total war'.

This kind of warfare had been foreseen in the seventeenth century by a prescient cleric, a Jesuit priest called Father Francesco de Lana-Terzi who, in 1670, published a scientific treatise, *Prodromo*, which was an illustrated proposal for an 'aerial ship' to be used for mass bombing of an enemy:

> *. . . it may overset them, burn their ships by Fireworks and Fire balls and this they may do not only to Ships but to great Buildings, Castles, Cities, with such a security that they which cast these things down from a height out of Gun shot, cannot on the other side be offended by those below.*

An RAF bomber crew of the Second World War flying into action. This stylized painting by Laura Knight gives a compelling impression of the cramped crew positions and restrictive clothing, Mae West life-jackets and parachute harnesses of a typical heavy night-bomber crew *c.* 1944. The four crew members depicted are: pilot and co-pilot, navigator and flight engineer. In addition there would be a bomb aimer, radio operator and mid-upper and rear gunners.

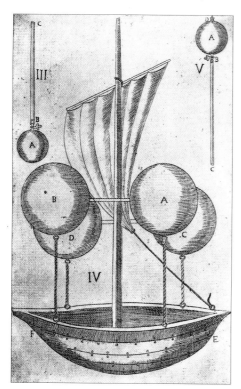

ABOVE **The 'aerial ship', the ingenious though impractical proposal put forward in 1670 by Father de Lana-Terzi. Though his aerial ship was never to fly, the cleric's dire prediction of the bombing of cities was to become reality during the First World War.**

Although the prophecy was correct, the priest's proposal for his 'aerial ship' was seriously flawed. De Lana-Terzi had envisioned a sailing vessel borne aloft by four copper globes from which all the air had been evacuated by the then newly developed vacuum pump. The theory was sound, but unfortunately any large copper vessel strong enough to withstand implosion from atmospheric pressure would be far too heavy to achieve any lift at all. When this was pointed out to the Jesuit he took solace in remarking that: 'God would not suffer such an invention to take effect.' Alas, he was mistaken again . . .

In 1794, the fulfilment of de Lana-Terzi's dire prophecy began. The French army used a gas-filled observation balloon during the war against the Austrians at Fleurus. This was the first known application of an aircraft in war. The stratagem must have been considered satisfactory because, during the early nineteenth century, the French became the undisputed leaders in military ballooning, forming the world's first army balloon corps. The use of military balloons became international; during the American Civil War both the Unionists and the Confederates used observation balloons. The British army, rather late in the day, became interested in observation balloons after a tentative start in 1862 when a sceptical War Office contracted demonstration flights from a noted balloonist, Henry Coxwell, who made several ascents at Aldershot with army officers carried as passengers during the tests. However, it was not until 1882 that the War Office commissioned a small balloon factory and training facility at the School of Military Engineering at Chatham in Kent, training officers and other ranks in the handling and use of tethered and free-flight balloons.

By the turn of the century the War Office had established a Balloon Section of the Royal Engineers, based on Laffan's Plain, the location of present-day Farnborough in Hampshire. The section had been formed to exploit the obvious military reconnaissance potential of man-lifting balloons which enabled commanders to 'see over the hill' and

RIGHT **The first use of aerial reconnaissance as Captain Coutelle's tethered hydrogen-filled French Army balloon rises above the battlefield at Fleurus on 26 June 1794. Although the contemporary print places the balloon well in Austrian musket-shot range, in reality it probably flew a good deal higher and was launched well behind the front lines. The observer in the balloon signalled the fall of shot and troop movements with flags. Despite the evidence of the print, it required twenty men to hold the balloon once it was fully inflated.**

French 'postal' balloons being inflated at the Gare d'Orléans in 1871 when Paris was under Prussian siege, inflated with town gas from the municipal gasworks at Villette. Early crews were recruited from circus acrobats on the reasonable grounds that they had no fear of height. (In fact several demonstrated this capacity by releasing sufficient gas soon after take-off for the balloon to descend, then shinning down ropes to the ground, leaving the now lightened balloon to ascend with passengers and dispatches carried aloft to their fate.)

allowed observers to report, by semaphore, both enemy troop movements and 'fall of shot' for artillery gunners. A limited number of British army balloons were deployed operationally during the Boer War at Paardeberg and during the siege of Mafeking, mainly as spotters for artillery. Despite, or because of, the experience gained in South Africa, in Britain military balloons came to be regarded as capricious, weather-dependent, frail and expensive devices that required a large ground crew and ideal conditions to perform well, if at all. The same ideal conditions unfortunately also provided an irresistible target for the newly invented (by Krupps of Germany) anti-balloon guns. The Germans had produced the guns to counter the 'postal' balloons escaping from beleaguered Paris during the Franco-Prussian War. Some sixty balloons, constructed in Gare d'Orléans and inflated by town gas, had escaped the siege, taking off at night to avoid the Prussian artillery. By the time of the armistice in January 1871, the balloons had carried a total of 150 passengers and 3 million dispatches and letters over the heads of the enemy troops laying siege to the city. One of the Paris balloons, *Jacquard*, was sighted over the Lizard, Cornwall, speeding westwards in the teeth of an easterly gale with the *pilote*, a sailor named Prince, dutifully dropping a pouch of letters overland before disappearing out over the Atlantic heading for America, never to be seen again. One cannot resist wondering how far he got . . .

Although balloons were used principally by the military as tethered observation platforms, from time to time there had been proposals for balloons to be used as bombers. Clearly they had, at best, a distinctly limited application as such; because no balloon can be navigated except by the wind, any bombing sortie would, unless exceptionally fortunate, be one-way. As early as 1799, the Royal Navy had considered and rejected a plan submitted, most improbably, by a Chelsea dancing master, Charles Rodgier, to fly 1,000 unmanned balloons, armed with incendiary bombs, to be released by clockwork mechanisms in order to act as aerial fire-ships over the combined French and Spanish fleets then blockaded by the Royal Navy at Brest in France. There were other similar proposals; one, advanced in 1849 during the Italian War of Independence, was put into effect. The Austrian army besieging Venice used unmanned hot-air balloons, each armed with a 30lb bomb to be dropped by time-fuse as they drifted over the beleaguered city. Several bombs released did cause damage – one exploded in St Mark's Square –

RIGHT **This painting by Kenneth McDonough captures the Edwardian atmosphere of ballooning. Two scarlet-clad Royal Engineers of the balloon section fly sedately over Hampshire at about 1,000ft during an army exercise c. 1870. The painting accurately shows the sand-ballast bags and fully inflated balloon. The balloon had possibly been launched from Laffins Plain, Farnborough. This British Army balloon is of the type used to a limited extent during the Boer War.**

BELOW **Seventy-five years on. A Japanese Fu-Go bombing balloon, recovered intact at Alturas, California in January 1945, is reinflated by the US Navy. The paper envelope has many gores and nineteen shroud lines attached to the weapon-carrying gondola. The nearly 300 Fu-Go balloons that are known to have reached the United States must have ascended to over 30,000ft to take advantage of the then little-known jet-stream winds.**

although they created panic rather than casualties. There was also panic when the wind changed direction and the attackers had to flee from their own balloon bombers, blown overhead with their bomb-release fuses hissing away.

Ninety-five years later, the Japanese, lacking any aircraft remotely capable of bombing the American mainland, were to revive the idea of unmanned balloon bombing, launching a little-known concentrated attack on the west coast of the United States and Canada. From November 1944 to August 1945 no fewer than 285 unmanned Japanese balloons, each armed with incendiary and anti-personnel bombs, were reported or recovered within North America from the west coast to as far inland as Michigan; a few were reported in Alaska and Mexico. The balloons, made of paper and inflated with hydrogen, were released from several bases around Sendai on the east coast of Honshu, the main island of Japan. The balloons on release quickly rose up to 40,000ft and were driven by the prevailing westerly jet stream across the Pacific to the United States, taking on average three days to reach the target area. Because of strict censorship, intended to deny to the Japanese any knowledge of the success or otherwise of the 'Fu-Go Weapon', as the

Japanese called the balloons, few, if any, American civilians knew of the attack. There had been no official warning; the sad but predictable result was that a picnic party in the Gearhart Mountain woods in Oregon discovered a deflated Fu-Go balloon entangled in trees; in clustering around to try to move it they caused the 30lb anti-personnel bomb to detonate, instantaneously killing a woman and five children aged from eleven to thirteen. That tragedy, in May 1945, caused the only American casualties on the United States mainland due to direct enemy action during the Second World War. Nearly all the Fu-Go balloon bombs that descended over North America landed in either open country or woodland but one was more on target than the Japanese attackers could possibly have hoped – it caused the loss of electrical power to the atomic energy plant at Hanford, Washington State, delaying briefly the production of fissionable material to be used in the Hiroshima atomic bomb.

The Hanford incident apart, even the relatively advanced Japanese Fu-Go balloons of 1945 achieved little. Of the estimated 9,300 launched from Japan, only 285 are known to have fallen over North America – an immensely large target. Up to the turn of the century, when balloons were the only practical method of flying, dependence on the winds for direction was acknowledged as a limitation to further progress. The arrival, around 1900, of lightweight petrol engines with an excellent power-to-weight ratio was to offer the limitless prospect of what the early pioneers longed to achieve: powered flight. Internal combustion engines had enabled the dirigible, a steerable non-rigid airship, to become a practicable proposition. All the Western powers were at once attracted to what they saw as a navigable balloon, which was all most of the early efforts amounted to. Albert Santos-Dumont, a 28-year-old Brazilian living in France, astonished Parisians by piloting his cigar-shaped airships over the city of Paris, circling *la Tour Eiffel* in his 1901 airship with insouciance, 'No. 6', which was powered by a

ABOVE **Santos-Dumont piloting his 1901 airship No. 6 around the Eiffel Tower on his way to claim his prize for the seven-mile flight from the Parisian suburb of St-Cloud.**

BELOW **Santos-Dumont in the wickerwork basket of No. 6, one of the fourteen airships he constructed. This photograph shows the engine just behind the aviator with a large fabric-covered rudder at the rear. One would like to think that Santos-Dumont wore his starched collar and bowler *en volent*.**

The third of Count Zeppelin's civil airships, the *LZ 3*, is launched over Lake Constance in 1906 watched by an admiring crowd. The next Zeppelin, *LZ 4*, was wrecked and the count was facing certain bankruptcy when the German government stepped in and rescued the company with substantial orders for military Zeppelins. Thus the night bomber was born.

15hp air-cooled engine mounted on a vestigial framework and suspended by ropes from the gasbag above. The intrepid pilot, clearly visible to all, was precariously perched in a small wickerwork basket at the front, with the engine amidships driving a pusher-propeller at the rear. The whole vehicle was steered by a large rudder aft of the airscrew. The flight was a successful attempt to win a prize of 100,000 francs offered by a wealthy financier, Henry Deutch de la Meurthe, for a flight from the Aero Club at St Cloud around the Eiffel Tower and back, a distance of 7 miles, in half an hour, requiring an average speed of 14mph. In fact, because of a misfiring engine and a headwind on the return journey, Santos-Dumont was forty seconds over the time limit, but an outcry lasting two weeks in the popular press more or less forced the Aero Club to award the prize money to the Brazilian, who donated most of it to charity.

Santos-Dumont had demonstrated the possibilities of the dirigible, and in Britain both the army and the navy began to build experimental airships with, it must be said, distinctly moderate results. It was in Germany that astonishing progress was revealed when, in 1900, Count Ferdinand von Zeppelin, a retired army general (he was sixty-two years old at the time) unveiled his *LZ 1*, or *Luftschiff Zeppelin Eins*. This machine was a quantum leap. The fabric envelope was over an aluminium-framed self-supporting rigid structure pointed at each end; 420ft in length and 40ft in circumference, it contained fifteen ballonets made from gas-impenetrable rubberized cotton, each inflated by hydrogen gas to provide a total of 399,000cu ft of lift. Two gondolas suspended beneath the airship held a five-man crew and there were two 16hp Daimler-Benz petrol engines, each driving two tandem propellers. When the giant aircraft was slowly eased from the hangar on Lake Constance and took to the air for the first time, it required little imagination for those below that sinister shape sedately droning above the placid lake to foresee that the very name 'Zeppelin' would become synony-mous with terror. Those who did were correct: with the flight of *LZ 1*, the nascent bomber had arrived along with the new century.

Impressive though the Zeppelin undoubtedly was, the first flight of the Wright broth-ers *Flyer* at Kittyhawk, North Carolina, in 1903, began an era of progress in aviation which was to excite the military establishments of the Western powers. Some were more excited than others. In 1909, Louis Blériot flew the English Channel; in that same year an American pilot, Eugene Ely, had both landed and taken off from US Navy ships and, early in 1911, another American, Glen Curtiss, flying an aircraft of his own design, had (to the fury of some American admirals) successfully dropped dummy bombs on the outline of a battleship marked out with buoyed flags on Lake Keuka in New York State. In November the first live bombs to be dropped on an enemy target were released from an Etrich Taube (*taube* is German for 'pigeon') monoplane flying over Turkish positions at Taguira, North Africa. The pilot was an Italian officer, Lieutenant Gavotti. That same year the French held a 'Concours Militaire' at Reims; in Britain, an aviation meeting at Hendon was attended by representatives of the War Office and Admiralty, among them the young Winston Churchill, who expressed confidence in the future of aviation, a con-

'Frightening the horses'. The effect of aircraft on horses is one of the favourite clichés of aviation. These horses photographed in 1909 at the Wright brothers' French *école de pilotage* at Pau do appear about to inspire the saying. Also possibly frightened is the intrepid student pilot in the 'flyer' alongside Wilbur Wright; he is recorded as being a M. Paul Tissandier.

S.E.5as of *No. 1* Squadron of the newly formed RAF photographed at Claremarais, France in April 1918. The squadron had been formed in 1912 and had a continuous history from that date. The squadron would fly Hurricanes during the Battle of Britain. The 1918 pilots are wearing a mixture of uniforms; some with RFC 'maternity' jackets; one with an army tunic with the three pips of a captain on the sleeve; and others with the newly introduced RAF uniform. All, with one exception, are commissioned officers; the exception is the warrant officer observer with service cap and stick. The pet dog, goggles and silk scarves were traditional and would remain so among RAF fighter pilots for many a year to come. The 'erks' who maintained the aircraft are confined to the background.

fidence that was by no means universal in Whitehall. The British Secretary of State had stated only the previous year that: 'We do not consider that aeroplanes will be of any possible use for war purposes.' Sir Walter Raleigh, the official historian, was unwittingly to coin the phrase that has been quoted ever since when he wrote, in 1922, in *War in the Air* of the attitude of the army towards aviation: 'The cavalry, in particular, were not friendly to the aeroplane, which it was believed would frighten the horses.' The escalating cost of military aviation, once the simple balloon phase had passed, was frightening the British War Office, which had decided to call a halt to such pointless extravagance despite reports that the Germans had reputedly spent over £400,000 in 1909 – an enormous sum at that time – on military aviation.

The depressing consequence was that when the First World War broke out in August 1914 the Royal Flying Corps (RFC), which had only been formed two years previously, had on charge a total of 63 mixed, very moderate front-line aircraft, all intended for the same role as the earlier balloons: reconnaissance and artillery spotting. The question of bombing hardly arose; the total British bomb arsenal at the outbreak of the war consisted of just twenty-six 20lb bombs. That small measure was due, at least in part, to the Hague Declaration of 1907, which banned the dropping of explosive missiles or bombs from balloons, airships or aircraft. No fewer than twenty-seven nations, including Britain, were signatories; significantly, Germany was not, a fact that was to cause concern for, in contrast to the 63 British RFC's aircraft available at the outbreak of the war, the Germans had 285; that figure did not include 11 Zeppelins. These were much-developed versions of *LZ 2*, which had caused such disquiet when first flown in 1900.

From the outset of the war, the Germans had intended their Zeppelins to be used as bombers, though the first war sortie, flown against French military targets, was a disaster: three army Zeppelins were lost, two were shot down by French artillery and small arms fire; a third, *LZ 8*, was shot down by the 'friendly fire' of trigger-happy German troops. The Imperial Navy, undeterred by what they considered to be the army's partly self-inflicted losses, accelerated their airship construction programme under the energetic drive of the commander-in-chief of the Imperial Navy airships, *Fregattenkapitan* Peter Strasser, who began to use his Zeppelins to shadow the Royal Navy's every movement. Useful as this maritime reconnaissance undoubtedly was, Strasser was keen to bomb England. The army declined to participate, not because of ethical objections but simply because the German air force was committed to the tactical support of troops in the field.

The question of the bombing of England had been put at the outbreak of the war to the Kaiser by the German naval staff who had recommended the action. The Kaiser, after changing his mind several times finally agreed to the bombing so long as the targets were 'restricted to military establishments, and that London itself was not to be bombed'. This last stricture was for fear that the British Royal Family might become casualties – after all, King George V was the Kaiser's cousin.

The road to hell, so it is said, is paved with good intentions. No doubt the Kaiser's strictures were known to the commanders of the three Imperial Navy's airships, *L 3*, *L 4* and *L 6*, as they set out on 19 January 1915 from their bases at Fuhlsbüttel and Nordholz. The operation was to be at night; the possibility of anti-aircraft gunfire and the loss of the three army airships was uppermost in Strasser's thoughts. Flying at night did not pose undue difficulties for airships because they, unlike aircraft, have a high degree of inherent stability and could therefore fly just as well by night as by day, the only problem being navigation as the crews relied on dead reckoning and visual fixes to verify their position. Unfortunately, the weather on the night of the raid was very bad, with rain and snow squalls and low cloud over the North Sea, where the Zeppelin *L 6*

ABOVE **Two German Zeppelins, *LZ 11* (left) and *LZ 17* in their hangar.**

BELOW *Fregattenkapitan* **Peter Strasser, the commander-in-chief of the German navy Zeppelins. He was to lose his life when *L 70* was shot down in August 1918.**

An historic photograph of three of the four Avro 504s of the RNAS being prepared at Belfort, near the Swiss border, before taking off on the first strategic bombing raid of the First World War: the attack on the Zeppelin sheds at Friedrichshafen 120 miles away. The Avros were 873, 875, 874 and 179, the latter the first Avro ordered by the Royal Navy; it had to abandon the flight due to a broken tail skid. The remaining three Avros, each dropping four 20lb bombs, attacked the sheds and destroyed a gas-generating plant and a Zeppelin. 873 was shot down over the target and the pilot, Commander Briggs RN, was taken prisoner. The other two 504s made it back to Belfort after a 250-mile flight.

developed engine trouble and had to return to base. The remaining two, *L 3* and *L 4*, became separated but both sighted the lights of English coastal towns. There was no blackout in force as it never occurred to anyone in Britain that the Germans would attack defenceless civilians in their homes at night, hundreds of miles from the fighting front in France. They were soon to be disabused of this notion. At 8.30pm *L 3* dropped several 110lb bombs on the fishing port of Great Yarmouth; soon after, *L 4* bombed on and around King's Lynn. Both airships returned to Germany without a shot being fired at them. That night, it was reported, four civilians had been killed and sixteen injured. No military installations had been hit, damage being confined to civilian property, mostly houses. A shocked British government realized that a new dimension to war had been defined. The chilling prophecy of Francesco de Lana-Terzi had become a reality.

The reaction to this new display of German 'frightfulness', or *schrecklichkeit*, was outrage: the still neutral *New York Herald* demanded '. . . what can Germany hope to gain by these wanton attacks on undefended places and this slaughter of innocents?' The British press, as obsessed then as it is now with royalty, claimed that the target had been the Royal Family, who were staying at Sandringham over which, probably unknown to the crew, *L 4* had flown. (In fact, King George V and Queen Mary had left Sandringham that morning.)

Undeterred the German naval Zeppelins continued with the attacks; there was little that the Royal Naval Air Service (RNAS), charged with the defence of Britain, could do against the German airships. Although the early Zeppelins had a modest ceiling of only 6,000ft and a maximum speed of under 50mph, they were nevertheless difficult to locate at night and, if sighted, they could – by jettisoning water ballast – climb at a rate three times that of the lumbering two-seater Short biplanes which were all that the RNAS had at their disposal. The public outcry against the Zeppelin raids grew: London, Hull and Newcastle, as well as many towns on the east coast, were regularly raided. Avro 504s of the RNAS made bombing raids on the airship bases, and four Zeppelins were destroyed in this way. Meanwhile, the army provided searchlights and anti-aircraft guns in increasing numbers. In the end the courage of young fighter pilots defeated the Zeppelins by flying at night in single-seater day fighters. There were S.E.5a and Sopwith Pups and Camels, aircraft which, by the standards of the day,

had high performance and high landing speeds but lacked any blind-flying instrumentation, radios or oxygen systems; the pilots also had no parachutes.

The later *L 30* class of Zeppelins, introduced in 1916, could fly at 13,000ft, at which altitude they had been considered immune from fighters and anti-aircraft guns. The fighters waited on the ground on their small grass airfields. When an enemy airship was sighted – or more likely was heard above the cloud base – the fighters would be scrambled to patrol a given line at maximum altitude, usually 15,000ft. At that height, in open cockpits that lacked any heating, it was intensely cold. The best hope for the fighter pilots was that the target airship would be caught by a searchlight; once one had found its mark others would join and the enemy Zeppelin would be 'coned'. When it was coned the airship, lacking speed and manoeuvrability, had little chance of evading the lights other than by jettisoning ballast and climbing into the clouds, if there were any. The fighters would then attack by diving through their own anti-aircraft fire and firing 'Buckingham' incendiary ammunition from machine-guns synchronized to fire through the propeller arc; some aircraft were armed with solid-state rockets fired from tubes attached to the interplane struts. Usually a good burst was sufficient to ignite the hydrogen from the punctured gasbags.

The first indication of victory the attacking pilot had was a deep red glow within the airship that was 'like a Chinese lantern', one pilot reported. This was followed by a gigantic ball of burning hydrogen gas which usually consumed the entire airship within forty-five seconds, the pilots having to dive steeply to avoid the falling wreckage. They then had to find the dimly lit flare-path of the aerodrome as, down to the last reserves of fuel, they returned to base. Many crashed in the attempt. Very few of the airships' average twenty-man crew survived, and then only if the airship have been forced down more or less intact.

Five Zeppelins fell to fighters over England in September and November 1916, plus two more were accounted for by anti-aircraft guns. A desperate contest of technology then followed as the designers of the airships tried to out-perform the defending fighters. The Germans produced 'height climbers'. These new airships were capable of reaching 21,000ft, an altitude matched by S.E.5a fighters and DH-4 fighter bombers of the Royal Air Force (the RAF had been formed from the RFC and RNAS on 1 April

1918, a date many thought significant). The last Zeppelin raid on targets in England was mounted on 5 August 1918. Five airships took part; *L 70*, the latest super-Zeppelin, with *Fregattenkapitan* Strasser himself on board, was intercepted and shot down in flames by a DH-4 just off the coast at Wells-next-the-Sea. There were no survivors. The DH-4, flown by Major E. Cadbury with Captain Leckie as his gunner, was probably one of a number built by Westland Aircraft of Yeovil in 1918 which were fitted with a 375hp Rolls-Royce Eagle engine, offering a service ceiling of 23,000ft. The DH-4 had taken off from Yarmouth heading for the North Sea; the *L 70* was sighted at 17,000ft. Cadbury climbed hard, jettisoning his incendiary bombs used to drop on airships, in order to gain height, sighted and closed in on the target, keeping clear of possible long wireless telegraphy (W/T) aerials that Zeppelins often trailed; he positioned the DH-4 abeam to port, coming under machine-gun fire from the airship's gunners. Ignoring the enemy fire, Leckie opened fire with his Lewis gun, loaded with 'ZPT' explosive ammunition, aiming at the lower half of the envelope amidships. Fire immediately started internally, quickly spreading along the length of the giant Zeppelin which raised its nose before plunging into the sea in a blazing mass. Cadbury felt no elation; as he wrote to his father: 'Another Zeppelin has gone to destruction, sent there by a perfectly peaceful live-and-let-live citizen, who has no lust for blood or fearful war spirit in his veins. It all happened very quickly and very terribly.' Cadbury was recommended for the Victoria Cross (VC), Britain's highest military decoration: he got a Distinguished Flying Cross (DFC), as did Leckie. Four other RAF pilots were killed that night in landing crashes.

Witnessing the fate of *L 70*, the other four airships turned for home. It was the last Zeppelin sortie over England. From the first to the last, the Germans had built 88 Zeppelins during the First World War years; they had made a total of 55 night raids over Britain, during the course of which over 5,000 bombs had been dropped containing about 200 tons of explosive. These bombs killed 557 people, injured 1,358 and caused extensive damage to property. In all, 22 Zeppelins had been shot down, and another 22 lost in accidents, mostly caused by bad weather.

The Zeppelins had, in four years of war, achieved little of military consequence except that, as a direct result of the raids, the British government had been forced by public opinion to deploy twelve fighter squadrons for home defence and a large number of anti-aircraft guns with ammunition and searchlights requiring the services of no fewer than 12,000 men. This large, purely defensive force, could otherwise have been with the armies in France.

Despite their limited success in material terms and the disappointing failure to instill mass terror into the population – if anything, the raids stiffened the resolve of servicemen and civilians alike, a fact which was to be overlooked by both sides during the Second World War – the developed *L 30* class of Zeppelins must be included as 'classic bombers' in that they represent a very considerable aeronautical engineering achievement, being constructed from the then newly developed light aluminium alloys at a time when Allied aircraft were made from wood. The *L 30* class were 650ft in length and were powered by six 240hp Maybach water-cooled engines. They had a range of nearly 5,000 miles at 46mph with a bomb load of 11,000lb. The *L 30*s could have crossed the Atlantic; indeed it had been Peter Strasser's ambition to bomb New York. In retrospect, if the Germans had inert helium at their disposal instead of explosive hydrogen as the lifting gas and if they had concentrated on London instead of diluting the attack on coastal cities, the outcome could have been very different for the Allies.

The German Zeppelins remain the first heavy, long-range strategic night bombers and have the dubious distinction of being the pioneers of indiscriminate bombing in order to terrorize, as a deliberate target, civilians in their towns and cities. This was a

proposition dismissed as barbaric by the Allies who, at the time, had limited means of reprisal but one which, when long-range Allied heavy bombers became available in 1918, they would embrace without any qualms.

As the Imperial Navy's Zeppelins were withdrawn from the attack on London, the German air force took up the role of bombing England, not with airships but with heavy bombers named by the British press – not always correctly – 'Gothas'. The first heavy bomber raid against England, in contrast to the Zeppelins' night offensive, was in daylight. It was mounted on 25 May 1917, and the formation was led by *Hauptmann* Ernst Brandenburg. The target was London but dense cloud cover over southern England caused the formation to turn back when it was over Gravesend, and the unfortunate target of opportunity sighted as they flew east was the seaside resort of Folkestone. It was a heavy raid with no fewer than twenty-one of the large biplanes bombing seemingly unopposed. Ninety-five people were killed and 195 others injured. The daylight raid by aircraft had come as a surprise; belatedly, fighters took off and succeeded in intercepting the bombers over the sea flying back to their Belgium base but the fighters attacked without visible results. After the war it was learned that two bombers had been hit and damaged; one crashed in the Channel, the other in German-occupied Belgium.

Further daylight raids followed: in June there was a raid on Shoeburyness where one bomber was shot down by anti-aircraft fire. On 25 June, to the acute embarrassment of the British government, eighteen Gothas defiantly flew over London in broad daylight and in perfect formation, dropping seventy-two bombs on Liverpool Street Station and others elsewhere in the city. It was the worst raid of the war, leaving 162 dead and over 400 injured. All eighteen German bombers escaped without loss. When it was learned that no fewer than ninety-two fighters had scrambled without shooting down a single raider, there was an unprecedented public outcry against the defending forces. This row was, in part, to lead to the formation of the independent RAF to replace the divided

This picture is something of a mystery. The aircraft is a German Gotha bomber, apparently named 'Lori 2 the Great', with crewmen and presumably maintenance staff. The significance of the bomb crater in the foreground is unknown. Perhaps the airfield had been bombed by the Allies?

This Hawker Hart is flying under false colours. Although it is carrying an RAF serial number it was never on RAF charge. J 9941 was one of the initial batch of fifteen Harts ordered. The original J 9941 served from 1929 with No. 33 and No. 57 (Bomber) Squadrons when stationed at Netheravon, Wiltshire in 1931. It was the first Hart to log 1,000 flying hours, which it achieved in just two-and-a-half years – an RAF record. The Hart depicted is actually G-ABMR, believed to be the 13th Hart airframe, which was retained by the Hawker company as a communication aircraft and photographic mount for many years. Here it is being flown up from Dunsfold in the 1970s by Hawker test pilot Duncan Simpson. G-ABMR has been grounded for some years and is now preserved on permanent static display in the RAF Museum at Hendon.

responsibilities of the RFC and RNAS. The defensive forces were reorganized and, after one more daylight raid on the capital and three against coastal targets, the German bombers discovered that fighters were intercepting them with ease – to the extent that, in September 1917, the Gothas, like the Zeppelins before them, shifted to night operations to reduce interception by fighters and accurate anti-aircraft fire. Altogether there were to be fifteen night-bomber raids on Britain, nine of them on London. Night fighter pilots, flying Sopwith Camels – which were considered tricky to fly even in daylight – had nevertheless improved their technique, for the losses suffered by the lumbering bombers rose to a point in May 1918 where 7 heavy bombers out of the 43 attacking were shot down, mostly in flames. In all, 48 Gothas had been lost on sorties over Britain: at least 8 were known to have been shot down by fighters and 12 by anti-aircraft gunfire, the remainder crashing from causes including battle damage, faulty navigation, bad weather, pilot error and mechanical failure. The loss rate was unsustainable; the air raids on Britain ceased. In the final grim audit of war, the Gothas had been more effective than the Zeppelins, releasing 2,772 bombs containing 196 tons of explosive. Altogether 857 people had been killed, 2,058 had been injured and damage to property was estimated at £1,500,000 (equivalent to £1 billion today). There had been large-scale disruption to the working day and the commercial life of cities and towns. In strictly military terms the raids – other than the diversion of forces – amounted to little. Nevertheless, they had engendered a vociferous press and public demand for reprisals against 'Hun' towns by RAF bombers. There was, too, a lasting consequence of the air raids: a revulsion of Germany and the Germans that was to smoulder in Britain for a generation, until the embers were fanned into flame by the Second World War.

What kind of aircraft were the Gothas? The prototype bomber had been built by the rather appropriately named Gotha Wagonfabrik – the source of the generic name – and was produced as a number of differing subtypes, the version used in the attacks on Britain being the G-IV, the 'G' standing not for 'Gotha', but *Grossflugzeug*, which literally means a great or large aeroplane. Most were produced by the Siemens-Schuckert company. The G-IV was powered by two 260hp Mercedes D IVa engines, enabling just over

90mph to be achieved. They were wood and fabric biplanes with a wing-span of 77ft and could carry a bomb load of 1,000lb, partly internally and partly suspended externally. The service ceiling was an excellent 21,300ft, though it must have been distinctly chilly for the crew in their open cockpits and gun positions. When attacked by fighters the Gothas proved surprisingly agile for their size, which was fortunate as they were inadequately defended against intercepting fighters by just two hand-trained 7.92mm Parabellum machine-guns firing from positions in the nose and on the upper fuselage just aft of the top wing. There was no defence against fighters attacking from below.

Towards the end of the Germans' night-time bombing offensive on London, a very much larger four-engined bomber also took part. Although called 'Gotha' by the British press and public, this was in fact the Staaken, so-called because it was produced by the Zeppelin company at Staaken near Berlin, and was known to the Germans as the *Staaken R-VI Gigant* (*gigant* means 'giant'). The type was built by Avatik and Schutte-Lanz. There seems to have been a good deal of latitude in the specification as few machines of the total of eighteen in service were identical. The Staaken has the distinction of being the largest aircraft produced by the fighting powers during the war years. The wing-span was an impressive 138ft, the all-up weight (i.e. including fuel, oils, etc.) was, at nearly 12 tons (26,066lb) also impressive. The truly heavy bomber could carry a 1-ton bomb load at 12,500ft for 500 miles and one of 2 tons over a shorter range. The four engines were arranged as twin tandem pairs driving tractor and pusher-propellers; the still-air endurance of the R-VIs was ten hours. Defensive armament consisted typically of three 7.92mm machine-guns in positions in the nose, upper fuselage, and a third ventral position able to fire below the aircraft to protect against fighters attacking from beneath. The pilots (two were normal), a navigator, wireless operator and an engineer were, uniquely for wartime bombers, ensconced in a capacious enclosed cabin, though the gunners' positions were still in the open. Although to modern eyes the Staakens look archaic, in 1918 they represented highly advanced technology and aeronautical engineering.

At the zenith of the Gotha raids in 1917, the public and press clamour for reprisal bombing raids against the German capital, Berlin, though understandable, was simply not possible. A British bomber raiding the German capital, even when flying from a base in northern France, would have a return trip of over 800 miles; this meant ten hours of flying over hostile territory. German bombers, on the other hand, taking off from bases at Ghent in occupied Belgium, only had to fly 120 miles to London, most of the route being over the sea with the unmistakable River Thames to guide them to the heart of the capital.

By 1918, the Handley Page O/400s became operational as the principal night bombers of the newly formed RAF. They had an endurance of eight hours and thus it was at last possible to mount strategic bombing raids on Germany, though Berlin remained out of range. The O/400 heavy bombers equipped seven of the RAF strategic bomber squadrons which, in October 1918, were ordered by General (as he was then) Hugh Trenchard to: '. . . mount an extensive and sustained bombing offensive against German munitions industries'. The only German munitions factories attainable by O/400s were in the Ruhr and Saarland. Several industrial towns in the Ruhr valley were bombed at night, some of the bombers being armed with massive 1,650lb bombs, the heaviest dropped by either side during the war. Although official communiqués claimed heavy damage to munitions factories, without doubt heavy collateral damage and civilian casualties occurred. The cost was high: in the last five months of the war, sixty-nine RAF heavy bombers were lost, either to direct enemy action or in flying accidents, a consequence of night operations in winter with few landing aids other than a flickering paraffin lamp flare-path to guide down exhausted pilots.

This naval officer is dropping a 20lb bomb from a small 'coastal airship' around 1915. A similar casual and foolproof method was used by observers when flying in early RFC aircraft. Before long, however, bombs were carried on special racks beneath the aircraft's wings and aimed with bomb-sights which made allowance for the aircraft's airspeed and the prevailing wind.

Although welcomed by the British popular press, these raids on provincial German towns, munitions factories not withstanding, were regarded as a poor substitute for the German capital, Berlin. The incessant press demand to avenge the 'Hun' attacks on London by bombing the German capital continued. By late 1918, the RAF had at last the means of reaching Berlin. The designer of the O/400, George Volkert (who would design the Halifax bomber of the Second World War), had in 1917 revised his O/400 design to produce the Handley Page V/1500, the epitome of the 'bloody paralyser' which Murray Sueter, when chief of the Royal Navy Air Department, had demanded four years earlier.

The V/1500, built in Cricklewood, London, was big. It was the first four-engined bomber in the RAF Order of Battle (even the Staakens were not the first four-engined bombers; that palm must go to the incredible Sikorsky *Ilya Mourometz* of 1913, designed by Igor Sikorsky before he left Russia to found the American helicopter industry). The 'Super Handley', as the V/1500 was known, had a wing-span of 126ft; four 375hp Rolls-Royce Eagle VIII engines offered a maximum speed of 99mph and an 80mph cruising speed at 10,000ft when carrying a bomb load of thirty 250lb bombs – a total load of 7,500lb. The bomber had a seventeen-hour endurance, sufficient to give a still-air range of 1,300 miles, and could have bombed Berlin from an English base, though the open cockpits and gun positions would have been a severe test of the crew's endurance. It was the first RAF aircraft designed from the outset as a strategic bomber, a role which it was destined never to fulfil. Three V/1500s of No. 166 Squadron were standing by on 11 November 1918 to take off for Berlin from their base at Bircham Newton in Norfolk when the news arrived of the signing of the Armistice ending the four-year First World War. Although 255 of the V/1500 big bombers were on order, only eight had been placed on RAF charge when the war ended. The remainder of the contract was cancelled.

In the immediate postwar years of disarmament and RAF retrenchment, the V/1500s, costly to operate and service, did not long survive. However, in December

1918, one, named for the occasion HMA *Carthusion*, did make a record-breaking flight from Martlesham Heath, Suffolk to Karachi via Rome, Malta, Cairo and Baghdad. The celebrations attending this landmark flight to India were compromised slightly by the aircraft landing at Karachi on just two of the four engines. Another V/1500, F 7140, just missed immortality, being shipped to Newfoundland in 1919 to attempt the first Atlantic crossing by an aircraft. However, Alcock and Brown, flying a Vickers Vimy, another war-surplus RAF bomber, beat them to it. The Handley Page Atlantic flight and a place in aviation history was abandoned.

At the end of the First World War the RAF, the world's first independent air force, was by a considerable margin also the largest. It had 188 front-line squadrons, plus another 75 training units. There were 22,647 aircraft of all types on charge and an establishment of over a quarter of a million officers, men and women. Almost overnight this vast force was reduced to just twelve front-line squadrons, of which only two were for home defence. Thousands of aircraft, many straight from the factories, were sold for scrap and a wholesale reorganization began to fit the RAF for a peacetime role. In fact, the very existence of the RAF was in doubt. It was formed as a wartime expediency; now that the war was over, and Germany was defeated and disarmed, the army and the navy wanted 'their' aeroplanes back. Viscount Trenchard, not to become known as the 'Father of the RAF' for nothing, fought his corner with vigour and political skill. His chance to save the RAF as an independent force came about because Britain emerged from the First World War not only with the Empire intact but also, as a consequence of the dismantling of the Turkish Ottoman Empire, with considerable extra territory. The League of Nations had mandated Mesopotamia (Iraq), Transjordan and Palestine to Britain. These proposals were never accepted by either Turkey or many of the populations of the countries concerned: British law and government ran contrary to their Islamic customs. Clearly a very large standing army, estimated at two divisions, would be required to keep the peace. In view of the recent four blood-soaked years of war and the huge casualty lists, the British public was in no mood for the idea of protecting – as the public then perceived it – arid and worthless deserts thinly populated by ungrateful natives. Trenchard astutely saw a new role for the RAF: 'Air Control'. He boldly proposed that the army infantry and artillery divisions were not necessary and that, as an alternative, eight RAF squadrons based in what was by then Iraq with an army brigade composed of British and Indian troops and a small force of armoured cars manned by the RAF could effectively, without incurring heavy casualties, maintain the peace and law and order. The proposition was dismissed as impracticable by the War Office but it had one irresistible feature that appealed to the government of the day: it was very inexpensive. Air Control was adopted in October 1922.

In practice this worked in a very simple way: when the 'natives', usually warlike Kurds, were causing trouble, typically by attacking another village, the known leaders would be summoned to trial. If they refused to attend – which they usually did – they would be informed by leaflets dropped from the air that on a given day their village would be bombed. On the due date this would happen. The strategy was effective: the prior warning ensured that there were no people or animals in the village attacked, so only material damage occurred. Air Control was so successful that it spread to all British possessions and mandated territories in the Middle East and on the North-West Frontier area of India and Afghanistan, though there the army insisted on retaining a major role. Air Control was to produce two truly classic tactical light bombers; the De Havilland DH-9A and the Hawker Hart, the latter being one of the most adaptable aircraft the RAF was ever to possess.

The DH-9A, known to the RAF as the 'Ninak', was a very successful light day bomber that first entered service with No. 110 Squadron in June 1918. By the Armistice, that squadron alone had dropped 10 tons of bombs on German targets with only light losses. The DH-9A was an Anglo-American collaboration. It had a British biplane airframe powered by American-built Liberty engines jointly manufactured by three major US car makers: Ford, Lincoln and Packard. The V12 water-cooled Liberty power plants were rated at 400hp and gave the two-seater bomber a top speed of 114mph at a respectable 10,000ft. A bomb load of 450lb was carried externally. The pilot had a single .303in Vickers gun, synchronized to fire through the propeller arc. The rear gunner was armed with a single hand-trained .303in Lewis gas-operated machine-gun with 96-round drums of ammunition; the gun was mounted on a Scarff ring that enabled it to be quickly trained. This excellent weapon was to remain in RAF service for over fifty years. Westland Aircraft of Yeovil built 390 DH-9As; hundreds more were built by subcontractors and the total number produced by the end of hostilities was nearly 900. In the postwar period, 400 airframes were withdrawn from store with maintenance units to be rebuilt by various manufacturers, plus eighty new aircraft. The last batch, thirty-five new aircraft, J 8460–J 8494, were ordered from Westland and Parnell in January 1927. Though a few DH-9As had a Napier Lion or Rolls-Royce Eagle engine, the original 400hp US Liberty engine was standard, probably because the RAF held huge stocks of engines and spares left over from the war years; 2,252 Liberty engines with spares had been delivered to the UK – 1,272 after the war – at a cost of nearly $16,500,000, or $7,300 per engine.

It is doubtful whether the DH-9As used for Air Control by nine RAF squadrons overseas were able to attain the types' 'brochure' maximum airspeed of 114mph, festooned as they were with an assortment of survival equipment: a spare wheel to cope with emergency landings on rock-strewn desert strips, and occasionally even a spare propeller lashed to the fuselage for the same reason; tools, emergency rations and water, often carried in a goatskin container hanging over the side of the rear cockpit to keep it cool; and medical kit and an additional radiator beneath the nose to cope with tropical temperatures. The DH-9As operating over hostile territory, and that included most, worked at least in pairs so that in the event of a forced landing one aircraft could circle to provide cover while the crew of the downed machine struggled to get it airborne again, if at all possible. Lacking radio, signalling between aircraft was by coloured flares fired from a

E 8804, an airco-built DH-9A. This Ninak was one of a late batch of 400 aircraft ordered in 1918, many of which were exported to the USA. The machine is flying on 'Air Control' duties in the 1920s in either the Middle East or India, with a spare wheel bolted under the fuselage; the gunner has a solar topee hat and beneath the engine cowling a secondary radiator can be seen. The streamers on the elevators probably denote a section leader.

Very pistol. This was not without risk; on at least two known occasions, the pilot signalling 'all is well' to his airborne colleague neglected to note the wind direction before firing the Very pistol and the falling flare set fire to his wooden, fabric-covered aircraft. Even without the aid of pyrotechnics, DH-9As had a reputation for catching fire when crashed; this was due to the 45-degree angle of the V12 Liberty engine which made the provision of the usual magneto very difficult. Consequently Delco coil and contact-breaker ignition was employed; this required a lead-acid battery, a fire hazard if petrol tanks were ruptured in a crash landing. Although a system of prepared, though rough, emergency landing strips was available, forced landings were to be avoided for another urgent reason: the desert tribesmen had a tradition of castrating any prisoners, especially any RAF bomber crews, who were unfortunate enough to fall into their hands. For this reason no RAF pilot engaged on Air Control duties cared to fly lower than 3,000ft because the tribesmen were renowned shots and the DH-9A, with its external radiator and associated plumbing, was vulnerable to small-arms fire. If forced down, the best hope was that the circling aircraft could land and pick up the stranded pilot and gunner, taking off as quickly as possible with the rescued crew crammed into the rear cockpit or, as it is known to have occurred more than once, clinging to the struts and bracing wires on the lower wings, with the shots from tribesmen ripping through the fabric structure. If rescue was impossible then the last resort was the famed RAF 'goolie chit'. This was a document written in the vernacular which promised that if the holder was returned to a British outpost, if not undamaged at least intact, a substantial cash reward – no questions asked – would be paid. Once it had been proved that the British honoured the promise, the chit was believed by the airmen to be their salvation, provided of course that the tribesmen holding the prisoner were not all illiterate, which many were. Be that as it may, no airmen would fly without his chit and the practice continued throughout the Second World War and up to the Gulf War when all RAF air crews were issued with a 1990s' version of the goolie chit.

The DH-9A remained in front-line service with the RAF both at home and overseas until it was superseded in 1928 by the Westland Wapiti – known to Servicemen as

A flight of Westland Wapiti Is of No. 601 Squadron of the Auxiliary Air Force, the part-time 'weekend flyers' up from Hendon in the 1930s. The DH-9A ancestry of the Wapiti is clearly seen by comparing these aircraft with the DH-9A on the opposite page. The Wapiti used the tail, wings and fin of the earlier aircraft. J 9101 was the penultimate Wapiti I of a Westland-built batch of twenty-five aircraft delivered to the RAF in 1929. The Wapiti served with the RAF in India until 1939.

'what a pity'. (A wapiti is the American elk, *Cervus canadensis,* and the word wapiti means 'white deer' in the Shawnee native American language). The Wapiti was ordered under the terms of the 'ten-year-rule': this assumed that no major war was probable within ten years. It provided the Treasury with an excellent reason for keeping the RAF from indulging themselves in profligately ordering new aircraft. The Westland Company must, therefore, have been pleased, not to say surprised, to receive an order for the new type to replace the venerable DH-9A: this was to be the Westland Wapiti. However, when they read the small print of the contract the Yeovil-based company realized that the only 'new' features of the Wapiti were the unusual name, an enlarged fuselage, which would be for carrying the survival gear and spares, and a new engine, a 550-hp Bristol Jupiter air-cooled radial. The order stipulated that as many parts as possible of the obsolete DH-9A were to be used in the construction of the Wapiti. These 'parts' eventually consisted of the wings, struts, tail assembly, control surfaces and undercarriage to be drawn from the large stock of DH-9A spares the RAF had in store, sufficient for the first fifty aircraft. The old Ninak therefore did not die: it became, at least in part, a Wapiti. It must be said that the Westland Wapiti fulfilled the Air Control tasks of the late DH-9A with distinction. Sadly, no airworthy examples of either aircraft remain, although there is a static DH-9A on display in the RAF Museum at Hendon, and a Wapiti airframe is believed to exist in India.

The Wapiti was itself to be supplanted in the Air Control role by a genuinely new design and one of the great aircraft of the RAF, the Hawker Hart. This was a true classic, with a design so adaptable that this elegant biplane led to a total production of nearly 3,000 Hawker Hart aircraft in seven major variants and scores of subtypes, which served the RAF and the Fleet Air Arm (FAA) for a decade and was to be exported for service with many foreign air forces. Yet the type came into existence in a most roundabout way.

With RAF aircraft that had been built or designed in the last years of the First World War being outclassed in 1925 by such high-performance machines as the 225mph Gloster IV Schneider Trophy seaplane, which was 70mph faster than the front-line RAF fighters of the day, it was clear to the Air Ministry that unstoppable progress both in aerodynamics and aero-engines, together with the impressive – and cost-effective – results of Air Control, enabled funds to be prised from a tight-fisted Treasury for long overdue modern replacement aircraft for the RAF. To that end the Air Ministry in 1926 issued Specification 12/26, which called for a newly designed single-engined light day bomber. The provenance of the specification was unusual. The industry in those days was run by a small number of very hard men who totally controlled their aircraft companies; one of these was Sir Richard Fairey, who had obtained an agency import, an excellent American V12 aero-engine, the 400hp Curtiss D-12, which he was also to build under licence in England as the Fairey Felix to power a new Fairey Fox light bomber. The Air Ministry were placed in a quandary as there was no doubt that the Curtiss D-12 was in advance of any home-produced unit, as the astute Sir Richard was well aware. The Air Ministry did not want the RAF to rely on imported, foreign engines, not even if they came from the United States, still less to have an additional British aero-engine builder at a time when the four old-established manufacturers had barely sufficient orders to survive. There was only one solution: a new British aero-engine would have to be designed that would at least be the equal of the American unit. To this end the Napier Company was first approached but declined, and then Rolls-Royce, who agreed. In July 1925 work began on the engine that was to become the Rolls-Royce Kestrel; a supercharged liquid-cooled V12 of just over 21 litres offering 525hp for take-off. The Kestrel, which first ran in 1926, possessed a striking resemblance to the Curtiss

D-12, passed all Air Ministry tests. Brochures were sent by Rolls-Royce to the principal British airframe makers. Hawker's chief designer, Sydney (later Sir Sydney) Camm, designed his tender to Specification 12/26, to be powered by the new Rolls-Royce Kestrel engine. The prototype, named Hawker Hart, J 9834, first flew from Brooklands in June 1928. After competitive trials conducted by the Air Ministry against a Fairey Fox (with a Curtiss D-12) and Avro Antelope, the Hawker Hart was selected for immediate production for the RAF, which began with orders for fifteen development aircraft. After a full Service evaluation, further unprecedented peacetime orders for 483 Hawker Hart bombers, beginning with K 1417, were to follow.

No. 33 Squadron, based at Eastchurch in Kent, received their first operational Hawker Harts in April 1930. The squadron quickly demonstrated the excellent properties of the new bomber: during the annual air exercises RAF Siskin fighters tried, in vain, to intercept them. This was hardly surprising as the Hart bomber, with a maximum level flight speed of 184mph, was a good 30mph faster than the Siskin, a frontline RAF fighter of the day. Other bomber squadrons followed No. 33; between 1930 and 1936, seven home-based bomber squadrons flew the Hawker Hart; in 1936, as the RAF expanded, three out of every four new aircraft delivered to the RAF were Harts or Hart variants. The Auxiliary Air Force squadrons flew the type until 1938, when many Harts were converted to advanced trainers (a number were built as such). An RAF inventory made at the outbreak of the Second World War in 1939 revealed a total of 547 Harts still on charge with many flying as trainers or on communication duties as late as 1942. One Hart, K 5861, a trainer, was still serving with No. 7 Flying Training School (FTS) until January 1944; possibly the last airworthy Hart on RAF charge. (One Hart died of shame; abandoned intact on Mirville airfield in May 1940 during the retreat to Dunkirk it was impressed into the *Luftwaffe*, and was the only Hawker Hart known to fly in full German military markings.)

Hawker Harts served with RAF squadrons overseas: 'tropicalized' Harts (Harts India) served with Air Control units in Iraq, on the North-West Frontier of India, in Egypt and Palestine. Flying over 'The Grim', as RAF pilots called the mountainous North-West Frontier region of Afghanistan, with the near impossibility of surviving a forced landing, the reliability of the Rolls-Royce Kestrel engine and the Harts' service ceiling of 21,300ft was appreciated. The Hart was well liked by all who flew the type. One Hart pilot, John Nesbitt-Dufort, writing in his book *Open Cockpit*, recalled his impressions on seeing a Hart for the first time in the 1930s:

> . . . it was one belonging to 12 Squadron from Bister . . . An old pupil of No. 3 FTS Grantham had flown up the gleaming beauty to show it off to an admiring ring of as yet, wingless acting Pilot Officers on Probation. I can still remember gazing at what was to us the most beautiful machine we had ever seen. Its staggered and slightly swept back wings, brilliantly polished aluminium cowlings with a big golden '12'; and the Squadron crest of a fox's mask painted on it . . . I can also recall the gasps of admiration (unwarranted) at the steep clambering swerve the pilot made on his take-off after lunch, which fortunately for him, none of the instructors witnessed.

The Hart was a delightful aeroplane to fly and, though a bomber, was fully aerobatic; however, before indulging, as John Nesbitt-Dufort remembered:

> . . . the radiator had to be laboriously wound in prior to any aerobatics involving negative 'G'. Failure to do this resulted in a frighteningly loud 'clonk' as the radiator fell inboard, during a slow roll for example.

Hawker Harts of No. 11 (India) Squadron, RAF, flying over the 'Grim'. This mountainous region of the North-West Frontier of India was well named and typical of the country over which the RAF flew on 'Air Control' sorties during the 1930s. Engine failure over such inhospitable terrain would invariably prove fatal even if the crew survived the forced landing. However, the trust that the pilots and observers placed in their single Rolls-Royce Kestrel engines and the men who maintained them was rarely misplaced.

The pilot's 'office' in a Hart of the 1930s. The old curved level with its capricious bubble has been supplemented by the then new Reid & Sigrist 'turn and bank' indicator as an aid to blind flying. The other instruments from left to right are: altimeter, airspeed indicator (ASI), oil pressure, engine RPM canted so that cruising revolutions appeared at 'twelve o'clock', oil temperature, radiator temperature and manifold boost gauge measured in inches of mercury (Hg). The large white-faced instrument is a fuel contents gauge. Below is the knob for the 'Ki gas' engine primer pump. The two brass domestic-looking switches are for the magnetos. The compass slung between the pilot's feet is a P6 course-setting model which was to survive into and beyond the Second World War, and above the compass is the mechanical indicator for the radiator position. The hand wheel at the bottom right of the picture is the control for raising or lowering the radiator. A similar wheel, on the left-hand side (not in the photograph) controlled the fore and aft trim. Below the rudder pedals is the cellar into which the bomb aimer crawled to aim the bombs. The 'spade' control column has two thumb controls for the differential wheel brakes. It is instructive to compare this 1930s front line RAF aircraft's sparse instrumentation with that of the Cessna 172 light aircraft of the 1990s on page 121.

Negative 'G' could also shower the pilot with dried mud and other detritus – even, on occasion, hand tools from within the deep fuselage beneath the pilot's feet, there being no floor as such, just two aluminium troughs on which to slide his booted feet to the adjustable rudder bar.

Since the Hawker Hart and its many variants represent the transitional technology of the 1930s, bridging between the low-powered, wooden aircraft of the First World War and the all-metal monocoque monoplanes of the Second World War, it is worthwhile to examine this very successful aircraft in some detail. Although the fashions of the 1930s still favoured the biplane, the major engine makers – Napier, Rolls-Royce and Bristol – were producing a generation of new aero-engines in the 450–600hp class which enabled the manufacturers of military aircraft to design airframes to exploit the enhanced performance available from these powerful and reliable engines.

Sydney Camm's design had been finalized in close collaboration with Rolls-Royce. The slender fuselage of the Hart had a cross-section no wider that the fitted Kestrel engine; the primary structure of the aircraft was a seamless steel tube, the sections being bolted, not welded together, to aid maintenance in the field. Wooden formers defined the shape of the top of the fuselage, which was covered with fabric. This form of construction was a Hawker speciality and one that would be utilized by all the Hart variants and, eventually, the Hurricane. The wings of the Hart were of mixed construction with steel main spars in a dumb-bell configuration; the ribs were made from duralumin, and the whole of the wing covered in fabric. The biplane wings were also staggered, the 37ft 3in top wings being slightly swept back to improve the pilot's upward view and also to give a clear exit should he be forced to bale out. The right, starboard half of the centre section incorporated a secondary 19-imperial-gallon gravity-fed fuel tank (the main fuel tank of 68 imperial gallons formed the top of the fuselage between the engine bulkhead and the pilot's cockpit). Ailerons were only fitted to the top wings, which also had automatic Handley Page slats. The pilot's cockpit was comfortable and, though open, was surprisingly draught-free. The usual instruments of the time were fitted: air-speed indicator (ASI), a sensitive altimeter and a P4-type magnetic compass, though the only aid to blind flying was a Reid & Sigrist gyroscopic turn-and-slip indicator, itself then a new addition, and the familiar curved tube and bubble cross-level, which could indicate a bank up to 20 degrees from level, but which – like the pilot – was subject to errors caused by acceleration and deceleration forces. Today, even in a light aircraft, those two blind-flying instruments would be regarded as a dangerously limited panel. They were inadequate for instrument meteorological conditions (IMC) which comprise blind flying, that is flying without visual contact with the ground or horizon.

In the 1930s, few pilots flew on instruments from choice, but if a pilot was caught out in bad weather and dense cloud, the best advice available was simple: 'Rudder for the compass; stick for the wings', banked turns or changes of attitude to be avoided or, if essential, to be made very, very gently to avoid the dreaded 'leans'. This meant disorientation, which in the absence of a reference to the ground or horizon, real or artificial, could rapidly lead to what the RAF euphemistically termed – and still do – 'a departure from controlled flight', typically into a spin. (Research in the late 1920s showed that, without the turn-and-slip instrument, even the most experienced pilots flying 'blind' would invariably fall into spins within a few minutes.) The inherent stability of the Hart was an aid to counter this hazardous and potentially terminal departure when flown in bad weather.

The Hawker aircraft had the familiar British military 'spade'-grip control column; the engine throttle and mixture controls were on the port side of the cockpit and there were the usual engine instruments with the addition of a boost gauge, reminding the pilot that he had a 'blown' or supercharged power plant up front. The propeller, a wooden Watts, was of fixed pitch. A dated feature of the cockpit was the .303in Vickers gun to port, with the breech in the cockpit as it had to be manually cocked by the pilot who also had to clear any stoppage. Spent cartridge cases and the disintegrating ammunition feed-belt were ejected overboard from a chute. The gun was aimed by a 'ring-and-bead' sight, firing through the propeller arc via a deep blast trough indented in the port engine cowling.

When the prototype Hart was flown by service test pilots at the Aircraft and Armament Experimental Establishment (A & AEE), then at Martlesham Heath in Suffolk, about the only criticism they could find after three months intensive flying was the 'cramped' gunner's cockpit. The gunners had a busy time aboard the Hart; they had to stand to fire their single Lewis gun, though the patent Hawker rotating gun mounting made it easier to track a target because it had a powerful compensating spring which aided the gun when trained against the slipstream. The gunner was tethered to his aircraft by a 'G-string', a strong wire clipped to his parachute harness and a hard point on the floor of the cockpit. The Lewis gun had the classic 97-round .303in ammunition drums, eight being stowed on the starboard wall of the cockpit. The drums were usually loaded with tracer rounds in a ratio of 1:3. When *en route*, the gunner had a tip-up seat facing into the aft fuselage, towards the twin high-pressure oxygen cylinders and, if fitted, a vertical camera. If the sortie the aircraft was engaged on required wireless telegraphy (W/T), an HF (high-frequency) W/T set with transmitter, receiver and batteries would be fitted on the port side of the gunner's cockpit. When operating W/T, the gunner had manually to winch the long trailing aerial up or down. Though W/T was not a standard fit, all Hawker Harts had screened ignition and a bonded structure (signified on RAF aircraft of the 1930s by a 3in ringed 'WT' stencilled on the fin) and standard W/T crates accessible via a removable panel in the fuselage to allow the squadron W/T fitter to install and adjust the set on the ground. Whether radio was fitted or not, the gunner, who doubled as the bomb aimer, had to tip up his seat to get to the bomb-aiming position, unhook his safety wire, oxygen feed and Gosport tube (the acoustic voice intercom that enabled him to communicate with his pilot) and then turn around and crawl under the pilot's seat. He also had to do all this when encumbered by a parachute and heavy flying clothing. Some, though not all, Harts had a small rectangular window to light the bomb-aiming position.

When in place, lying prone in front of the bomb-sight with his oxygen and Gosport tubes reconnected, the gunner, having carefully adjusted his goggles, slid back a square panel in the fuselage floor to reveal the 'bombing aperture' and was offered a view of the ground undistorted by glass or perspex.

The 'tools of the trade' in the lower position consisted of the standard RAF bomber 'Mk VI course-setting bomb-sight'; an instrument panel with an altimeter and air-speed indicator to give the numbers required to set up the bomb-sight; and there was also a cross-level to ensure that the aircraft was not yawing at the moment the bombs were released as this would impart an unwanted 'sling-shot' impetus to the bombs. The bomb load of a Hart was a maximum of 500lb carried on the lower wings, which were selected and dropped manually by the bomb aimer with a bomb-release lever.

The excellence of the Hart airframe enabled Hawkers to adapt it to perform dedicated roles other than bombing, with little modification. All the Hart-variant prototypes were first flown as converted Harts. The inability of existing RAF fighters to intercept Harts during the 1930 air exercises caused the Air Ministry to issue Specification 15/30 which revived the concept of a two-seater fighter, a configuration dormant since 1918. Hawker offered the Demon, the prototype being a converted Hart (J 9933). This, despite the two forward-firing guns and ammunition and a revised rear gunner's cockpit to improve his range of fire, was only 2mph slower than the Hart, with a service ceiling of 27,500ft. It was ordered into production and issued either to all-Demon units or in mixed formations, flying with Bulldog and Gauntlet fighters, to no fewer than twelve fighter squadrons at home and overseas. Later (1936) production Demons had an experimental hydraulic turret and a 640hp Kestrel VI to compensate for the additional drag of the turret; 190 Demons were built, the type flying operationally until 1939.

In 1931 another Hart (K 1438) was modified for 'Army Co-operation' duties. The name given was Audax (Latin for audacious) and production, which ended in 1937, amounted to 652 aircraft built by the Hawker, Gloster, Bristol and Avro aviation companies. The Audax could be identified by long exhaust pipes beyond the gunner's cockpit and a retractable hook suspended from an undercarriage spreader bar; this was for picking up a message pouch, a feat that called for very precise flying as the pouch was suspended between two 8ft poles. The success of Air Control led to another Hart variant, the Hawker Hardy; only forty-eight were built, all serving in Palestine, Iraq and Kenya. The Hardy differed from the standard Hart in having low-pressure 'doughnut' tyres, with fully braked wheels for rough landing strips, and was equipped for close co-operation with ground forces, having either bomb racks or supply containers below each lower wing.

Because of the widespread use of Harts and their variants through the RAF, the need arose for a dual-control trainer for these high-performance aircraft of their day. The Hawker Hart Trainer was devised, with the gunner's and bomb-aiming positions deleted and replaced by an instructor's cockpit with full instrumentation and dual control. The prototype Hart Trainer (K 1996) first flew in 1932. In all, 417 dedicated Hart Trainers were built and many more converted from redundant Hart bombers as the type became the standard advanced trainer of the RAF during the expansion years, beginning in 1936. Many RAF pilots who flew into action in the early years of the Second World War had

gained their wings on Hart Trainers. The Royal Navy also had a Hart variant, the Hawker Osprey, which was embarked on five pre-war naval carriers: HMS *Eagle*, HMS *Ark Royal*, HMS *Glorious*, HMS *Hermes* and HMS *Courageous*. The role of the Osprey, which had folding wings, flotation gear and could be fitted with floats as a seaplane catapulted from cruisers, was fighter-reconnaissance. Altogether 193 Ospreys, from Mk I to Mk IV, were built and the type served with FAA (Fleet Air Arm) units afloat and ashore until 1939.

When, by 1936, it was clear that the German *Luftwaffe* was a reality and the Nazi government in Germany posed a threat to peace, there was a near panic expansion of the RAF. The hurried change from biplanes to new all-metal monoplane types was to prove difficult and, as a stopgap, the front-line role of the Hart and its variants was extended beyond normal limits as an interim type. The Hart bomber was revised to become the Hawker Hind, which began to supplant Harts in front-line units from 1936. It is a measure of the extent of the RAF's expansion that no fewer than 528 Hinds, including trainers, had been built when production ceased in 1938. The Hind bomber differed from the Hart in having an uprated 640hp Rolls-Royce Kestrel V engine with flame-damping 'ram's-horn' exhaust stubs to aid night flying, the gunner's cockpit was revised and a tail-wheel replaced the Hart's simple skid as paved runways were now appearing on the traditional RAF grass airfields. The Hind, the last Hawker biplane for the RAF, served with twenty-two front-line Bomber Command squadrons and eleven Auxiliary Air Force squadrons, as well as numerous advanced flight-training schools into the first months of the Second World War.

The last Hart variant is the odd man out: the Hawker Hector. Although it was first flown in 1933 as a converted Hart (K 2434), the Hector, a replacement for the Audax in army co-operation squadrons, differed from all others of the Hart family in having a 24-cylinder Napier Dagger air-cooled engine of 805hp. This made the Hector the fastest Hart-based aircraft, with a maximum speed of 187mph and a service ceiling of 24,000ft. Hectors were easy to identify: the Dagger engine, being lighter than the

One of the many variants of the accommodating Hart airframe was the Hawker Osprey, a fighter-reconnaissance aircraft for service with the Royal Navy. K 3615 was the first of a batch of 39 Osprey IIIs delivered in 1934. It is being flown here by Hawker chief test pilot 'George' Bulman whose bald head was seen above the cockpit of many Hawker aircraft, including the Hurricane. K 3615 never served with the Royal Navy as it was delivered to the Marine Aircraft Experimental Establishment (MAEE), Felixstowe, where it was to remain. Ospreys differed from the Hart in that they had a stainless steel structure (to resist the ravages of salt water), folding wings and flotation gear, and could be rigged as seaplanes with floats replacing the wheeled undercarriage. The type served on all the pre-war Royal Navy carriers and, as seaplanes, were catapulted from cruisers at home and abroad, replacing aged Fairey IIIFs.

FACT FILE

HAWKER HART

Type
Two-seat light day bomber.

Builders
Hawker/Vickers/Armstrong Whitworth.

Power plant
(Typical) one 525hp V12 Rolls-Royce Kestrel IB.

Dimensions
Wing-span 37ft 3in
Length 29ft 4in.

Performance
Maximum speed 184mph
Service ceiling 21,320ft.

Armament
One 0.303in Vickers gun forward, one Lewis gun aft.

Bomb load
500lb

Number produced
Over 3,000.

Kestrel, required a straight top wing to compensate for the changed centre of gravity; all others in the family had a swept-back top wing (except the Fury biplane fighter, which was not a Hart variant although it was a Hawker design). All the 193 Hectors built came up from Somerset, from Westland at Yeovil. The type served well into the Second World War; Hectors of No. 63 Squadron dive-bombed German units attacking Calais, and dropped supplies for the troops defending the town. The Hector ended its service days late in 1942 towing training gliders for the nascent British airborne forces.

The Hawker Hart and the other aircraft of the Hawker family played a vital role in the RAF of the interwar years. Apart from their active service on Air Control overseas, at home these elegant biplanes, with highly polished cowlings, taut silver-doped fabric, adorned with the colourful squadron heraldry, were very much instrumental in consolidating Trenchard's young and initially insecure independent air force into an equal third service with the two older ones. To the crowds attending the annual RAF pageants at Hendon and Tern Hill, the squadrons of Hawker aircraft, by far the most numerous RAF machines for the 1930s, displaying impeccable 'wing drill' and formation aerobatics impressed all, public and air attachés alike, exhibiting as they did the highest standards of military flying. Many Hawker Harts were built for export to foreign air forces; at least one survives in a Swedish museum. Swedish and other exported Harts had a Bristol Pegasus radial engine and lacked the visual elegance of the RAF's classic Kestrel-powered aircraft.

The thousands of Hawkers are now sadly diminished: just two Harts and two Hinds are preserved in the UK. The RAF Museum at Hendon has a Hart (G-ABMR), believed to be the thirteenth airframe of the first production batch. Although it now carries RAF marks, it was never an RAF aircraft but civil registered. A G-ABMR was retained by the company as an engine test bed and photographic chase plane with the famous bald-headed Hawker test pilot 'George' Bulman in command. It survived the war years and was impeccably flown at postwar air displays piloted by a later, jet-age, Hawker test pilot, Duncan Simpson. Although a civil aircraft, G-ABMR displayed the RAF marks and the serial number J 9941, which indicated a Hart of No. 57 Squadron. Was this a tribute to the wide variety of roles the type played? It went, still airworthy, to the RAF Museum where it is permanently exhibited alongside a Hind. This machine, too, was never on RAF charge. In 1938, the Royal Afghan Air Force, impressed no doubt by the performance of RAF Hinds on Air Control, bought eight new Hinds from the makers. They flew, unbelievably, until the 1970s when two survivors were discovered in a Kabul hangar and brought to the UK. The Hind in the RAF Museum still carries its original Afghan markings; the second is airworthy and in the collection of the Shuttleworth Trust at Old Warden in Bedfordshire; it flies during the summer shows as K 5414 of No. 15 Squadron, RAF. It is ironic that, for a type which so dominated the RAF for a formative decade, neither the preserved Hart nor the Hind in the RAF Museum ever served with the RAF. There is, however, a third: K 4972, an ex-RAF Hart Trainer on static display at the Cosford Aerospace Museum, West Midlands.

By the outbreak of the war in September 1939, the Hawker Hart and Hind bombers had vanished from Bomber Command's front-line strength, to be 'struck off-charge' or converted to trainers. They had been replaced by new all-metal monoplane types: the Fairey Battle, Bristol Blenheim, Handley Page Hampden, Armstrong Whitworth Whitley and, the only RAF bomber to prove really effective in the early years of the war, the twin-engined Vickers Wellington designed by Barnes Wallis. This was always known simply as the Wimpy. The others, in official assessments, would turn out, one way or another, as disappointing – one bomber, the Fairey Battle, tragically so. All the 1939 generation of RAF bombers were designed for high-level bombing but the enemy, the German *Luftwaffe*, had a bomber in front-line service in 1939 that excelled at a very specialized form of attack, dive-bombing. It bore the chilling name Stuka and its place as a true 'classic aircraft' is secure. No warplane before or since has a reputation for terror even approaching that of this rather moderate aircraft as it ruthlessly spearheaded the German *Blitzkrieg* (lightning war), blasting a path for the German armoured divisions as they crushed all Allied opposition in 1940.

The name Stuka (the Junkers Ju 87) is derived from the German *STUrzKAmpfflugzeug* meaning literally 'diving warplane', also the German word for any dive-bomber. The Stuka has the dubious distinction of dropping the first bombs of the Second World War. In fact, bombs were dropped on a Polish target before any formal declaration of war.

The history of the Stuka is international. Design on the bomber began in 1933 by Hermann Pohlmann, the Junkers designer working at Dessau. Pohlmann was clearly an engineer rather than an artist, for the aircraft that emerged from his drawing-board is acknowledged as the most ugly, angular and evil-looking aircraft of the Second World War. Its cranked wing, great maw of radiator and long fixed undercarriage legs bestowed, either by accident or design, the appearance of some monstrous bird of prey with talons extended.

Secretly, in 1928, the German Junkers aviation company, forbidden by the terms of the Treaty of Versailles to build military aircraft, had used their Swedish subsidiary to design and build the Junkers K 47, a prototype dive-bomber in all but name. The bomber was a robust and workmanlike metal monoplane which was tested and awarded airworthiness certification by the Deutsche Versuchsanatalt fur Luftfahrt (DVL), the German research institution for aviation. In 1931, as the Germans' covert plans for the creation of the *Luftwaffe* were crystallizing, the former First World War German fighter ace and renowned aerobatic pilot, Ernst Udet, was in the United States, probably for other than purely sporting reasons, for Udet attended a demonstration of dive-bombing by the US Navy's Helldiver display team. Udet was impressed both by the team's Curtiss O2C biplane bombers and the very high degree of bombing accuracy the navy pilots achieved. On his return to Germany, Udet, soon to hold high rank in the *Luftwaffe*, became the champion of the tactical possibilities of dive-bombing. Two American Curtiss Hawk aircraft were bought and test-flown by Udet, and the Junkers company was contracted, still secretly, to pursue development work on a German dive-bomber development of the Swedish Junkers K 47. Work proceeded slowly because of restrictions imposed by conditions of strict secrecy. Thus it was not until 1935, with the Nazi party secure as the legal government of Germany, that the prototype Junkers Ju 87 Stuka was ready for flight-testing. The first prototype aircraft was powered by a 525hp V12 Rolls-Royce Kestrel V engine. It was revealed as an angular monoplane which, when first test-flown, still lacked the essential dive brakes that prevent a steeply diving bomber from exceeding its 'Vne': the 'never exceed velocity (speed)' of the airframe. The first Ju 87, lacking the essential dive brakes, exceeded its Vne when pulled out of a test-dive, flutter set in and the tail plane collapsed, the aircraft crashing to destruction.

The accident caused a delay in the programme and it was not until late in 1935 that the second and third prototypes were ready for testing, both with a revised tail assembly and hydraulic dive brakes that limited the maximum speed in a dive to under 375mph, considered to be the prudent 'Vne' by Pohlmann's stress office. The revised design included a change of engine; the Kestrel was replaced by a Junkers Jumo 210, 610hp inverted V12 engine. By the time the flight tests took place, the existence of the *Luftwaffe* had been publicly revealed, the Versailles Treaty repudiated and all pretence of secrecy dropped although, still being a private venture, the Ju 87 Stuka prototypes carried civil German registration marks. (The third prototype is known to have been D-UKYQ.) The testing and evaluation of the Ju 87s was conducted at Rechlin, the German military test centre near Berlin.

There were two other serious contenders for the contract to supply the rapidly expanding *Luftwaffe* with a dive-bomber: the Arado 81 and the Heinkel He 118. Unfortunately the He 118 crashed when being flown by Udet himself, due to his mismanagement of the variable-pitch propeller which actually parted from the engine. This disaster did not endear the machine to the influential Udet and perhaps explains, in part, why the Ju 87 became the aircraft chosen to equip six of the newly formed *Stukagruppen*.

The Ju 87 A-1 that was put into production was certainly ugly: it had a 'trousered' fixed undercarriage and cranked wing to allow a maximum load of a single 1,102lb bomb to be carried externally under the centre section of the fuselage. (When this load was carried the crew was restricted to the pilot.) With a bomb load of 550lb the normal crew of two, the pilot and the gunner/radio operator, sat back to back under a long glazed canopy, the pilot having a roomy cockpit and a single MG 17 7.9mm gun in the starboard wing, which fired clear of the propeller arc. The gunner had a single hand-trained MG 15 7.9mm gun firing to the rear, with a flexible mounting. Production Ju 87 A-1s were not fast: the maximum speed with a 550lb bomb was 183mph at 10,000ft, slightly slower than the contemporary RAF Hawker Hind biplane bomber. The Ju 87 had a service ceiling of nearly 23,000ft and a still-air range of 620 miles. The moderate performance of the bomber caused some doubts to be raised by senior officers of the *Luftwaffe* though Udet was still adamant that the accuracy of dive-bombing was cost-effective. He correctly claimed that a small number of well-piloted Ju 87s could knock out a tactical target on a single sortie, which could well require several sorties if attacked by high-level bombers. That question of cost-effectiveness swung the argument; Hermann Göring, now the head of the *Luftwaffe*, was discovering that creating the world's most powerful air force from zero was a costly undertaking in any currency.

It is important to understand that the German *Luftwaffe*, although an independent air force like the RAF, had from the outset been planned as an adjunct to the army on the ground. All the bomber types ordered or in service were tactical, long-range artillery; no four-engined strategic bombers were envisioned. Close support of a rapidly advancing army required bombing of great accuracy, if only to forestall unfortunate friendly-fire incidents. Uniquely, dive-bombing provided such accuracy. Bombing from a high level could never be as accurate. The high-level bomb aimer had to solve a number of conflicting parameters to set up his bomb-sight: airspeed, altitude, the heading of the aircraft and the wind speed and direction. All this information was subject to error. Once a free-fall bomb had been released its fall path towards the intended target was irreversible. Even if all the numbers fed into the sight had been correct, the falling bombs were still subject to wind shear and even the ballistic properties of the individual bombs – these can be significant when dropped from above 12,000ft. Level bombing, until the arrival of the first 'smart bombs' (i.e. radio-controlled) towards the end of the Second World War, was literally hit and miss. For example, to be certain of destroying a bridge across a river in a town, a number of high-level bombers would be required; their wayward bombs would flatten most of the built-up area around the target and still very possibly miss it. The higher the bombers flew, to avoid anti-aircraft fire and fighters, the lower the accuracy of the bombing. To be certain of hitting a small tactical target, such as a town bridge, dive-bombing was seen, correctly, to be the answer.

The pilot of a dive-bomber simply dived his aircraft straight at the target, usually employing his gun-sight for the purpose; the angle was very steep, nearly vertical (German dive-bombers had lines representing dive angles painted on the side of the canopy and all

the pilot had to do was align the selected line with the horizon). The dive brakes, as has been discussed, were deployed to avoid too high an airspeed which, apart from compromising the structure, would make accurate flying difficult, the controls becoming immovable because of aerodynamic forces. In effect, the dive-bomber was carrying the bomb down to the target, which the pilot kept in his sights all the time. At a given height, which could be as low as 800ft, the bomb was released to carry on to the target, the free fall being reduced to the minimum; a very high degree of bombing accuracy was then guaranteed. Of course, there was a downside: when diving towards a well-defended target the bomber would come under progressively heavier anti-aircraft fire, including even infantry weapons. A point would then be reached when the bomber, pulling up from the dive, presented a full plan view of the aircraft to the gunners. Dive-bombing was hazardous, though the number of bombers required was low because they were accurate.

The role originally envisaged for the Stuka by the German Staff was tactical bombing of targets in the rear echelons of the enemy: supply dumps, reinforcements, airfields and command centres. To explore these and other ideas, three Ju 87 A-1s were sent, in late 1936, to Spain to test-dive bombing techniques under fire as part of the German *Legion Condor* on the side of General Franco's Nationalists. The three dive-bombers were flown by a large number of crews on a rota basis so that as many pilots and gunners as possible could gain operational experience. The sorties were, in the main, intended to help the Nationalist drive to the Mediterranean coast from Catalonia. The targets were railways, major road crossings, bridges and shipping, mainly in the harbours of Valencia, Tarragona and Barcelona. Such was the success rate enjoyed, in the absence of effective fighter opposition, and without loss, that additional, improved Ju 87 B-1s were dispatched to the Condor Legion. The Ju 87 B-1 was the definitive Stuka of the glory days of 1940. It had a more powerful Junkers Jumo 211 engine of 1,100hp and a revised airframe, incorporating changes deemed necessary from the lessons learned over Spain. The cockpit canopy was redesigned, the tail unit enlarged, a second forward-firing MG 17 machine-gun in the port wing increased fire power and the bulky 'trousered' mainwheel housing was replaced by much neater streamlined wheel 'spats'. The bomb load, with a two-man crew, was increased as a consequence of the raised engine power to a single 1,000lb bomb under the fuselage, or a

One of the infamous Stuka dive-bombers that spearheaded the *Blitzkrieg* of 1940. The Stuka above is a rarity, a Junkers Ju 87R, the final 'R' standing for *Reichweite* ('range'). There were a small batch of these specialized bombers, which had long-range tanks including two 66-imperial-gallon drop tanks under each wing. The additional fuel capacity reduced the offensive load to a single 551 lb bomb. Ju 87Rs were used on Operation *Weserubung*, the invasion of Norway and Denmark in April 1940. The aircraft above was photographed in December 1940, landing on an airfield that could be Rechlin, the German equivalent of Farnborough. The aircraft in the background is a Dornier Do 17.

single 550lb bomb with four 110lb bombs under the wings. Thus armed, the maximum speed of the Ju 87 B-1 rose to 232mph at 13,000ft with a range of 370 miles.

Despite the success – or perhaps because of that success – there remained opposition in the senior ranks of the *Luftwaffe* to the technique of dive-bombing; a scepticism reinforced by an appalling incident in August 1939. A demonstration of dive-bombing was laid on at the training range at Neuhammeraid at a top Stuka unit, 1/St.G.76, to sway the doubters. Among the top brass invited were *Generalleutnant* von Richtofen and *Generalfeldmarschel* Hugo von Sperrl, who had commanded the German Condor Legion in Spain. The weather was poor but, keen to impress, the thirty Stukas had been briefed to dive from 12,000ft through broken cloud cover and pull out at 1,000ft to release practice smoke bombs. Between take-off and the arrival over the target, the cloud base had lowered and thirteen of the Stukas crashed into the ground with the loss of twenty-six aircrew. Despite the very public display of the reliance on the weather that dive-bombing clearly entailed, Ju 87 *Stukagruppen* were considered to be prepared for action.

On the eve of the outbreak of the war in September 1939, the *Luftwaffe* had an operational strength of no fewer than 335 Ju 87 B-1s deployed in nine *Stukagruppen*. At 0426 hours on 1 September 1939, three Stukas of 3/St.G.1, led by *Oberleutnant* Bruno Dilley, flew from Elbing to bomb a target on the approach to a vital bridge across the Vistula at Dirschu. The sortie was to destroy a building which was known to contain the detonators for Polish sappers to blow up the bridge on the outbreak of war and deny it to the invading German armies. The detonator building was destroyed by the Stukas at 0434 hours and the Second World War had begun – eleven minutes before Germany declared war on Poland.

The subsequent role of the Ju 87s in the defeat of the Poles has become legendary: some 300 operational Stukas were as foxes in a hen coop. The use of the dive-bombers was widespread – against shipping, railways, airfields and troops. It was against troops that the Stuka became the most dreaded weapon of the short campaign. The Stuka, due to the dive brakes and fixed undercarriage, emitted a high-pitched scream when it was diving steeply, and it was discovered that this had a profound psychological effect on troops already demoralized by artillery and bombing. The Germans added air-driven sirens, called Jericho trumpets, to some Ju 87s to increase the terrifying noise. The 'terror weapon' aspect of the Stuka was increased when 240 Stukas made almost unbroken attacks on the virtually undefended city of Warsaw. By the end of the Polish invasion, the Ju 87 Stuka was proved to have been the major weapon in the ruthless twenty-seven-day destruction of Poland. This destruction was the first, and to observers in the West, unbelievable application of *Blitzkrieg*.

It was to be the same story, though with tactics refined, as the German armies swept through the Low Countries, Belgium and finally, in May 1940, France. The brilliant integration of air power with fast panzer units was to overwhelm the defensively minded French who were secure, they imagined, behind the supposedly impregnable Maginot Line. This turned out to be nothing of the kind. The Stukas were used with devastating effect as artillery, directed by radio by the troops on the ground; seemingly endless waves of low-flying Stukas pounded targets, fortifications, artillery, even individual tanks, with precision and at times only yards ahead of German troops. The rugged aircraft were able to remain serviceable to fly up to seven sorties a day operating from makeshift strips. When not blasting a path for the speeding armour, Stukas flying at tree-top height machine-gunned the marching troops on the retreat and the streams of civilian refugees, causing panic and choking the roads, making it virtually impossible for troop reinforcements to arrive at the rapidly shifting fronts. The effect on the French and Allied troops was devastating; the screaming Stukas became the harbingers of the rapidly advancing panzer columns just behind the aircraft. Some troops stood and fought with great bravery, while elsewhere the panic spread contagiously; retreats became routs and led the British Expeditionary Force (BEF) to Dunkirk. The first of 340,000 British and Allied soldiers walked across the sands to the 'little ships' at Dunkirk on 26 May 1940. The war in France was lost and the French army capitulated on 22 June 1940. France had been defeated in just forty-three days.

The Battle of France had been a stunning victory for the proponents of *Blitzkrieg* and the Stukas had played a major role. The next major engagement, the Battle of Britain, was to be an assault from the air, a prelude to invasion. The opening attack, *Adlertag* (Eagle Day), was delayed by bad weather until 5 August 1940. It was not until 13 August that 280 Stuka bombers were included in the German Order of Battle, to attack, for the first time, targets in Britain. No doubt the Stuka crews were confident that the unbroken successes of their aircraft would continue over the British Isles as everywhere else. They were mistaken. For the first time the *Stukagruppen* pilots were intercepted by radar-directed fighters of the highest quality flown by determined RAF pilots who were aware that they were fighting for the very survival of their country. The inadequate defensive armament of the Stuka was starkly revealed; within six days forty-eight Stukas had been shot down by Spitfires and Hurricanes. On 16 August nine were lost when attacking Tangmere airfield; two days later sixteen Stukas were lost in raids on Thorney Island and Ford airfields. The loss rate was unsustainable; the Ju 87 Stuka, the bomber that had terrorized Europe and defined modern warfare, was withdrawn from the battle.

The Ju 87, though defeated over Britain in the summer of 1940, flew on other fronts; the Ju 87 B-1 gave way to the C and D subtypes which looked leaner, though had essentially the same predatory outline as the earlier bomber. A Ju 87-T was produced for service on board the projected German aircraft carrier *Graf Zeppelin*, the 'T' standing for *Trager*, the German word for carrier. A batch of Ju 87-Ts was produced; they differed from the B-1s in that they had the usual tail-hook arrester of carrier aircraft, and the wings' outer sections could be folded manually. The Ju 87-T was stressed for catapult launching, had flotation gear and provision for the undercarriage to be jettisoned in the event of a forced landing in the sea. The proposed carrier was never commissioned and the few Ju 87-Ts built were converted back to Ju 87 B-1 standards.

In 1942, on the Russian front where German air superiority obtained, Ju 87 G-1s appeared; they were anti-tank aircraft armed with two 37mm flak (anti-aircraft) guns mounted under the wings, and were very successful. *Oberleutnant* Hans Ulrich Rudel is credited with destroying no fewer than 519 Russian tanks with his Ju 87 G-1. He was to survive the war as well.

The Royal Navy was to experience attacks from Stukas during the desperate battles in the Mediterranean in 1941, as the British endeavoured to keep Malta supplied as a base from which to attack the German convoys supplying Rommel's *Afrika Korps*. As many as 150 Stukas of *Fliegerkorps X*, based at Cosimo and Catania in Sicily, were ordered to attack the convoys and if possible to sink a Royal Navy Fleet carrier. On 6 January 1941 a Malta-bound convoy passing through the Sicilian Narrows between Sicily and Cape Bon was reported by a German reconnaissance aircraft and the Stukas took off to intercept. Forty-three Ju 87s dived from 12,000ft; ten broke away to attack other ships in the convoy but thirty-three continued their near-vertical dive on the carrier HMS *Illustrious* just as she had turned into the wind to recover fighters which had been scrambled to intercept SM 79 Italian high-level bombers. On the carrier the crew watched fascinated as the Stukas, ignoring intense anti-aircraft fire put up from all the ships in the fleet, split into a clover formation displaying great airmanship. Watching from the bridge of his flagship, HMS *Warspite*, Admiral Cunningham was to write of the attack in *A Sailor's Odyssey*:

FACT FILE

JUNKERS
JU 87-B1 'STUKA'

Type
Two-seat dive-bomber.

Power plant
One 1,200hp Junkers Jumo
211 V12 liquid-cooled engine.

Dimensions
Wing-span 45ft 3in
Length 36ft 5in.

Performance
Maximum speed 238mph.

Armament
Two forward-firing 7.9mm
MG 17 guns in the wings
One 7.9mm MG 15 hand-
trained gun in the rear
cockpit.

Bomb load
One 1,102lb bomb, or one
550lb bomb and four 110lb
bombs.

Number produced
(all subtypes)
Over 5,000.

One was too fascinated in this new form of dive-bombing attack to be frightened, and there was no doubt that we were watching complete experts . . . we could not but admire the skill and the precision of it all. The attacks were pressed home at point blank range, and as they pulled out of their dives some [Stukas] were seen flying along the flight deck of the Illustrious *below the level of the funnel.*

Illustrious was directly hit by six bombs and suffered mining damage from three near misses. One 1,000lb bomb pierced several decks and started large fires below; five 500lb bombs hit the armoured flight-deck and aircraft lifts, and two exploded inside the hangar, setting fire to many aircraft. Within minutes the carrier was blazing from stem to stern. Incredibly, the armoured decks protected the machinery spaces and the vital aircraft fuel bunkers. *Illustrious* could still steam and was thus able to go on to the United States for repairs, remaining out of action for nearly a year.

By 1943, the Ju 87 was able to operate as a bomber only where the Germans had air superiority; this was a rapidly diminishing area, and the surviving Stukas were employed on second-line duties, such as glider towing. No one now knows exactly how many were produced but the figure is around 5,000. None remain airworthy and very few are in static exhibitions. The RAF Museum in North London has one Stuka, a Ju 87 D-5; it was discovered in Russia and its history is obscure. Viewed today, sixty years on, it is difficult for the casual visitor to the museum to understand how this ungainly aircraft could have altered the strategy of war and terrorized a continent.

The Fairey Swordfish, a biplane in the monoplane era, might not at first glance seem to be in the running for consideration as a classic aircraft. However, few military aircraft of the Second World War have earned the affection felt by the crews of this dated aeroplane. The Stringbag, as the Swordfish was universally known, was a naval torpedo bomber. A three-seat fabric-covered biplane powered by a single 690hp Bristol Pegasus air-cooled radial engine, its maximum speed of 139mph was exceeded by many contemporary RAF trainers. Yet this aircraft, obsolescent at the outbreak of the war, having seen off at least two intended replacements, was still in front-line service at the end of the war.

The Swordfish, like the Junkers Ju 87 Stuka, was to influence the nature of warfare, in this case war at sea. It launched the first carrier-borne torpedo attack during the Norwegian campaign of 1940, carried out the assault on the Italian fleet at Taranto and disabled the German battleship *Bismarck*, considered to be one of the most powerful naval units afloat. In 1940 a Swordfish sank the German U-boat *U-64*, the first of many to be destroyed by Swordfish which, at the war's end, had sunk a greater tonnage of enemy shipping than any other type of Allied aircraft.

The origin of the Swordfish goes back to 1933. Orders being few, the Fairey company produced, as a private venture, a three-seat torpedo-spotter-reconnaissance aircraft, T.S.R.1, a biplane powered by a Bristol Pegasus radial engine. The single example was test-flown in March 1933 from the company's grass, Great West aerodrome, now rather better known as Heathrow. After showing considerable promise during initial test-flying, in September 1934 the T.S.R.1 entered into a spin from which the well-known test pilot, Chris Staniland, found it impossible to recover; he was lucky to be able to parachute to safety but the aircraft was totally destroyed.

Despite this loss, the encouraging nature of the flying characteristics – spin recovery apart – was such that a second, replacement, aircraft was built, revised to meet a recently issued Air Ministry specification, S/15/33, which called for a multi-role naval aircraft. The T.S.R.2, which had a redesigned tail assembly and a longer fuselage, first flew in April

1934, with the Fairey test pilot Chris Staniland again at the controls. The company test-flying programme was successful and the prototype, carrying the service serial K 4190, was extensively evaluated by service test pilots at Martlesham Heath both as a land plane and, with floats replacing the land undercarriage, as a seaplane; the aircraft was catapulted from the battleship HMS *Repulse*. At the conclusion of the service trials the name Swordfish was bestowed on it and an initial order for three pre-production Swordfish, K 5660-1-2, was followed by an order for sixty-eight Swordfish Mk Is, the first emerging from the Fairey works at Hayes, Middlesex, in early 1936. The type began to replace obsolete Blackburn Baffins and Blackburn Sharks in the FAA, the Swordfish becoming the main torpedo-bomber embarked aboard Royal Navy carriers.

By the outbreak of the war in 1939, thirteen front-line FAA squadrons ashore and afloat were flying the type. Swordfish served on all British carriers, including the small escort and merchant aircraft carriers (MACs), which were merchant ships carrying a full cargo but with the superstructure removed to provide a short flight-deck. Carrier-borne Swordfish fought in the bitter Battle of the Atlantic from the first day of the war in Europe until the last; their excellent slow-flying ability and general crisp handling made them ideal for the task, as one wartime Swordfish pilot, Terence Horsley was to write in *Find, Fix and Strike*:

> *You could pull a Swordfish off the deck and put her in a climbing turn at 55 knots. It would manoeuvre in a vertical plane as easily as it would straight and level and even when diving from 10,000 feet her ASI never rose much above 200 knots. The controls were not frozen rigid by the force of the slipstream and it was possible to hold the dive within 200 feet of the water . . . The approach to the carrier deck could be made at a staggeringly low speed, yet response to the controls remained firm and insistent. Consider what such qualities meant on a dark night when the carrier deck was pitching the height of a house.*

This photograph was taken aboard the escort carrier HMS *Tracker* at the peak of the Battle of the Atlantic in 1943. The Swordfish II, HS 158, 'B' of No. 816 Fleet Air Arm Squadron, has just 'landed on' and the deck party are struggling to fold the 'Stringbag's' wings, while the Pegasus is ticking over; when the wings are secured the pilot will taxi the aircraft to the lift and be 'struck down' to the hangar below, guided by the deck officer who already has his signalling flags raised. This Swordfish has 'Yargi' radar antennas on the interplane struts for the 1½m air-to-surface vessel (ASV) search radar. The four visible rocket launching tubes are empty, suggesting that they were fired on an anti U-boat strike. The open, wet, windswept and freezing flight-deck of a typical escort carrier operating in that cruel sea, the North Atlantic, is portrayed well.

Production Swordfish Mks II and III, used in action during the war, were made by two companies: the Fairey Aviation Co. Ltd of Hayes and, from December 1940, all Swordfish production was by the Blackburn Aircraft Co. Ltd of Sherburn in Elmet, Yorkshire. The latter Swordfish were known in the navy as Blackfish; they were virtually identical to the Fairey-built machines. The 45ft 6in wings could be manually folded to a mere 17ft 3in when aboard a carrier. The engine was a single Bristol Pegasus 30 radial developing 750hp, maximum speed 138mph, with a 1,610lb torpedo slung externally between the fixed undercarriage legs. Its range was 546 miles on normal tanks but, for reconnaissance duties with extra tanks (236 gallons) in place of a third crewman, the range was increased to 1,030 miles – nine hours in open cockpits! Swordfish had a single .303in Vickers gun for the pilot and the TAG (Telegraphist/Airgunner) in the rear cockpit had a single .303in Lewis or Vickers gun on a flexible mounting.

It would be tedious to chronicle a detailed account of the wartime history of the Swordfish: the type served with no fewer than twenty-five FAA and two RAF front-line squadrons and a further twenty-three Fleet requirements units, on training and target-towing. However, two epic engagements have contributed to the almost legendary wartime reputation of the Stringbag: Taranto and the sinking of the *Bismarck* must be told.

The Battle of Taranto took place on the night of 11 November 1940; the victory is still celebrated in the Royal Navy by an annual Taranto Night dinner. It is rightly held to have been the turning-point in the history of naval warfare – the first time aircraft alone had crippled an enemy fleet, the fleet in question being that of the Italian Navy, a sizeable portion of which (six major battleships, together with cruisers and destroyers) was discovered by reconnaissance to be at anchor in the port of Taranto. In fact, Taranto was an attack waiting to happen; it had been seen as a profitable target in staff studies in 1938 just before the war. The Commander-in-Chief (C.-in-C.) Mediterranean had requested a feasibility study from the commander of the carrier HMS *Glorious* which had remained on file. When Italy declared war on the Allies in June 1940, the Taranto attack plans were dusted off and updated. It was decided that the attack could only be successful if it came as a surprise, which meant that it would have to be made under cover of darkness. Flying from carriers was never easy; at night it was considered

An 'air tail' fitted to a torpedo being loaded on to a Swordfish for the attack on Tarranto. The air tail flattened the angle at which the torpedo entered the water of the shallow Tarranto harbour; a standard torpedo could have dived into the mud and exploded prematurely. The success of this concept impressed the Japanese who copied the idea when attacking Pearl Harbor.

suicidal (the US Navy never trained for night-carrier operations during the Second World War). Intensive night-flying training took place to bring the Swordfish to a very high degree of efficiency. The nature of the Swordfish – and a strong undercarriage – must have made a very substantial contribution to the success of the venture.

The Royal Navy, being traditional, planned the attack for the anniversary of Trafalgar Day, 21 October, but it was delayed due to a hangar fire on the carrier that was to mount the operation, HMS *Illustrious*. The fire had damaged several Swordfish, which had to be replaced. The attack finally took place on 11 November 1940 when a three-quarters full moon became available. Twenty-one Swordfish from four FAA squadrons made up the attacking force. Nos. 815 and 819 embarked in *Illustrious*; Nos. 813 and 824 were from *Eagle* which had been damaged by bombing – her aircraft were therefore embarked in *Illustrious* for the attack. The initial strike force comprised twelve Swordfish led by the commanding officer of 815 Squadron, Lieutenant Commander Kenneth Williamson. Six Swordfish were armed with torpedoes with wooden 'air tails' fitted to allow them to enter the water at a shallow angle as the depth of water in Taranto harbour was restricted. The tails, really small winglets, were designed to break off as the torpedo entered the water. The torpedoes had magnetic and contact pistols and were set to run deep enough to detonate under the hulls of the warships, as it was known that anti-torpedo nets would be in place. Of the remaining six aircraft, four were armed with six 250lb armour-piercing (AP) bombs, and the remaining two carried bombs and parachute flares to illuminate the targets.

At 2030 hours, *Illustrious* turned into wind and the twelve Swordfish took off for Taranto, 170 miles away. Since it was considered very unlikely that enemy fighters would be encountered, the TAGs were left behind and long-range fuel tanks were carried in the rear cockpits along with the observer/navigators. A second wave of nine aircraft took off from *Illustrious* an hour after the first. At 2256 hours the first flares were dropped from 7,500ft exactly over the harbour. The flare-dropping Swordfish then dived and bombed an oil farm, and a large fire lit up the harbour. The second flare-carrying Swordfish in the first wave was piloted by Charles Lamb, who watched the Swordfish attack 5,000ft below:

> . . . *flying into the harbour only a few feet above sea level, so low that one or two of them actually touched the water with their wheels as they sped through the harbour entrance. Nine other spidery biplanes dropped out of the night sky, appearing in a crescendo of noise in vertical dives from the slow moving glitter of the yellow parachute flare.*

The second wave, led by Lieutenant J. W. Hale, comprised seven Swordfish and arrived to find the harbour well alight, 'like Piccadilly Circus' one pilot reported, with flares, fires and gunfire, and some of the ships were firing at each other in the confusion. The tactics of the first wave were repeated, and the ships and harbour installations were bombed. In all, two Swordfish were shot down, although two of the crew survived and were taken prisoner. All the remaining Swordfish had landed on *Illustrious* by 0250 hours.

Photo-reconnaissance revealed next day just how effective the raids had been. The battleship *Conte di Cavour* was sunk, the new Italian battleship *Littorio* had been hit by three torpedoes and would be out of action for a long time; three cruisers and a destroyer had been hit and were either beached or sunk in shallow water, and there was extensive damage to oil storage tanks and other harbour installations. It was a famous victory. In a little over an hour, with the loss of only two men and two aircraft, twenty Swordfish biplanes had shifted the balance of power in the Mediterranean, inflicting more damage on an enemy fleet than the entire Grand Fleet had achieved at Jutland in 1917 with over 6,000 men killed and the loss of fourteen ships of the Royal Navy. The Taranto raid was greatly admired in Japan; a detailed study of the raid was ordered for the Imperial Navy staff officers who were engaged in the planning of a similar surprise airborne attack on a naval base – Pearl Harbor . . .

On 24 May 1941, in the North Atlantic, the 41,700-ton German battleship *Bismarck* engaged, at a range of 15 miles, one of the Royal Navy's most powerful battleships, the 42,000-ton HMS *Hood*. After the opening salvoes from both ships' 15in guns, the German ship scored a direct hit. *Hood*'s magazines exploded and the British battleship disintegrated. Of the 1,419 crew, three survived. The weather in the North Atlantic was appalling; there were blizzards of snow and sleet, driving gale-force winds and mountainous seas. Visibility was down to just yards at times and only radar enabled the ships to keep in contact with the enemy. Then even that was lost; for some days it seemed that *Bismarck* had eluded the armada of British battleships, including the brand-new HMS *Prince of Wales* and the carrier HMS *Victorious*.

Swordfish, from 825 Squadron, took off from *Victorious* in weather that exceeded the prudent limits for flying with young pilots who had never yet seen action, for the squadron had only recently been formed. At least one of the Swordfish was equipped with air-to-surface-vessel (ASV) radar; contact was established and *Bismarck* was attacked with torpedoes. Two hits were made amidships, which merely shook the heavily armoured battleship, but damage had been caused to the massive hull. The effect made by these hits combined with the evasive manoeuvres at high speed to 'comb' the Swordfish torpedoes in heavy seas which had caused fuel bunker damage earlier in the gunfire action led to more serious damage with fuel oil leaking from the hull. To contain this problem, the German ship slowed to 18 knots. However, the weather closed in and once again *Bismarck* escaped. The Admiralty correctly considered that the German ship, damaged, would be heading for the safe harbour of Brest which was only 200 miles away. Confirmation came on 26 May when an RAF Coastal Command long-range reconnaissance Catalina radioed that she had sighted *Bismarck* and was shadowing her. Swordfish, from HMS *Ark Royal*, were ranged to attack the ship which, from the position given by the RAF aircraft, was 80 miles north-west of the carrier.

The resultant action is the stuff of fiction: a full gale swept green seas over the carrier's flight-deck as fifteen Swordfish were ranged and took off. Because of faulty intelligence the first ASV radar contact they attacked was the British cruiser HMS *Sheffield* which the aircrew did not know was in the area; it is said that an alert signaller on board used his lamp *en clair* to signal 'F*** off' and the pilots realized it was a British ship. That attack was without casualties and was fortunate in that the magnetic pistols fitted to the Swordfish torpedoes had fired prematurely as soon as the weapons hit the sea, due to the effect of the tremendous seas on the magnetic pistols.

The Swordfish returned to the carrier, were rearmed – with contact pistols in the torpedoes – and all fifteen took off again for the *Bismarck*. This time they found her. The ASV radar enabled the strike to be made in subflights from cloud cover although, because of the cloud, the flights became separated. Even so, in the face of intense gunfire from the German ship, at least two torpedo hits were seen. One torpedo had detonated under the ship's stern, jamming the rudder 20 degrees to port. *Bismarck* could now only steam in left-handed circles and, as the British fleet with two battleships and a carrier steamed into action with all hands determined to avenge the *Hood*, the German ship was clearly doomed. After disabling *Bismarck*, all fifteen Swordfish returned to *Ark Royal*. Most of the aircraft had been damaged in the attack and the carrier's flight-deck was measured as plunging up to 60ft, yet all of them landed. Deck-handling parties of forty men grabbed each aircraft as it slithered to a standstill, for the wind over the deck was sufficient to get a Swordfish airborne.

What had saved the Swordfish in the face of heavy, accurate anti-aircraft gunfire was their very slowness. German anti-aircraft guns had predictors that assumed that no attacking aircraft would ever be flying at less than 100mph, and that was the minimum setting. In the teeth of the 60-knot gale the Swordfish were making good, relative to the ship, about 70 knots. To the amazement of the British crews all the shells were bursting harmlessly, well ahead of them. Unable to shoot the Swordfish down, their torpedo attack was to prove fatal. *Bismarck*, unable to steer, was caught by the battleships HMS *Rodney* and HMS *King George V* and pounded by gunfire into a blazing hulk, then torpedoed at point-blank range by the cruiser *Dorsetshire* which signalled the commander-in-chief: 'I torpedoed *Bismarck* both sides . . . she had ceased firing but her colours still flew.' As *Bismarck*, with her crew dead or wounded and the hull red-hot up to the water-line, slowly rolled to port to sink into the North Atlantic, her gallant end also marked the end of the battleship as the principal ship of the fighting powers. That role had passed to the aircraft carrier.

In all, 2,391 Swordfish had been built when production ceased in December 1944. A number survive in museums and private hands. At least two are currently airworthy, both with the Royal Navy Historic Flight at Yeovilton in Somerset. These are Blackfish Swordfish Mk IIs: W 5856 and LS 326, which delight visitors to the summer airshows. The LS 326 has the distinction of being the last Swordfish ever to take off from a carrier. This event occurred on 13 November 1962, when the Swordfish had been placed aboard HMS *Hermes* alongside at Portsmouth, for the Taranto Night dinner. Lord Louis Mountbatten, the guest of honour, suggested that the Stringbag be flown off. The pilot was Lieutenant Commander John Wrayford, and I was in the TAG's cockpit handling not the Lewis gun, but a BBC film camera. The memorable flight took one hour and five minutes from the ship to Lee-on-the-Solent. It was a calm sunny day, even so, one wondered at the men who flew in these single-engined wire-braced biplanes with open cockpits, far from land over the North Atlantic in winter, searching hour after freezing hour for U-boats and then, with dwindling reserves of fuel and in fading light, finding their way back to their distant carrier.

The Avro Lancaster bomber is not just a classic, for many consider this four-engined British 'heavy' to be one of the great military aircraft of all time. Its origins, like so may wartime RAF machines, can be traced back to 1936, that landmark year when the politicians realized that the defences of the country were at an all-time low when compared with what was happening in Hitler's Germany. The RAF between the wars had neglected the heavy bomber. There were several valid reasons for this. For example, the funds grudgingly provided by the Treasury for the 'Air Estimates' were inadequate other than to maintain the remit of the RAF, which was primarily to defend the country from bomber attack and to provide aircraft suitable for policing the British Empire, that 'Empire beyond the Seas' on which the sun had yet to set. The result was some excellent fighters, such as the Hawker Fury of 1931 which was the first fighter anywhere to exceed 200mph in level flight, and the efficient light day bombers actively engaged in Air Control.

Bomber squadrons of the RAF therefore had lumbering biplane bombers of which the 108mph Vickers Virginia of the late 1920s was typical, and which was little more than a moderate development of the aircraft used at the close of the First World War. It was not until 1937 that the RAF got an all-metal monoplane bomber, the 155mph Fairey Hendon, and only fourteen of these were ever built. Part of the problem stemmed from the League of Nations, which was trying – in an era of general disarmament – to abolish all bombing. This was a laudable aim, which the Treasury supported, but unfortunately Germany was not a member of the League. When, by 1936, the RAF was allowed to expand, the Air Ministry

An Avro Manchester IA. This was officially acknowledged to be 'disappointing' – a masterly understatement. It was a flying disaster from the day it entered service with No. 207 Squadron in November 1940 to June 1942 when the type was withdrawn from Bomber Command's Order of Battle. There was nothing wrong with the airframe; the trouble lay with the two 1,760hp Rolls-Royce Vulture 24 cylinder 'X' engines, which suffered endless crankshaft and other failures, to the extent that when the airframe was revised by designer Roy Chadwick to be powered by four Rolls-Royce Merlins, the projected name 'Manchester III' was changed to 'Lancaster I' to avoid any connection with its ill-fated predecessor.

issued outline specifications for heavy bombers to supplement the medium bombers then being built. Under Specification B.12/36, contracts were issued to Shorts and Supermarine, and these resulted in the Short Stirling, Britain's first monoplane four-engined 'heavy'. The Supermarine prototype to Specification B.12/36, designed by R. J. Mitchell who had designed the Spitfire, was destroyed, unfinished, during an air raid on the Woolson factory in Southampton in 1940. By that time Mitchell had died and the project was abandoned. Avro and Handley Page had been asked to build twin-engined heavy bombers to a second specification. This was P.13/36, to be powered by two of the new 1,760hp Rolls-Royce Vulture engines. The Vulture, a complex 42-litre, 24-cylinder 'X' engine was one of the few that Rolls-Royce built which was to prove to be unsatisfactory, to say the least. Frederick Handley Page, the autocratic head of the company that bore his name, seemed to have foreseen this as he refused to use the Vulture, and the HP 56 (L 7244), soon to be named Halifax, was built around four proven V12 Rolls-Royce Merlins. The Avro company, however, bowed to Air Ministry pressure and used two Vultures to power the prototype Avro Type 679 Manchester heavy bomber (L 7246) which first flew in July 1939. With war imminent, the type was passed by the Air Ministry test pilots at Boscombe Down, in Wiltshire; the acceptance tests were something of a formality as the Manchester had been ordered 'off the drawing-board' and production of the first 200 was well under way.

The Manchester was designed by a gifted team under Roy Chadwick. It was an aerodynamically clean midwing monoplane with a 33ft long unobstructed bomb bay; the maximum speed was a very respectable 265mph at 17,000ft, with a range of 1,630 miles carrying an 8,100lb bomb load. The service ceiling was 19,200ft. The large aircraft had a 90ft wingspan, this being the maximum permissible due to the restricted width of the doors of the standard brick-built RAF hangars of the time. The defensive armament consisted of power-operated turrets in the nose, dorsal and rear positions; all the guns were .303in. Test pilots reported pleasant and vice-free flying characteristics and the aircraft was considered acceptable for operational use. The first production Manchester (L 7247) was delivered in May 1940. The first Bomber Command squadron to be equipped with the type was No. 207 based at Waddington, Lincolnshire who received their Manchesters in November 1940. The first operational sortie, a raid on Brest, was on the night of 24/25 February 1941. It was soon clear that the Manchester was to be dogged by endless failures, with more aircraft and crews being lost to that cause than to enemy action. The seven RAF squadrons so equipped continued to fly the Manchester but it had rapidly acquired a bad reputation and was very unpopular with the crews unfortunate enough to have to fly it.

Roy Chadwick knew that Rolls-Royce, which were responsible for the Vulture engines, was finding it hard to eliminate the faults that were only too apparent. The company was fully extended in developing the Merlin and Griffon engines, which were powering most of the fighters then in RAF service or projected. The Vulture was becoming a 'one-off' type powering only the Avro Manchester. The Hawker Tempest fighter, which was to have been Vulture-powered, had changed at the design stage to a Napier Sabre. It has, unkindly, been said that Rolls-Royce aero-engines were a triumph of engineering over design and that they therefore relied on detailed development to get the best out of them. Be that as it may, the Vulture engines of the Manchester had serious connecting rod and crankshaft troubles that were going to require a lot of time and development effort to rectify. This was something that Rolls-Royce simply could not afford.

Roy Chadwick's design team had, like Handley Page, been doubtful about the reliability of the Vultures and, even before production of the Manchester was under way, had a proposal on the drawing-boards for a Manchester II to be powered by either two Napier Sabres or two Bristol Centaurus engines; a third position was to revise the wings to accept four Rolls-Royce Merlin Xs like the Halifax. This latter proposition, known as the Manchester III, was the one adopted; a Manchester airframe (BT 308) was taken from the production line and a new centre section was built to accommodate the four Merlin engines. The modified aircraft was test-flown in January 1941, still called Manchester III. It was flown to Boscombe

A squadron of Lancaster heavy bombers at dusk stand on their Lincolnshire airfield, bombed up with crews on board awaiting the hour to 'start engines' and take off on a night raid against a target deep inside Germany. This was just one of the 156,000 sorties flown by Lancasters during the war years. The loss rate of the Lancaster was the lowest of the three RAF 'heavies', but the chances of crew members surviving a standard 30 operational 'tour' was only one in three. The average life of an operational Lancaster in the winter of 1944/45 was forty hours flying time.

Down and service test pilots of the A & AEE flew intensive acceptance trials. These were highly successful and BT 308, which had a top speed of just over 300mph, went to No. 44 Squadron for four-engine crew training. The Air Ministry altered the existing contracts to allow the remaining twin Vulture Manchester airframes to be completed as four Merlin-powered Manchester IIIs; however, it was considered desirable, in the light of the unpopularity of the Manchester, that the name be changed, so Manchester III became the Avro Type 683, Lancaster I. The first true production Lancaster was L 7527 and, as production got under way, evidence of the Manchester conversion vanished.

The Lancaster was a remarkable aircraft that required surprisingly little development throughout its wartime service. The long, 33ft bomb bay inherited from the Manchester, together with great structural strength, enabled the type to carry astonishing bomb loads – eventually including the Barnes Wallis 22,000lb 'Grand Slam' earthquake bomb, by far the heaviest bomb carried by any wartime bomber. To carry that bomb some modification to the bomb bay was required; that apart, about the only major change to the standard production airframe throughout the war years came about with the introduction of the Lancaster II, designed to be powered by four 1,750hp Bristol Hercules XVI air-cooled radial engines, as a precaution in the event of Rolls-Royce Merlins being in short supply due to enemy bombing. In fact, this never occurred and, because of the availability of American Packard-built Merlins, only 300 Lancaster IIs were built, flown mainly by Royal Canadian Air Force (RCAF) squadrons in the UK. Altogether 422 Lancasters were built in Canada; the pattern Lancaster I was flown across the Atlantic to Montreal.

Four Lancasters of No. 44 Squadron made the first Lancaster operational sortie when mines were laid off Heligoland, an island off Schleswig-Holstein, in March 1942. That first sortie was followed by 156,000 others. Soon Lancasters equipped fifty-nine Bomber Command squadrons in addition to Coastal Command and conversion-training units.

The Lancaster, despite its size, was a pilot's aeroplane; it was very light and responsive on the controls – at least one is known to have survived being looped – and it could safely take effective evasive action when attacked by fighters. If hit, it could sustain a lot of damage and still make it home – many Lancasters limped back on two engines. The normal crew was seven and consisted of the pilot, irrespective of rank (and many were sergeants), who was the 'skipper', the flight engineer, the navigator, the wireless operator, the rear gunner, the mid-upper gunner and the bomb aimer, who also operated the front guns. No co-pilot was carried and operational Lancasters did not even have dual controls. However, most prudent captains gave their flight engineers sufficient informal instruction to allow them to fly the aircraft 'straight and level' back to the UK to enable the crew to bale out should the pilot be incapacitated. Some flight engineers and other crew members actually did this; they probably had the aid of 'George', an efficient – up to a point – autopilot with which all Lancasters were fitted.

By 1944 all Bomber Command standard Lancasters carried H2S 10cm radar and the electronic navigational aid called Gee. Pathfinders were also fitted for blind bombing with the electronic aid, Oboe. Lancasters were equipped to take part in electronic counter-measures (ECM), and the weapons to fight the secret electronic war were played out in the night sky over Germany with whispered code-names: Tinsel, Perfectos, Monica, Corona, Jostle and Window. They were all designed to counter the enemy radar defences that vectored the deadly German night fighters on to the bombers. (There was a small number of a little-known Lancaster variant, the Mk VI, powered by Merlin 87 engines driving four-bladed propellers which, in 1944, with nose and dorsal gun turrets deleted, joined the bomber streams loaded not with bombs but with sophisticated radar-jamming equipment operated by the highly specialized crews from No. 635, ECM Squadron.)

The Avro Lancaster was the main night bomber of the Allied offensive against German industrial targets. The Stirling was late into production and, with a divided bomb bay, could only carry bombs of up to 4,000lb; its service ceiling was restricted to 17,000ft, well within the range of German flak. The early Halifax was underpowered and plagued with a complex rudder-stalling condition that caused many fatal accidents until it was rectified following a protracted investigation by the A & AEE at Boscombe Down. With revised fins and rudders the Halifax III became a successful partner to the Lancaster, although it remained overshadowed by the Avro aircraft. A 1943 RAF operational research analysis showed that 132 tons of bombs had been dropped for every Lancaster lost on operations; the figures for the Halifax were 56 tons and for the Stirling 41 tons. After the war, the wartime commander of RAF Bomber Command, Sir Arthur Harris, summed up the Lancaster at that time by saying:

The Lancaster far surpassed all the other types of heavy bomber. Not only could it take heavier bomb loads, not only was it easier to handle, and not only were there fewer accidents with this than other types, the casualty rate was also consistently below those of other types.

No fewer than nine VCs were awarded to RAF Lancaster crews during operations and it is difficult to single out individual sorties – there were so many that were epic. Whole books have been published on the subject. The 'dam-busting' raids and the sinking of the German battleship *Tirpitz* as she lay, supposedly out of bomber range, in Tromsø Fjord, by Lancasters from Nos. 9 and 617 Squadrons flying a thirteen-hour sortie, with each carrying a 12,000lb Tallboy armour-piercing (AP) bomb, are the best known.

The Lancaster was primarily a night bomber but one early raid, that required precise accuracy, was made in broad daylight. In April 1942, just a month after the type commenced operations, twelve Lancaster Is of Nos. 44 and 97 Squadrons were briefed to attack the M.A.N. factory at Augsburg, then the major manufacturer of the marine diesel engines for the U-boats that were then threatening to sever the convoy routes to and from America. The flight was to be made at low altitude to lessen radar detection and in late afternoon so that the return trip could take advantage of darkness. The distance was 500 miles, nearly all over German or German-occupied territory. The hope that low altitude would confuse German radar was soon proved misplaced. As soon as the French coast was crossed, at least twenty-five German fighters attacked. An incredible running battle began between relays of fighters and the bombers, and this continued for over an hour. The Lancasters flew so low that individual bombers could be seen lifting to clear chimneys, even trees, as the formation roared with engines flat out, throttles 'through the gate' to combat boost down to absolute minimum height and all gunners firing at the fighters, which were also flying, at times, below the rooftops. Four Lancasters were shot down on the way to the target; eight fought their way to it and bombed the M.A.N. factory, which was directly hit by seventeen bombs. The run-up to the factory was so low that crews reported that flak and fighter cannon-shells were ricocheting off the streets and squares of the town. Three more Lancasters, with their crews, went down over the target; the remaining five, all damaged, fought their way back to base. That incredible daylight raid, which even the Germans conceded had been 'precision bombing of the highest quality', had been led by a South African, Squadron Leader J. P. Nettleton, DFC, of No. 44 Squadron, who was awarded a VC. All the surviving crews were granted immediate DSOs, DFCs and DFMs. The loss rate had been 50 per cent of the attacking force. It was one of the first Lancaster operations and is considered to have been one of the finest.

For future night bombing, Lancasters were formed into the Pathfinder squadrons, which marked the targets with great precision using coloured flares. Lancasters flew on

FACT FILE

AVRO
LANCASTER MK I

Builders
A.V. Roe & Co. Ltd/
Armstrong Whitworth/
Austin/Metropolitan Vickers/
Vickers Armstrong.

Type
Heavy bomber; crew of seven.

Power plant
Four Rolls-Royce
1,460hp (V12 Merlin 20, 22),
or 1,640hp 24 engines.

Dimensions
Wing-span 102ft
Length 69ft 6in.

Performance
Maximum speed 287mph at
11,500ft
Cruising speed 210mph
Range, with 14,000lb of
bombs, 1,660 miles
Service ceiling 24,500ft.

Armament
Twin 0.303in guns in nose and
dorsal turrets; four 0.303in or
twin 0.5in guns in the tail turret.

Bomb load
One 22,000lb bomb or
14,000lb of a selection of
smaller high-explosive or
incendiary bombs.

Number produced
7,366

all the major RAF raids over Germany from 1942 to the end of the war and equipped the Coastal Command squadrons engaged on anti-U-boat patrols over the Atlantic. Bomber Command Lancasters ended the war bombing, in daylight, the VI and V2 rocket sites in France and Holland. As many as 7,374 Lancasters had been built when, in February 1946, the last one, TW 910 – still a Mk I – was delivered by Armstrong Whitworth. During the war years Lancasters of Bomber Command dropped 608,612 tons of bombs, 51,513,106 incendiaries and 12,733 mines on German targets.

The last RAF sortie of an operational Lancaster was made in February 1954 when RF 273 was flown back from Malta to be struck off charge and scrapped. A number of ex-RAF Lancasters flew after the war with the Egyptian, Swedish and Argentine air forces and the French naval air arm. Lancasters were also used postwar as flying test beds for early jet engines; a number were also used by Flight Re-fuelling as development aircraft and some were converted as makeshift, and hopelessly uneconomic, airliners called Lancastrians. Lancasters are preserved as static exhibits in Canada, Australia and the UK. The RAF Museum has R 5868, which served as aircraft 'PO-S' of No. 467 Squadron and is credited with having flown 137 operations over Germany, the second highest total, though at least eleven 'Lancs' exceeded (against all the odds) over 100 operations. The RAF still maintains one airworthy Lancaster, PA 474, which flies in the summer months with the Hurricanes and Spitfires of the Battle of Britain Memorial Flight from RAF Coningsby in Lincolnshire. The Coningsby Battle of Britain Flight hangar is open to the public on selected days.

To a generation far removed from the killing fields of the Second World War, the bombing of Germany by Lancasters and other Allied aircraft may now seem barbaric and indefensible. All war is intrinsically barbaric. When viewed by later generations, secure in a continent at peace, wars can be perceived to demean both the victor and the vanquished. But to the young men who flew the bombers in the 1940s it was a war against a manifestly evil tyranny; it should not be forgotten that 47,268 aircrew of RAF Bomber Command alone, all volunteers and all young, died fighting what they believed to be a just war. The preserved Lancasters are their memorial.

The 'wireless op' in his cramped crew position just behind the navigator, both men on the port side of the bomber. The standard radio of British-built Lancasters was the HF 1154/55 transmitter and receiver. The set was used for wireless telegraphy (W/T, or Morse code); however, many operators went through an entire tour without touching that Morse key on the right of the table, due to strict radio silence.

The Boeing B-29 Superfortress was the ultimate heavy bomber of the Second World War, if only because B-29s dropped the atomic bombs on Hiroshima and Nagasaki, ending the war in the Pacific and ushering in the atomic age. When that war began, with the Japanese surprise attack on Pearl Harbor, Admiral Yamamoto, commander-in-chief of the Imperial Navy, simply said to the war cabinet: 'You have woken a sleeping giant.' He knew that, once in the war, the United States had production resources that no other nation could begin to challenge. The Boeing B-29s illustrate the point to perfection; the largest bomber of the war, and the one which would compel the Japanese to surrender, was designed, built and in operational service in substantial numbers in just four years. In comparison, the Lancaster and the Halifax, smaller aircraft, took six years from drawing-board to squadron service – although, of course, British factories were subject to the strictly enforced blackout and air raids which did not affect American aircraft plants. That said, 4,221 B-29s were built, each one containing sufficient material and man-hours to manufacture eleven P 51 Mustangs – a remarkable achievement.

The history of the B-29 began in 1938, when the Boeing company of Seattle was asked to submit proposals for a pressurized version of the Boeing B-17 Flying Fortress then in production, to maximize that aircraft's existing unpressurized high-altitude capabilities. The design study submitted was of a tricycle undercarriage bomber powered by four R-2180 Pratt and Whitney radial engines with an estimated maximum speed of 307mph at 25,000ft carrying a 10,000lb bomb load. It was rejected by the United States Army Air Corps on the grounds that funds to build a prototype would have to come from money committed to the existing B-17 programme. There followed a series of proposals for a high-altitude pressurized bomber, including one powered by four Allison V12 liquid-cooled engines. This was ruled out due to the poor high-altitude performance of the Allison engines. There were four or five more Boeing proposals for what was becoming known as the 'hemisphere defence' concept; there was an appreciation that the growing strength of the *Luftwaffe* and the bellicose position adopted by Nazi Germany could, in the not-too-distant future, result in a long-range bomber threat to the eastern seaboard of the United States – New York being a likely target.

The preserved Lancaster PA 474, stationed at Coningsby as part of the RAF's Battle of Britain Memorial Flight, flies regularly during the summer months. It is fitted internally as a wartime Lancaster with the period radio and radar equipment, though modern flying conditions require up-to-date VHF radios in addition. Unlike the wartime Lancasters, PA 474 has dual control: it is too valuable to risk with just one pilot! The Lincoln tail fins are the only clue that would differentiate this Lancaster from a wartime bomber – that, and the immaculate paintwork.

The several private-venture designs made by Boeing were tending to veer away from the original remit; an improved, pressurized version was the B-17 Fortress, moving towards the completely original Superfortress. This was a consequence of original Boeing research into a new high-lift, aerofoil high-aspect-ratio wing which, at a projected span of 124ft, would make the idea of a bomber with an estimated speed of an incredible 405mph at 25,000ft practical when powered by four 2,000hp Pratt & Whitney radial R-2800 engines. The range was estimated at 7,000 miles with a ton of bombs. The proposal was designated Boeing Model 341. A Model 341 brochure was probably circulated to the War Department. In November 1939, the European war now having started, General 'Hap' Arnold requested the War Department to issue a specification calling for a 'superbomber' eventually to replace the Boeing B-17 Fortress and the Consolidated B-24 Liberator bombers then in service. The specification, Data R-40B, was issued to selected manufacturers in December 1939 and called for a true 'superbomber': speed at 400mph, plus a range of 5,000 miles with a minimum bomb load of 2,000lb. As a consequence of confidential combat reports from US air attachés in Europe, features new to the Americans, such as self-sealing fuel tanks and upgraded defensive armament, were added to the remit.

Two prototypes were built to Data R-40B and both flew; these were the Consolidated XB-32 and the Boeing XB-29. In the event, the XB-32, the first to fly in September 1942, encountered serious problems; these took a long time to solve and few were completely solved by the end of the war. The War Department had to take a gamble with the Boeing B-29 proposal and order the aircraft into large-scale production 'from the drawing-board' before the prototype was even built, much less test-flown. There was no alternative: even if all had gone perfectly, B-29s were not to be operational until 1944 at the earliest.

The prototype XB-29 made its maiden flight from Boeing Field, Seattle, on 21 September 1942 with the Boeing chief test pilot Edward Allen in command. The flight was uneventful, but on a test flight in February 1942 the second prototype XB-29 had a serious engine fire and crashed into a factory building while trying to land at Seattle, killing the eleven-man crew, including test pilot Allen, and twenty Boeing workers on

The flight-deck of a Boeing B-17G Flying Fortress No. 42-97213. Like wartime RAF aircraft, Boeing adopted a version of the 'basic six' blind-flying panel set between the two pilots. The command pilot sat on the left and the co-pilot on the right where the engine instruments were placed. The central pedestal has the four-engine throttle and mixture controls. The propeller pitch levers are just below the throttles. Although out of shot, the roof of the flight-deck had radio and other electrical controls; the magnetic compass can just be seen at the top centre of the photograph. The B-17 seen here is 'factory fresh', and the pristine condition of the paintwork did not survive long once the bomber was issued to an operational station.

the ground. This appalling accident caused a set-back to the B-29 programme. However, it did not stop it and the third XB-29 prototype, bearing the service tail number 41-18335, with revised engine fire precautions and with all the acquired experience gained from the testing to date, began flight-testing in June 1943. While being flown by service test pilots, the third XB-29 also crashed but by that time flight-testing and experience of operational B-17s flying in Europe had enabled definite armament and performance requirements to be finalized on the production B-29s.

Seven pre-production YB-29s were delivered to the US Army Air Force (USAAF) by July 1943 and, as they were representative of future B-29s, these operational aircraft were to train what were then known as 'very long-range' (VLR) units. Production lines for the B-29 were at Seattle, Wichita, Renton and Marietta, the firms involved in the gigantic task of production of the massive bombers being a consortium of the Boeing, Martin and Bell aircraft companies. There were delays caused by doubts about the nature of the defensive armaments as the air war in Europe grew more intense but by the end of 1943 the B-29 was in full production. A B-29 Superfortress wing, comprising five heavy bombardment groups, was formed at Salina, Kansas (conveniently near to the Boeing Wichita factory). It had been decided in Washington that the original plan to base the B-29s in England with their Eighth Air Force should be abandoned and the type was to operate against Japan where its great range would make it a formidable proposition. The production B-29 had emerged as a very clean nose-wheel mid-wing bomber with a wing-span of 141ft and, typically, four Wright Cyclone R-3350-23 radial engines with G.E. Electric turbo-superchargers offering 2,200hp for take-off and a combat emergency rating of 2,300hp at 23,000ft. The maximum speed was 357mph at 30,000ft and it could cruise continuously with a full bomb load at 342mph, also at 30,000ft. The range, with a 10,000lb bomb load was a staggering 3,250 miles and the service ceiling was 35,000ft. (Interestingly, the maximum B-29 bomb load permitted was 20,000lb, 2,000lb less than the 'Grand Slam' that the Lancaster could carry).

The defensive armament of the B-29 was formidable. There were twelve .5in machine-guns, each with 1,000 rounds in four remotely controlled turrets – the fore and aft dorsal and fore and aft ventral – with, in addition, a 20mm cannon in the tail. The guns were laid and sighted by gunners in astrodomes, using optical integrated sights. The aircraft was fully pressurized fore and aft except for the bomb bay; to

A Boeing B-17G. The tail number, 42-97246, reveals that this aircraft was ordered from Boeing in the fiscal year 1942. By the time the aircraft entered service, the USAAF had abandoned the use of drag-producing camouflage paint and all new aircraft were unpainted as shown. As this B-17 carries no unit markings it must be on a factory test flight over Seattle in the United States. The -G Fortresses had heavier armament than the earlier subtypes, including the characteristic 'chin' turret of twin .50in guns to deter the head-on attacks that *Luftwaffe* fighter pilots were employing in Europe. The B-17G was the final development to see action and the subtype numbered 8,680 machines, out of the total of 12,761 B-17s produced by the Boeing, Douglas and Vega companies. About 47 B-17s survive worldwide in museums and collections, though only a fraction remain airworthy.

enable the crew to pass from one end to the other a small tunnel with a one-man trolley passed over the bomb bay, thus allowing communication.

The first operational B-29 was flown to England in March 1944 for a short tour of Eighth USAF bases as a ruse to lull the Japanese into thinking that the original intent to deploy the B-29 against Germany was about to be implemented. In fact B-29s began to arrive at Kwanghan, China, via the main base at Calcutta, India, from April 1944 and the build-up followed, though delayed by accidents to aircraft on ferry flights from the United States. Of the first 150 dispatched, five had crashed from engine failure and another four had suffered serious damage. The first operational mission of the B-29 was made on 5 June 1944 when nearly 100 Superfortresses of the 58th Bombardment Wing, flying from bases in India, attacked railway workshops in Bangkok. Five B-29s were lost. Operational use against Japan became possible in July with the capture by US marines of Tinian, Guam and Saipan in the Mariana Islands. The Americans built five huge airfields on the islands in record time for their newly formed 20th Air Force. Each of the five bases could accommodate a wing of 180 B-29s and the extensive fuel, bomb stores and the 12,000-man echelons required to defend, service and maintain the aircraft. Even records take time; it was not until 24 November 1944 that the first B-29 raid on Japan was possible. On that day eighty-eight Superfortresses took off and bombed Tokyo. The weather was bad and the results moderate. The raid had been made as a copy of daylight precision attacks on German targets being made daily by the US Eighth Air Force in Europe. In the Pacific theatre of war, the very long distances and the need to make long continuous climbs at near maximum gross weight with heavy bomb loads was exposing what was to prove to be the Achilles heel of the B-29: it was proving to be underpowered at high altitude and the engines, worked to the limit, were failing.

A Boeing B-29 bomber of the type which dropped the two atomic bombs over Japan in 1945 to end the war in the Pacific. This aircraft was photographed after the war at RAF Scampton where the USAF 77th Bomber Squadron was stationed in September 1948. The bomber was about to take part in an exercise with the RAF as a consequence of the threat of the newly developing Cold War with Russia.

Major General Curtiss LeMay, the commander of the Marianas-based wings, decided to try a different tactic against the flimsy, predominantly wooden, Japanese cities, switching from bombs to incendiary attacks. Incendiary bombs are far lighter than high-explosive iron bombs, so many more could be dropped from a lower altitude, easing the B-29 engine problems. Furthermore, since precision bombing was no longer required, the area bombing with incendiaries could be made at night with a reduced risk of attacks from anti-aircraft guns and fighters, it being known that the Japanese had practically no night defence organization on German or British lines. The first B-29 night fire attack, made on 9 March 1944, proved LeMay correct: 334 Superfortresses, each carrying 8 tons of M69 incendiary bombs fused to burst at 2,000ft, releasing thirty-eight separate incendiaries, burned out 16sq miles of Tokyo and burned to death an estimated 80,000 of the inhabitants. Four other major cities, including Nagoya and Yokohama, and oil refineries were also burned out. The Japanese mainland was now virtually defenceless as few, if any, fighters could intercept the high-flying B-29. As a consequence of this immunity, most of the drag-producing guns and their heavy ammunition were removed, enabling the Superfortresses to carry more incendiary bombs at a speed increased by 10mph to 367mph at 30,000ft, out of anti-aircraft range and making fighter interception all but impossible. There was a 1.9 per cent loss rate but most of the B-29 losses were due to flying accidents and forced landings because of engine failure rather than direct enemy intervention. Up to 600 B-29s bombed and burned Japan every day. In addition, B-29s laid 12,000 mines, which accounted for some 800,000 tons of Japanese shipping. The night incendiary attacks continued with Pathfinder B-29s dropping napalm-filled bombs to start the fires, with the main force dropping oil-filled incendiaries at the rate of 8,000 per square mile.

It was hoped that under this relentless day and night bombardment the Japanese would sue for peace. They did no such thing. It seemed depressingly clear that a major land and sea campaign would have to be fought yard by yard against the most fanatical soldiers in the world, with the prospect that US and Allied casualty lists would approach a million men. As we now know, this did not occur.

On 8 August 1944 a Martin, Omah-built B-29, 44-86293, one of fifteen special B-29s of the top-secret 313th Wing based on Tinian, was bombed up by a single 9,700lb bomb code-named Little Boy. The B-29, named *Enola Gay* after the pilot's mother, was to be piloted by Lieutenant Colonel Paul Tibbets USAF, who had flown B-17s with the 97th Bomber Group based in England in 1942. Alone among the B-29 crew, Tibbets had been fully briefed about the atomic bomb by a US Navy scientist, Captain William Parsons, who would be flying with him on the mission and who would arm the bomb. When told this, Tibbets had said to him: 'Good, if anything goes wrong, Captain, I can blame you.' Parsons replied: 'If anything goes wrong, Colonel, neither of us will be around to be blamed.' Seven B-29s of the 313th Wing were to fly on the mission with a reserve aircraft; three were on weather reconnaissance and two were special observation aircraft, known as Superdumbos, carrying recording equipment and scientists. The two observation B-29s were *The Great Artiste* and *Necessary Evil.* Tibbets had a hand-picked crew, two of whom had flown with him in B-17s in Europe. They were navigator Captain Red 'Dutch' Kirk and the bombardier Major Tom Ferebee; they would fly in the same crew stations aboard Tibbets' B-29. The targets list for the mission was in order of preference: Hiroshima, Kokura, Niigata and Nagasaki. The list was required because a clear sight of the target was essential.

Enola Gay took off from Tinian at 0245 hours on 6 August 1945. As the B-29 approached the 'IP' (the initial point from which the bomb run commences, with the bombardier flying the B-29 through his bomb-sight integrated with the auto-pilot) weather aircraft radioed the target to be clear. Captain Parsons, the navy scientific observer, then armed the bomb. At 0915 hours the B-29's ground speed was 324mph as Major Ferebee, the bombardier, released Little Boy at 31,600ft. The bomb detonated forty-three seconds later at 800ft above ground zero and Hiroshima and 70,000 inhabitants ceased to exist. The atomic age had dawned. The Japanese military government still did not sue for peace so, on the 9 August, a second B-29, *Bockscar*, piloted not by the usual commander, Captain Frederick Bock, but by Major Charles W. Sweeney, carried the second and sole remaining US atomic bomb, Fat Man, a plutonium device. Unlike the first atomic bomb, Fat Man had to be armed on the ground and carried 'live' to the intended target, the city of Kokura. That target was obscured by smoke and haze and, running short of fuel, Major Sweeney decided to attack the alternative target, Nagasaki, thereby killing 35,000 people. Five days later, after 804 B-29s had bombed other Japanese targets with conventional bombs, the Japanese surrendered. The Second World War was over.

During the war in the Pacific, B-29 Superfortresses alone dropped 171,060 tons of chemical bombs and the two atomic bombs over Japan. With the end of the war, 462 Superfortresses flew over the USS *Missouri* in Tokyo Bay as the surrender formalities were completed aboard the battleship on 2 September 1945. After the war this force was run down and contracts for 5,092 B-29s were cancelled, though many B-29s were stored 'cocooned' for possible future use in the Cold War. In all, 4,221 B-29s had been delivered when production – to be strictly accurate, all American production – ceased in May 1946. However, during the attacks on Japan, three B-29s, short of fuel, were forced to land near Vladivostok in Russia. The Russians repatriated the crews but kept the B-29s

---

FACT FILE

BOEING B-29 SUPERFORTRESS

Type
Long-range heavy bomber; normal crew of ten.

Power plants
Four 2,800 Wright Cyclone R-3350-23 18-cylinder air-cooled radial engines, each with G.E. Electric turbo-superchargers.

Dimensions
Wing-span 141ft 3in
Length 99ft
Height 27ft 9in.

Performance
Maximum speed 357mph
Range with 10,000lb bomb load was 3,250 miles.

Armament
Twelve 0.5in machine-guns in remotely-controlled turrets
One 20mm cannon in the tail.

Bomb load
Typically 10,000lb
Maximum 22,000lb.

Number produced
4,221

The crew of the B-29 *Enola Gay*, the bomber that dropped the atomic bomb on Hiroshima on 6 August 1945: day one of the nuclear age. The captain of the bomber, Colonel Paul Tibbets, is standing at the centre of the group smoking a pipe in this photograph taken at the 313th Wing's base on Tinian in the Marianas, possibly before the bomb had been dropped as all markings were removed from the aircraft taking part on the atomic missions. The other men are unidentified and three seem to be missing as the normal crew of a B-29 numbered ten. *Enola Gay*, B-29 No. 44-86293, is believed to be preserved in storage in the United States.

and copied them almost to the last nut and bolt as the Tupolev Tu-4 bomber and the Tu-70 transporter aircraft, which served the Russian air force from 1947 until the jet age.

USAF B-29s were based in England at Alconbury, Cambridgeshire as part of the West's deterrent posture during the early days of the Cold War. In July 1950 the RAF, pending the delivery of the 'V' jet bombers, were loaned 87 B-29s which, in British service, were named 'Washington'; they equipped No. 149 Squadron at Marham, Lincolnshire. One RAF pilot flying on an exchange posting with a B-29 squadron was surprised when, after an engine fire had been extinguished in the air, the crew seemed totally unbothered. The crew chief drawled by way of explanation: 'That's the ole B-29 – two a turnin', two a burnin'.' The B-29's engine problems were never fully sorted out.

There is an airworthy B-29, *FiFi*, flying with the Confederate Air Force in Texas. *Bockscar* is on exhibition at the USAF museum at Dayton, Ohio, as are replicas of both Little Boy and Fat Man. The *Enola Gay* is believed to be held in store. There are several other static B-29s in the United States. One other B-29 almost became airworthy: that was *Kee-Bird*, which had been forced to land on the ice 200 miles from Thule in Greenland in 1947. It stayed in that desolate spot preserved by the subzero temperatures and the absence of any people to loot or disturb the aircraft. In 1995, after forty-eight years, a group restored the B-29 out on the ice, replacing engines, propellers and systems. However, during a taxi trial before taking off for Thule a small petrol auxiliary power unit (APU) used to start the engines was left running; vibration fractured a fuel line and started a fire which could not be extinguished. Sadly, the whole aircraft went up in flames and was totally destroyed. Fortunately no one was hurt. It was a symbolic end to the piston-engined bomber which, within a generation, had created total war – the destroyer of worlds . . .

To counter the threat of the bomber, the industrial resources of the fighting powers were stretched to produce the fighters, reconnaissance and the other military aircraft described in the following chapters. The knowledge gained from the imperative of war eventually led to the development of present-day airliners, now taken so much for granted.

CHAPTER TWO

THE RISE OF THE FIGHTER

There's a dogfight going on up there; there are four, five, six machines. . .
BBC radio broadcast, 1940

ON 14 JULY 1940, Charles Gardner, a BBC radio reporter, broadcast a 'running commentary' of an air battle he was witnessing over Dover. The battle that Gardner described so vividly was the prelude to the Battle of Britain. The style of the broadcast – preserved in the BBC sound archives – was very much that of a sporting event:

> *. . . Oh boy! I've never seen anything as good as this. The RAF fighters have really got these boys taped. Oh boy! Look at them going; look how the Messerschmitts run . . . Oh! This is really grand and there's a Spitfire just behind the first two. He'll get them . . .*

The broadcast produced a flurry of letters. *The Times*, for example, printed one from a retired major-general who considered the BBC broadcast to have been 'revolting to all decent citizens'. Other correspondents complained that Gardner had treated the battle 'with human lives at stake as if it was a sporting event'. These correspondents were, however, in a minority. In the UK the popular press had always perceived RAF fighters as glamorous heroes from the moment they became aware of their existence. This perception began in the First World War when the press discovered that there was no glamour in trench warfare. Pictures of heroes covered in mud did not excite the public, nor did the immaculately accoutred generals on their well collected horses. British war correspondents, severely inhibited by order of the War Office, but goaded by their editors to find newsworthy icons, discovered (one might say created) the young 'aces' of the Royal Flying Corps. The gladiatorial fighter-to-fighter combat, the dog-fights and the 'score' (the number of enemy aircraft shot down) achieved by the successful pilots caught the public imagination during both the First and the Second World Wars. In the summer of 1940 it was the pilots and the aircraft they flew – Spitfires versus Messerschmitts – which gained the headlines and were the subject of BBC broadcasts, rather than the unfashionable Hurricanes. These largely attacked the bombers and, in fact, shot down more enemy aircraft than all the other defences, Spitfires included, put together.

The definitive fighter aircraft and the fighter pilot evolved in 1915 during the First World War. The role of the aircraft, when war began in 1914, was minor and was confined to reconnaissance by slow aircraft with an observer detailed to either report or to photo-

Gone for ever are the silk scarves and leather helmet. Today's fighter pilot needs clothing as specialized as a medieval knight.

graph (with massive plate cameras) enemy troop concentration and artillery emplacements. A few British aircraft carried heavy – 80lb – wireless telegraphy sets with the operators reporting the 'fall of shot' for the artillery. They were a nuisance rather than a menace to the enemy ground commanders who could do little to stop the flights; anti-aircraft artillery ('Archie' to the British airmen) was ineffective. If two opposing aircraft met, the pilots or observers might, for form's sake, take pot-shots at each other with their officer-issued side arms. The British pilots, typically, had .455in Mk VI Webley revolvers; the Germans could be armed with a 9mm Mauser Pistole 08. If so, a German pilot held a slight advantage; he had eight rounds against the British pilot's six. In fact, apart from a few holes in the fabric, it was rare for serious damage to be inflicted, though a lucky shot might hit the pilot or the vulnerable fuel tank. It was more likely, in the early days, for the pilots to wave at each other and go about their way. In 1915, when the Germans were still advancing into France and Belgium and threatening Paris, reconnaissance aircraft began to compromise the essential secrecy of large-scale infantry attack and counter-attack.

It was clear from the informal air-to-air handgun shooting that, to be able to inflict telling damage against the fleeting targets the two aircraft presented to each other, machine-guns, rather than pistols, were a necessity. The obvious ideal was a forward-firing machine-gun fixed to the fuselage of the aircraft so that it became, in effect, a flying gun. To achieve that ideal, there were two seemingly insuperable problems to overcome. The only available weapons were infantry machine-guns, of which the .303in belt-fed British Vickers was typical; these heavy guns were lightened by fretting away the water-cooling jacket to make the weapon air-cooled, but they had to be hand-cocked and were also subject to several stoppages due to defective ammunition which the pilot had to clear. This required the breech of the gun to be within the cockpit or at least within reach – after all, the pilot had to continue to fly the aircraft. The ideal position for the sighting, firing and clearing stoppages was to mount the gun fore-aft of the aircraft on the pilot's eye-line and with the breech within the cockpit. However there was a local difficulty: the propeller. Some pilots, notably Major George Hawker, had success with a Vickers gun mounted on a bracket to the left of his cockpit – known as a Strange mounting – arranged to fire at an angle that cleared the propeller arc of his Bristol Scout (Scout was the generic name for a fighter aircraft at the time), but this called for very difficult deflection shooting at which Hawker was a master. He was awarded the VC in July 1915 for shooting down three enemy aircraft in a single day.

It was the French aircraft designer, Raymond Saulnier, who had a brilliantly simple, though interim, solution. Saulnier was a friend of a noted French military pilot, Roland Garros, to whom he revealed his idea of mounting a machine-gun on the cowling of one of his Morane-Saulnier monoplanes, directly in front of the pilot, the gun firing straight ahead through the propeller arc, with the wooden blades protected by bolting on to them two steel deflector plates that had deep grooves to bounce off the small percentage off the bullets which struck the propeller. Garros duly bolted an infantry, air-cooled Hotchkiss machine-gun, which had 25-round magazines, on to his Morane. Thus armed, he took off early on 1 April 1915 and headed for the German front line. The date is worth noting because it was to define the arrival of the dedicated fighter aircraft, as opposed to armed reconnaissance machines.

Garros shortly sighted a German reconnaissance Albatros flying above him; he climbed hard and got the enemy aircraft in the sights of his machine-gun simply by flying his Morane straight at the unsuspecting German. Garros emptied the 25-round magazine in a long burst without visible effect; another magazine was rammed into the Hotchkiss. After the first few rounds, as Garros reported, 'An immense flame erupted

Roland Garros, standing in the cockpit of his Morane-Saulnier; a photograph probably taken on his return after a successful sortie in April 1914.

A Morane-Saulnier of the type flown by Roland Garros, the first aircraft with a machine-gun able to fire through the propeller arc, thus becoming a flying gun. This was the classic concept of the fighter aircraft.

from the German engine and engulfed the 'plane immediately'. The Albatros spiralled into the ground; its unfortunate pilot probably never knew what had hit him. In the next few days Garros shot down two more German aircraft, and then his luck ran out. He had flown low over the enemy lines and a single lucky rifle shot severed the fuel line. The engine failed, Garros was forced to land behind the German lines and he and his monoplane were captured. The secret of the Morane's success, the steel deflectors, was secret no longer. However, when the Germans tried the idea in the butts, using an infantry Spandau machine-gun, the propeller of the test plane disintegrated as soon as the gun was fired. The reason was simple: French Hotchkiss ammunition was lead, encased in copper, whereas the thorough Germans used 7.92mm chrome steel-encased ammunition which, instead of deforming on hitting the deflectors, shattered the wooden propellers. At this point Antony Fokker enters the story.

Fokker was a Dutchman who built military aircraft that bore his name for the German air service at his works at Schwerin. He was told of the unsuccessful plate trials and was asked if he could devise a system that would enable his M-type monoplane, which was very similar to the captured French Morane, to be able to fire through the propeller arc. After the war, Fokker claimed that he had found the answer within forty-eight hours. That is one version, the other being that although he took the credit it was two of his engineers, Heinrich Luebbe and Fritz Herber, who, working around the clock for two weeks, produced the definitive firing mechanism which enabled a standard German army Parabellum 7.92mm MG.13 to be synchronized to fire through the propeller arc without any bullets striking the blades.

Leaving the provenance of the development aside (there were other claimants; one, Franz Schneider, having patented a similar proposal in 1913, seemed to have been overlooked), the Fokker synchronizing system was elegant. It had a cam behind the propeller, working through a system of rods and cranks, that *interrupted* the fire of the machine-gun, allowing it to fire only when the propeller blades were clear. It was ground-tested on a wingless fuselage by temporarily bolting a plywood disk in front of the airscrew and turning it by hand as the gun was fired. The tell-tale bullet holes in the wooden disk allowed fine timing adjustments to be made, with a margin for the occasional 'hang-fire' round. Fokker introduced a refinement that was soon much copied: the gun's trigger was modified so that the pilot fired the gun from a remote thumb-operated trigger on the aircraft's spade control column, via a Bowden cable – exactly

The 'Fokker Scourge'. Max Immelmann was the first German pilot to utilize the potential of the synchronized machine-gun, diving out of the sun in his Fokker monoplane straight at his quarry: an unsuspecting, slow and ill-armed RFC observation plane.

the same as the ones operating the brakes on a bicycle – so that the pilot did not even have to take his hand from the control once the gun had been manually cocked.

The Fokker interrupted gear was fitted to an M.5K Fokker monoplane which became the E-1 in military service. The gun fitted to production machines, mounted on the pilot's eye-line to starboard, was a modified version of the standard German infantry 7.92mm Spandau LMG 08/15 which, like the British Vickers, had the water jacket fretted away to provide air cooling to the barrel. The first armed Fokkers were issued to a reconnaissance unit, *Fliegerabteilung 62*, to protect the slow two-seaters from the Moranes that the French were still using.

The Fokker E-1 was an instant success, defining the format of all future fighters. It was a flying gun which, in essentials, was to remain valid for the next fifty years, until the arrival of the air-to-air missile. Two Fokker pilots became almost overnight the first fighter aces: Max Immelmann and Oswald Boelcke. Although the Fokker E-1s had been ordered to keep close to the observation aircraft they were protecting from the Moranes, they and other E-1 pilots soon began to seek out Allied Morane fighters. The first one to be shot down fell to the Spandau of *Leutnant* Kurt Wintgens, though he was not officially given the credit as the Morane fell behind the French lines and could not, therefore, be confirmed. Soon there was confirmation in plenty; the slow, ill-armed Allied observation aircraft were shot down with no chance of retaliation.

Max Immelmann is credited with the manoeuvre that still bears his name, which he originally developed to exploit the synchronized machine-gun of the Fokker E-1s. Immelmann would dive from out of the sun, gun blazing; if that did not destroy the Allied aircraft he would make a steep climbing turn, then a half-loop with his fighter rolling level just behind the two-seater, its tail preventing the gunner from having a clear shot at the attacking Fokker. Diving from above, or just circling like birds of prey waiting their chance, Immelmann and Boelcke, followed by others, were the subject of press attention which whipped up a rivalry as to who held the highest 'score'. It was collectively high enough for the Allied command to call the winter of 1915–16 the time of the 'Fokker scourge', as it became almost impossible for the poorly armed and slow BE 2c RFC observation aircraft flying over the German lines to survive. Most telling was the virtual immunity with which two-seater German reconnaissance machines, escorted by Fokkers, could report and photograph the Allied troop disposition during the critical battles of Lens and Arras. The best advice available to Allied pilots flying near the front was simply: 'Beware the Hun in the sun'. Immelmann came to be known to British pilots as the Eagle of Lille as he often flew over that area seeking targets. Immelmann and Boelcke were both decorated by Kaiser Wilhelm personally with the coveted 'Blue Max' the blue-ribboned *Pour le Mérite*, Germany's highest award for valour. They were the first airmen to be so honoured in the long history of the order. The award had been established in 1740 at a time when French was the language of the Prussian court.

The advantage of the Fokker E-1 was spectacular. Immelmann once said that ten minutes after the appearance of the Fokkers there would not be an Allied aircraft in sight, except for the smoking wreckage on the ground. Throughout the winter, into 1916, the Fokker scourge continued. A single BE 2c on a reconnaissance sortie would have to be escorted by up to ten others with machine-gunners in the observer's seats, a tacit tribute to the effectiveness of the Fokkers. By 1916 improved versions had appeared; these were the E-II and III, which had 100hp engines and were armed with twin Spandaus, each with 600 rounds of ammunition. The British High Command took the depressing view that, unless the RFC gained machines as good or better than the Fokker, that is with synchronized guns, the German supremacy would continue. The restriction on Allied reconnaissance was underlined when, in February 1916, 1,400 German guns began to pound the French fortification at Verdun; this was a battle of attrition that was to last a year with terrible casualties on both sides.

The aircraft that gained such advantage was, in aerodynamic terms, distinctly moderate. It was small, with a 28ft wing-span, and used outdated wing warping instead of ailerons. The engine of the E-I was an 80hp Oberursel, by no means the best rotary of the era, with a maximum speed of only 82mph and a ceiling of 10,000ft. Figures vary, but it is doubtful if more than 100 were ever issued to active service units and they were never operated *en masse*, but in small numbers protecting observation aircraft.

A captured Fokker E-1. The British markings suggest that it had been test-flown and evaluated by Allied airmen. The single Spandau machine-gun with fretted water-jacket can be seen.

Later, in 1916, E-III Fokkers were formed into fighter squadrons known as *Kampfeinsitzerkommandos*. But it was now too late; in April 1916 a single-seater Bristol Scout was encountered with interrupter gear. The pendulum of technology had swung in favour of the Allies with the DH-2, which had a pusher-propeller with the engine behind the pilot, and with the Bristol and Nieuport single-seater fighters fitted with Allied Constantinesco synchronizing gear.

The see-saw battle for aerial supremacy continued with new aircraft from both sides with names that have become history: Fokker triplane, Sopwith Pup and Camel, the French Spad S.7 and Nieuport 28s. These single-seater fighters were the aircraft used by the British, French and, from 1917, American aces whose exploits were becoming known to thousands. By 1917 swirling aerial dogfights had become set pieces as the squadrons on both sides flew to fighter-against-fighter battles, which had no relevance to the grim trench warfare thousands of feet below that destroyed a generation of young men at Verdun and on the Somme. The German pilots scorned the drab khaki-green camouflage of the Allied machines, painting the fighters of their *Jagdstaffeln* in brilliant heraldic colour schemes like the blood-red Fokker triplane of Freiherr von Richthofen, the Red Knight. Von Richthofen led the top German fighter unit *Jasta II*, popularly known in the British press as the Richthofen Flying Circus. Richthofen was the highest-scoring German ace with eighty 'kills' credited to him before he, too, was shot down. The great air battles of 1918 produced a number of outstanding fighter pilots and fighter aircraft on both sides, of which two are truly classic: the German Fokker D-VII and the British S.E.5a.

The Fokker D-VII came about as a result of the Germans, in 1918, inviting manufacturers to submit prototype fighters to take part in a competitive trial at Johannisthal airfield, conveniently near Berlin. The rules were simple: all the aircraft submitted had to be powered by a single 160hp six-cylinder Mercedes water-cooled engine and all were to be flown, not by company test pilots, but by front-line fighter pilots who had recent combat experience against the best Allied fighters. The Fokker entry was the D-VII, designed by Reinhold Platz, who had originally joined the company as a gas welder.

A Fokker D-VII, considered by many as the finest fighter of the First World War. This, a late D-VII, is in the markings of the Dutch Army Air Service. A train load of late German D-VIIs was smuggled out of Germany to Holland at the end of the war by Antony Fokker. '251', shown here, is one of those bootlegged aircraft. The lack of bracing wires and the cantilever top wing can be seen clearly.

The twin 7.92mm Spandau machine-guns of a Fokker D-VII. The fretted water-jackets and the chute for ejecting spent cartridge cases are clearly visible.

Welding was the secret of the D-VII, for the fuselage was made from expertly welded steel tubing. To gas weld such a complex structure without distortion is a major feat which, if done correctly, results in a very light and strong airframe. The biplane's wings of unequal span were of cantilever form with a high-lift aerofoil; the wings were so strong that no bracing wires were used – indeed, the interplane struts of very thin steel tubing were only added because Fokker knew that pilots would not fly the aircraft without them. The Mercedes engine had a rather drag-producing car-type radiator which, nevertheless, was efficient and allowed the used of full throttle for extended periods without danger of overheating. When tested during the competition, the D-VII was found to handle very well, being stable and yet manoeuvrable. Not particularly fast, the D-VII had a 160hp engine with a maximum speed of just over 116mph, but it had a ceiling of 21,500ft and the thick wings allowed excellent control response even at high altitudes. It was a *rara avis*: a high-performance aircraft – for its day – which forgave the mistakes of the inexperienced and flattered the flying of the best.

The combination of agility and stability made the D-VII an ideal gun platform for the twin 7.92mm Spandaus, now synchronized to fire through the propeller arc by a much improved flexible interrupter drive from the camshaft, devised by Heinrich Luebbe. The pilots at the Johannisthal trials voted the Fokker D-VII the best prototype and it was ordered into immediate production with a preliminary order for 400. Fokker-built D-VIIs had the designation Fok. D-VII followed by the works number stencilled on the fuselage sides. The losing entrants to the competition had the mortification of having to build D-VIIs under licence. These machines were identified by being designated Fok. D-VII (Alb) in the case of those built by Albatros; other contractors had similar stencils. Large orders were placed and, to keep production flowing, later D-VIIs were fitted with 185hp BMW engines.

The first D-VIIs were in service by May 1918 and by the following August no fewer than 800 were serving with several *Jagdstaffeln*. There is a story about the relative merits of the Fokker D-VII and the rival Albatros D-III. The rules of air warfare during the First World War demanded a certain degree of chivalry: downed pilots who survived were invited to the victors' officers' mess for a formal dinner before being collected by the military and sent to POW camps. It seems that an English pilot, known only as Shaw, had been shot down by *Leutnant* Theo Osterkamp (later a colonel in the *Luftwaffe*). After the ritual dinner Shaw was invited to test-fly a Fokker D-VII and an Albatros D-III, both

A formation of RAF DH-4s is attacked by Fokker triplanes and D-VIIs in late 1918. The British aircraft were uniformly camouflaged in drab earth and khaki green colours, whereas the German fighter pilots enjoyed the latitude to paint their fighters in vivid personal colours with an element of medieval heraldry.

fighters presumably unarmed. He flew them both for ten minutes or so and when asked for his opinion answered: '*Leutnant* Osterkamp, the Fokker is very good, the Albatros is *scheissen!* [shit]'. That was a nearly universal opinion. The Allied assessment of the D-VII was such that it was the only German aircraft ordered specifically to be surrendered; 142 went to the United States and several were later flown and crashed in the Hollywood films *Hell's Angels*, *Wings* and *The Dawn Patrol* of the 1930s. After the filming finished, the whole lot were piled up and burned. The RAF have a genuine static D-VII in their museum and there are airworthy replicas in American collections.

The S.E.5 was designed by a team led by H.P. Folland of the Royal Aircraft Factory, Farnborough, in Hampshire, the letters SE standing for Scout Experimental. The prototype S.E.5, A 4561, first flew in 1916; it was revealed as a sturdy biplane with, like the Fokker D-VII, a car-type radiator, though not as well blended with the fuselage as that of the German aircraft. The S.E.5 fuselage was a strong, wooden, wire-braced, elongated torsion box which was covered in fabric, except for the plywood sections around the engine and cockpit. The biplane wings had an equal span of 26ft 7in with a marked dihedral, also of wooden construction with spruce ribs. The engine specified for the type was a 150hp 90-degree V8 French Hispano-Suiza, an engine of very advanced design which was, however, not without its faults. Its speed of up to 2,200rpm was high for the time and required trouble-prone reduction gears to attain propeller efficiency; the engine also had problems with the connecting rods and valves. That said, it was efficient and with an excellent power-to-weight ratio.

In early testing the S.E.5 prototype attained a speed of 120mph in level flight. Despite this promising beginning, during a recovery from a dive, the wings folded and the aircraft crashed, killing the Royal Aircraft Factory's test pilot Major F.W. Gooden. With re-stressed wings, the S.E.5 went into production armed with a single .303in Vickers gun mounted on the port side of the cockpit with the breech within easy reach. The Constantinesco gun synchronizing was achieved by an hydraulic impulse from a pump driven from the crankshaft, a system that was superior to the all-mechanical German method. The pilot had an Aldis optical sight on his eye-line. He also had a second gun, a .303in Lewis with 97-round drums of ammunition. This gun was mounted above the top wing centre section, thus clearing the propeller arc – just! The Lewis gun was fitted on a curved mounting known as a Foster mount after the RFC sergeant who invented it. The mount allowed the pilot to pull the Lewis towards himself to fire upwards and to reload the gun with a fresh magazine. There is a true story of one S.E.5 pilot struggling with both hands to remove a jammed drum when his aircraft rolled upside down; not being strapped in and without a parachute he found himself hanging on to the drum praying it would not unjam as he struggled to get his feet back into the cockpit to kick the stick over to right the inverted plane. He succeeded and lived to dine out on the story.

S.E.5s were first issued to No. 56 Squadron in April 1917. The fighter was well liked; it was fast, could climb to 22,000ft, was very strong and, with ailerons on all four wings, very agile, yet remained a good, stable gun platform. The fighter was so stable that one

A detail of the armament of an S.E.5a. The Aldis sight and an alternative 'ring and bead' for the single synchronized Vickers machine-gun, the muzzle of which can just be seen, was the main armament of the S.E.5a. The secondary armament was the Lewis gun on its Foster mounting on the top of the upper-wing centre-section, the gun firing over the propeller arc; the curved rail down which the gun was pulled to enable the pilot to change a magazine was the main purpose of the Foster mount.

FACT FILE

S.E.5a

Type
Single-seat biplane fighter.

Builder
Royal Aircraft Factory

Power plant
One 220hp Hispano-Suiza or
a 200hp Wolseley Viper.

Dimensions
Wing-span 26ft 7in
Length 20ft

Performance
Maximum speed 120mph at
5,000ft
Service ceiling 22,000ft.

Armament
One 0.303in Vickers gun
One 0.303in Lewis gun.

Number produced
Over 5,000.

FACT FILE

FOKKER D-VII

Type
Single-seat biplane fighter.

Builders
Fokkers/subcontractors,
including Albatros.

Power plant
One 160hp Mercedes or a
185hp BMW water-cooled
engine.

Dimensions
Wing-span 29ft 3in
Length 22ft 9in.

Performance
Maximum speed 116mph at
3,280ft
Service ceiling 21,500ft.

Armament
Twin 7.92mm Spandaus.

Number produced
Over 800.

squadron (No. 24) reduced the dihedral of their S.E.5s to increase agility even further. In June 1917 the S.E.5a was introduced; this had a more powerful Hispano engine of 200hp. Again, there were difficulties: engine production lagged behind that of the airframes and, when fitted, the uprated engine had frequent reduction gear problems and other mechanical failings, mainly due to poor quality control during manufacture. The British Wolseley company revised the engine, eliminating the troublesome reduction gears by employing a direct drive, arguing that the slight loss of propeller efficiency was more than offset by increased reliability. The Wolseley Viper, as the 200hp engine was called, was a complete success and was to power most of the 5,205 S.E.5a aircraft manufactured.

In combat, the S.E.5a, equipping 24 RFC/RAF squadrons, was considered to be superior to all enemy fighters with the exception of the Fokker D-VII which it superficially resembled and equalled. It was the aircraft of the top-scoring RFC aces. Mannock achieved seventy-three victories, Bishop seventy-two, McCudden fifty-seven and Beauchamp-Proctor fifty-four. All four men were awarded the VC. Although some might point out that the Sopwith Camel shot down more enemy aircraft than the S.E.5a, the Sopwith, by 1918, was a dated design, being powered by a rotary engine which was an engineering dead end. Furthermore, it was a tricky machine to fly; the gyroscopic forces generated by the rotary engine caused many inexperienced pilots to spin and crash, usually fatally. Since most replacement RFC pilots were inexperienced, the forgiving nature of the S.E.5s – which, incidentally, could fly higher and faster than the Sopwith – was welcomed by the hard-pressed squadron commanders. Viewed in retrospect, most would agree that the two classic fighters of the First World War are the Fokker D-VII and the S.E.5a. There is an excellent static S.E.5a in the RAF Museum at Hendon and the Shuttleworth Collection have an airworthy example that regularly flies during the summer months at Old Warden in Bedfordshire.

Interestingly, many S.E.5as that survived the end of the war were sold off for a few pounds and were bought by aerial skywriting companies. On a clear day in the 1930s one might look up to see the word Persil, or something similar, written in white smoke at high altitude. Some of the S.E.5s, thanks to soap powders, miraculously survived to be restored to their previous military identity for preservation.

Twenty-one years and a second world war later, the fighter aircraft had, of course, changed, though not beyond all recognition. The immense progress made in aircraft design and construction between 1914 and 1918 was not to be repeated during the six years between 1939 and 1945. Aircraft had become far more complex and the time between design and squadron service, even during the war years, was long. Most, but not all, the aircraft that saw active service between 1939 and 1945 had been designed or were flying before the war started. Aeronautical progress between the wars had been slow, due to financial restraints justified by the ethos of disarmament, and was principally confined to development of supercharged aero-engines in the 1,000hp class funded by private venture. This, together with the increasing attraction of the stressed-skin all-metal monocoque construction, was to result in the near-universal monoplane fighter. Only two biplane fighters fought in the 1940 Battle of Britain; these were the Italian Fiat CR 42 and the RAF's last biplane fighter, the Gloster Gladiator. Both had been withdrawn from front-line service by 1941 (the Gladiator was withdrawn after a glorious finale in the defence of Malta). Either of these aircraft could have been flown without difficulty by any 1918 fighter pilot. The second generation of fighters, the new monoplanes, would be a different matter.

The provenance of the monoplane fighter of the Second World War can be traced back to 1931. In that year, the Supermarine S6B seaplane, after winning the Schneider

The last biplane fighter of the RAF. The Gloster Gladiator gained immortality in the defence of Malta when three Sea Gladiators were the sole defenders until Hurricanes, flown off Royal Navy carriers, took over. The type was also flown in the defence of Greece against heavy odds. L 8032 is a civil aircraft, G-AMRK, though as it was originally on RAF charge as L 8032, it now carries those marks. It is preserved by the Shuttleworth Trust as the sole remaining airworthy Gladiator and flies from Old Warden during the summer season.

trophy outright, went on to create a new world speed record of 407.5mph (655.8km). This was nearly twice the maximum speed of the RAF's front-line fighter of the day, the 207mph Hawker Fury, the first RAF fighter to exceed 200mph in level flight. The Fury had been designed by Sydney Camm and was, in effect, a single-seat version of the highly successful Hawker Hart series of versatile two-seat aircraft that so dominated the squadrons of the RAF.

The consequences of the unbelievable performance of the Supermarine S6B were twofold. The first was that the stressed-skin monoplane was clearly the shape of the future. The second was that Rolls-Royce had produced a V12 'R' engine for the S6B with the staggering output of 2,550hp, at a time when the best military engines were in the 550hp class. Of course, the 'R' was a very highly stressed sprint engine but, nevertheless, a fourfold increase in power was impressive. In achieving that power and performance – due, it must be said, to the public spirit of Lady Houston who gave £100,000 for the S6B when the government of the day had declined to fund it – Rolls-Royce had been able to amass considerable experience from the 'R' engines. This experience was mainly gained empirically about metallurgy, cooling, fuel chemistry and, above all, the then almost black art of supercharging, which had been pioneered by J.E. Ellor of the Royal Aircraft Establishment in the late 1920s and which was therefore a still little-known science. The direct outcome was that Rolls-Royce confidently enlarged their successful 21-litre V-12, 530hp Kestrel engine to the 36-litre PV12, later to be named Merlin, a military engine that would offer 1,030hp for take-off. At Kingston, Surrey, Camm decided that this new Rolls-Royce engine was the one he was seeking for the monoplane fighter, to be named Hurricane, which was already taking shape on his drawing-board.

Despite the example of the Schneider Trophy S6B monoplane, there was a marked reluctance at the Air Ministry to abandon the biplane fighter. Most of the senior staff officers had been wartime fighter pilots and considered the undoubted virtue of high manoeuvrability of the biplane to be essential for a fighter. What they overlooked was that the future role of RAF fighters would be intercepting high-performance *monoplanes*, which would shortly replace the lumbering 120mph contemporary biplane bombers, and that a top speed of 200mph would soon be insufficient to offer a fighter any realistic hope

The first Hurricane. K 5083 was the prototype and was first flown on 6 November 1935, four months before the Spitfire took to the air. At the time of the first flight the Hawker aircraft was known as 'Interceptor Monoplane', a name soon to be changed to 'Hurricane'.

FACT FILE

HURRICANE IIB

Type
Single-seat fighter.

Builder
Hawker Aircraft Ltd.

Power plant
One Rolls-Royce Merlin XX
V12 of 1,850hp at 21,000ft.

Dimensions
Wing-span 40ft
Length 32ft 3in.

Performance
Maximum speed without
bombs or external stores
340mph at 21,000ft
Service ceiling 40,000ft.

Number produced in UK
12,780

Number produced in Canada
1,451

of successful interception. The Boeing 247 and Douglas DC-2 monoplane airliners had appeared by 1934 and RAF fighters of the day would have been hard-pressed to intercept them. Camm knew that, even with a 1,000hp engine up front, no practical biplane fighter could ever exceed a maximum speed of around 250mph in level flight due to the drag of the rigging and the aerodynamic interference created by the two adjacent biplane wings.

As a consequence, work on the new Hawker Fury monoplane fighter began in earnest in 1934. What emerged was an interesting 'halfway' between the new technology and the old: this was the monoplane Fury Interceptor, as it was by then known. It was just that; a monoplane version of the existing RAF biplane Fury Interceptor. The Hawker company, the successor to Sopwiths, stuck to the technology they knew best and which was proved beyond doubt in the 3,000 Hawker aircraft then serving the RAF and foreign air forces. The prototype monoplane fighter was to be constructed in the traditional Hawker manner. The fuselage was a strong yet light structure made from seamless steel tubing bolted together and the whole airframe was fabric covered, apart from the engine cowlings and the wing roots. The wings on the prototype were fabric covered as well. It was, by 1934, a dated form of construction for a front-line fighter but it was to hold two overwhelming advantages in battle: it was easy to build and repair and the structure could, and did, absorb an incredible amount of damage and still allow the Hurricane to get home – damage that would have proved fatal to other all-metal fighters which relied on the nearly total integrity of their monocoque structures not being compromised. Though the fabric covering was dated, the Hawker fighter had a modern canopy for the pilot and retractable undercarriage and flaps, together with other new features.

The Air Ministry, possibly as a consequence of the appearance of monocoque twin-engined airliners in the United States and German progress in military aviation, issued a new fighter specification written around the Hawker design; this was F.36/37, which called for a monoplane fighter armed with eight .303in machine-guns mounted in the wings and therefore clear of the propeller. This had been made possible by the US Browning company developing a machine-gun that did not require hand-cocking and was, with carefully screened ammunition, reliable enough to be removed from the cockpit and out of the pilot's reach. The Air Ministry, after inspecting a wooden mock-up, ordered a contract for one Hawker 'High-speed Interceptor Monoplane' according to the specification in February 1935.

The prototype, with the service serial number K 5083, first flew from Brooklands, the famous pre-war motor-racing circuit and airfield in Surrey, on 6 November 1935 in the capable hands of Hawker's chief test pilot 'George' Bulman. The aircraft was powered by a 1,189hp V12 Rolls-Royce Merlin 'C' engine. K 5083 proved to have a top speed of 315mph at 16,000ft and could climb at nearly 3,000ft per minute, to a ceiling of 34,500ft. The rate of climb was an important point when home-based RAF fighters were able to wait on the ground until enemy bombers came within range. They would then rapidly climb to intercept, the philosophy being to reduce both the number of aircraft and the high engine hours that 'standing patrols' at altitude required.

Such was the euphoria at Kingston when the test-flight reports were analysed, that the Hawker board, led by the redoubtable 'Tommy' Sopwith, sanctioned, in March 1936, the production of 1,000 of the new fighters without waiting for the Air Ministry to place any order. There is little doubt that this unprecedented act of faith in Sydney Camm's design saved at least three vital months during which production drawings and tooling were provided. The time saved was to play a major part in the Battle of Britain, which was then just four years away. In the event, Air Ministry orders were placed for 600 Hurricanes in July 1936. The first production Hurricane, L 1547, first flew in October 1937, powered by a 1,030hp Merlin II engine. The top speed was 320mph at 18,500ft; this excellent performance was with a two-bladed fixed-pitch propeller.

The first RAF fighter squadron to take delivery of the Hurricane was No. 111, stationed at Northolt, west of London; they exchanged their 230mph Gloster Gauntlets for the 320mph Hurricane 1s in December 1937. In February 1938 the commanding officer of the squadron, Squadron Leader J. Gillan, made the headlines by flying from Edinburgh to Northolt at an average speed of 408mph. Ever after, he was known in the RAF as Tailwind Gillan.

The last of many. PZ 865 was the 12,780th and final Hurricane to be built. PZ 865, a Mk IIC, was delivered to the RAF in September 1944. It is now preserved. The photograph shows the Hurricane as it took off with the undercarriage in the act of retracting. The Hurricane's wheels retracted inwards, offering a much wider track than that of the Spitfire, and thus resulted in the easier ground-handling of the Hawker fighter.

When the Second World War broke out in September 1939 there were 497 Hurricanes in RAF service. The type was progressively developed; the fabric wings became metal-clad, and the fixed-pitch wooden two-bladed propeller was replaced by a de Havilland, or Rotol, three-bladed constant-speed airscrew. Hurricanes bore the brunt of the early battles in Norway, Belgium and France that preceded the Battle of Britain, when the RAF Order of Battle included thirty squadrons of Hurricanes and nineteen squadrons of Spitfires. The Hurricanes of 1940 were slower than either the Spitfire or the German Messerschmitt Bf 109 E fighters, but the Hurricane proved time and time again to be more than the sum of its parts. It could outmanoeuvre any contemporary fighter, it was by far the better gun platform than the Spitfire, and the wide-tracked, inward-retracting undercarriage offered a greater margin to inexperienced pilots on landing and ground handling. It was easy and forgiving to fly; so forgiving that, whenever possible, a trainee pilot, before his first solo on a Spitfire, was given a few 'touch-and-go' circuits on a hack Hurricane , which of course shared the same Merlin engine with the Spitfire.

The wartime combat record of the Hurricane speaks for itself. During the Battle of Britain, Hurricanes took on the bombers, though they could more than hold their own against German fighters. Some notable Battle of Britain pilots flew the Hurricane, including Douglas Bader, Stanford Tuck and the top-scoring 'Ginger' Lacey, none of whom would hear a world against their Hawker fighters. When the smoke of that first decisive air battle in history had cleared, although they were overshadowed by the more glamorous Spitfire, it was discovered that Hurricanes had shot down a greater number of enemy aircraft than all the other defences, including Spitfires and anti-aircraft guns, combined. Hurricanes fought on all the fronts in which British forces were engaged; there was even a Sea Hurricane, although the lack of folding wings restricted their use on carriers. Hurricanes were put aboard catapult-armed merchant (CAM)

A Hurricane on its launching ramp aboard a catapult-armed merchant (CAM) ship. From 1941 the Hurricane merchant ship fighter units, equipped with reconditioned Mk I veteran Hurricanes, were placed aboard selected merchant ships plying the dangerous convoy routes across the Atlantic. When within range the convoys were often shadowed by long-range Focke-Wulf Condor Fw 200 reconnaissance aircraft, which radioed the course, speed and composition of the convoys to U-boat HQ at Loriant. The Hurricanes were catapulted off their ship to attack the Fw 200s. Several German aircraft were shot down and many more driven off. After the sortie the pilot, if the coast was out of range, had to ditch near an escort ship to be picked up.

ships, perched on the bow so as to be catapulted off to attack or drive away the sinister long-range Focke-Wulf Fw 200 Condor four-engined reconnaissance aircraft which shadowed the convoys for the U-boats. (After the engagement, if land was out of range, the Hurricane pilot had to ditch near an escort ship to be picked up.)

Hurricanes defended Malta, flying to the besieged island from the carrier HMS *Argus*. The rugged structure of the Hurricane was an asset on Malta in 1941. Hurricanes that any engineering officer in England would have struck off-charge with a single glance from the hangar doorway were deemed to be airworthy in Malta. Although their engines were worn out and, in the absence of linen, pages of The *Times of Malta* were doped over the fuselage fabric, although they were holed by German 20mm cannon fire, out-classed and out-numbered, they still flew and fought day after day, holding the island until new Spitfires were flown in from Royal Navy and US Navy carriers. Hurricanes flew in Burma and in the Western Desert. Hurricane IID 'tank-busters', the only RAF fighter armed with twin 40mm Vickers cannon, destroyed scores of Rommel's *Afrika Korps*' tanks and were also used as 'skip-bombers', carrying a 500lb bomb under each wing. Standard armament of the Hurricane IIb, which had a 1,280hp Merlin XX engine, was either *twelve* .303in Browning guns in the wings or four 20mm cannon. Finally, the Hurricane IV was armed with eight underwing rockets for ground attack following D-Day.

PREVIOUS PAGE, TOP **The Hurricane's rival, the Spitfire, was far more difficult to produce, being an all-metal monocoque structure; the complex shapes required did initially delay the entry of the Spitfire into RAF service. However, as this photograph testifies, difficulties were overcome. This batch of 1,000 Spitfire VBs (BL 251-BM 653) were being built at Vickers Armstrong at Castle Bromwich.**

PREVIOUS PAGE, INSET **During the Battle of Britain, Hurricanes mainly attacked bombers; the Spitfires took on the enemy fighters. This magnificent photograph shows a cannon-armed Spitfire making a maximum-rate turn, with full aileron deflection. No German fighter could out-turn a well-handled Spitfire, for the aircraft remained under full control however steep the turn (no doubt to the relief of the photographer taking this shot).**

BELOW **'Random Harvest'. Women of Berwick, near Eastbourne, crowd to get a closer look at a Bf 109 E shot down at the height of the Battle of Britain. The wounded German pilot had crash-landed in the corn field.**

The Hurricane was the most versatile fighter the RAF was ever to have; it was hardly altered and never seems to have failed its pilots. Hurricanes fought from the first day of the war to the last, equipping some 134 RAF squadrons; many Hurricanes were given to the Russians. It remains one of the great military aircraft of all time. The last Hurricane (PZ 865) of over 14,000 (including 1,451 built in Canada) was delivered to the RAF in September 1944. Few now remain. One that does is P 2617, preserved in the RAF Museum, which flew with No. 607 Squadron in 1940. The RAF Battle of Britain Memorial Flight at Coningsby also has two airworthy Hurricanes: LF 363 and PZ 865.

The Hurricane became a versatile aircraft through force of circumstance. It had been designed, as had most of the European fighters, for a specific role (it was what would today be called an Air Superiority fighter), which was to control a clearly defined airspace in order to deny it to the enemy air force. The Germans had similar aims, though with the emphasis on attack rather than defence. At the outset of the war in 1939 the Germans used Messerschmitt Bf 109 fighters to escort their tactical bombers as the army swept through Poland to the Atlantic coast. RAF Hurricanes and Spitfires were designed for home defence against bombers; both British and German fighters performed their designated tasks with distinction. In fulfilling their disparate roles, European fighters had high speed, good manoeuvrability, a high rate of climb to altitude and were well armed with excellent handling as stable gun platforms. They gave a good all-round performance with a relatively modest endurance on standard tanks, since the distances between the fronts, as then perceived, were not great. The 1940 Hurricane, Spitfire and German Messerschmitt Bf 109 all possessed the essential qualities – though in differing measure – of front-line fighters. The RAF had the two fighters because, from 1933, after Hitler came to power in Germany, the possibility of a future war with Germany turned inexorably to probability and, in Britain, it was decided by the farsighted that air defence, including early warning radar, should be prepared on the assumption that, if war came, Germany once again would be the enemy.

In the United States, aircraft designers had little experience of fighter design. In 1917, when the United States entered the war, US forces in France used French and British aircraft. Between the wars the American Army Air Corps had no obvious enemy; it was unlikely that either Mexico or Canada would suddenly attack the United States. As

a consequence, even the best indigenous US fighters of 1940 when bought or ordered by France and Britain (for example, the Brewster F2A Buffalo and the Curtiss P-40 Tomahawk) were found to be hopelessly outclassed in European air combat. (Buffaloes, in particular, had such a moderate performance that they remained unassembled in their transit crates even during the darkest days of the Battle of Britain.)

In April 1940, realizing that existing off-the-shelf US fighters were unsuitable for combat against the *Luftwaffe*, a British Purchasing Commission went to the United States to try to persuade an aircraft manufacturer there to build Spitfires under licence. By 1940 the American government was busy rearming its own forces and all the major aviation factories were fulfilling substantial orders for the US Army and Navy. However, one small company, North American Aviation of Inglewood, California, had production capacity – possibly because they had only ever designed and built one fighter for what was then Siam. The North American Aviation president 'Dutch' Kindelberger, on meeting the British Purchasing Commission, declined to build Spitfires but said he would design and build a better fighter. Possibly to call Kindelberger's bluff, the Purchasing Commission stipulated that if orders were to be forthcoming for the 'wonder' fighter, in view of the serious war situation in Europe, a prototype would be required for flight-testing within 120 *days*. When it is considered that it took Hawkers, a company with vast experience of fighter design and production, three years to produce the prototype Hurricane, the scale of the task confronting North American Aviation is apparent. In fact, 'Dutch' Kindelberger, unlike most American designers who relied on their 'Yankee know-how', had made an intensive study of the European air war and had formed an outline specification of a fighter that could compete on an equal footing with the best. The North American design team was led by Raymond Rice and Edgar Schmued; the latter's CV usefully included past work for Fokker and Messerschmitt. Working without a break, the North American Aviation prototype, designated as NA-73, was rolled out – on wheels bor-

In 1940 the need for Spitfires to keep pace with German fighters, particularly the formidable Fw 190, resulted in the interim 'clipped spit', which had its wing-tips removed to increase its speed at low levels at the expense of high-altitude performance. The Mk IX Spitfire redressed the balance against the Fw 190 and the North American Mustang initially took over the low-level attack role. The aircraft shown here, AR 501, is a VC LF Spitfire from the Shuttleworth Collection. In 1942 the clipped-wing Spitfires also had their supercharger impellers cropped to reduce engine loading and, as most Mk Vs were, by 1942, well past their sell-by date, LF V Spitfire pilots referred to their aircraft as 'clipped, cropped and clapped'.

AG 351, the first North American NA-73 Mustang I to undergo performance trials at the A & AEE. The fighter is seen at Boscombe Down in January 1942. The 'P' signified that the aircraft was a prototype. Mustang Is became operational with No. 2 Squadron on photo-reconnaissance duties in April 1942. When later Mustangs were re-engined with Rolls-Royce Merlin engines and the restrictive canopy was revised, the Mustang, as the P-51D, became the best Allied escort fighter of the war.

rowed from a light aircraft – in just 117 days. This was an incredible achievement. Unfortunately it had to wait for the engine, a V12 Allison V-1710-39, which was rated at 1,150hp. With the engine installed, the NA-73, soon to have the British name Mustang bestowed on it, was test-flown a few weeks later. It was a low-wing monoplane with drag-reducing laminar-flow 37ft wings, and square-cut tips to the wings and tail rather like the Messerschmitt, thus simplifying production. The fuselage was clean, though the pilot's canopy had rather thick frames. The radiator intake for the liquid-cooled engine was placed well aft under the cockpit to enable the designers to keep the fuselage depth to a minimum, thereby further reducing drag.

Extensive flight-testing of the prototype revealed remarkably few snags. Within the year Mustang Is were rolling off the North American Aviation's production line. The rate was restricted, British orders being relatively modest, as the Lend-Lease Act had yet to be passed and the aircraft had to be paid for in US dollars. Under American law, North American Aviation were obliged to give, free of charge, two representative production aircraft for evaluation by the USAAF. The two, designated as XP-51 and given the army serials 41-038 and 039, impressed the pilots; they had a maximum speed of 382mph, higher than any existing US test fighter and faster than the contemporary Spitfire V (374mph).

When the first Mustangs arrived in Britain, it was clear that they were, in many ways, outstanding fighters, the only disappointment being the American Allison engine's poor high-altitude performance. Since European fighter-against-fighter combat was, by 1942, taking place at 20,000ft and higher, the Mustang I was issued to Army Co-operation Command for ground attack, armed with either eight machine-guns or four 20mm cannon, and as a high-speed tactical reconnaissance aircraft using F.24 cameras arranged at an oblique angle behind the cockpit. An early Mustang operation was supporting ground troops during the disastrous Dieppe raid in July 1942. By 1942 the RAF had taken delivery of 620 Mustang I and IAs, operating with nineteen squadrons. It was a pointer to future deployment that a Mustang was the first single-seat RAF aircraft to enter German air space from the UK, a sortie made possible by the very long range of the aircraft, which had two internal fuel tanks (180 US gallons) allowing a still-air range of 1,000 miles. The contemporary Spitfire V on internal tanks could only achieve a maximum range of 400 miles. The two early production NA-73s tested by the USAAF led to orders for 150 of an American version of the Mustang, which were designated P-51 Apache. That version had US radios and provision for either bombs or drop tanks under the wings, which offered a ferry range of no less than 2,350 miles. (The name 'Apache' was soon dropped and the British name 'Mustang' adopted for the USAF's P-51s.)

In Britain, a Mustang I, AM 208, was flown to Hucknall, Nottinghamshire, to be fitted with a Rolls-Royce Merlin 61 engine driving a four-bladed airscrew. The fighter was tested at Boscombe Down where the A & AEE pilots discovered that the high-altitude performance of the Mustang had been transformed. Mustangs with Rolls-Royce engines were progressively developed by 1944 to become P-51Ds, which were without question, the greatest escort fighters of the war. The Mustang P-51D had a cut-down rear fuselage and a bubble hood. It was powered by a Packard-built Merlin 1650-7 engine, offering 1,450hp for take-off, with a two-stage supercharger which could boost the engine to a combat rating of 1,700hp at 10,300ft. The maximum speed was 437mph at 25,000ft with a service ceiling of 40,000ft. Issued in large numbers to the USAF fighter squadrons of the Eighth Air Force in Europe, P-51Ds were in natural aluminium without heavy and drag-producing green camouflage paint, the only paint on the P-51D airframe being a matt black anti-dazzle finish to the top of the engine cowling on the pilot's eye-line. The usual 1944 squadron and national markings were carried as well as the inevitable 'nose art' beloved of American pilots. P-51Ds with two 90-gallon compressed paper drop tanks, escorted B-17 and B-24 daylight bombers to Berlin and back with sufficient fuel to fight *en route*.

P-51Ds could outfly any piston-engined German fighter, including the formidable Fw 190, the Butcher Bird. On one sortie, a single P-51D shot down two Messerschmitt 262 jet-engined fighters. P-51D armament varied according to the mission flown but typically consisted of six Browning .50in machine-guns with up to 400 rounds per gun, with the British K-14 gyroscope gun-sight known to the pilots as 'No miss 'um', or two 1,000lb bombs on underwing hard points, or ten rockets. This made a total weapon load of up to 4,000lb. The final version, the P-51H, which had a top speed of 487mph, was too late for the war in Europe but was used in limited numbers in the Pacific until the Second World War ended. As many as 1,700 P-51Hs were delivered to the USAF. The Commonwealth Aircraft Corporation of Australia had been granted a licence to assemble the P-51D as the CA-17, although the company had sufficient parts for 100 aircraft, only eighty had been built when the Pacific war ended.

The P-51H is, by common consent, considered to be the ultimate piston-engined fighter. As late as 1967, well into the jet age, the P-51 was back in limited production by Cavalier as a 'Coin' (counter-insurgency) aircraft. In 1975 a turbo-prop version, the Enforcer, was produced for forward air control (FAC) for the USAF to combat guerrilla air rebel forces who could have been flying piston- or early jet-engined fighters, acquired from Third World air forces. Excluding the postwar production, the total number of the wartime versions of the Mustang amounted to 15,586 aircraft. Many ex-USAF, late P-51Ds, were reconditioned, some with dual control, to serve with no fewer that fifty-five air forces. Because of the number available from surplus stocks in the 1970s, and the very high performance attainable, many Mustangs have survived to be restored and compete regularly in air races in the United States. In July 1983 a modified P-51D raised the straight-line speed world record for a piston-engined aircraft to 517.06mph (832.12kph).

If the United States in 1940 was lagging behind the best European fighters, it was a position quickly remedied with the P-51 Mustang and other fighters. In one sense the US designers enjoyed an advantage: there were two years of the European air war, including the Battle of Britain, which gave them an unrivalled overview of the combat techniques of the protagonists. Britain welcomed the still neutral US Army and Navy officers to active RAF airfields to talk to pilots and aircrews, and also made combat analysis available. No doubt US air attachés in Axis countries could form a fairly accurate picture too, once the inevitable propaganda had been nullified.

A US Navy F4F Grumman Wildcat, flaps and tail-hook down, is waved away from a landing on a US carrier at the time of the Battle of the Coral Sea in 1942. Though outclassed in manoeuvrability by the Japanese Zero, the Wildcat was a rugged carrier-fighter that served with distinction until the end of the war with both the Royal Navy (as the Martlet) and (as the Wildcat) on US escort carriers.

American naval fighters in 1940, though better than British types on Royal Navy carriers, did not have a performance as good as the best European land-based fighter aircraft. It was, of course, true that naval aircraft, encumbered by wing-folding gear, additional radio and flotation equipment, and with airframes stronger and therefore heavier to withstand the stresses of repeated arrested landings on the heaving decks of carriers, always had a lower performance than a land-plane equivalent. When the war in the Pacific began on 7 December 1941 the best US Navy fighter was the F4F Grumman Wildcat. The Royal Navy had been using the Wildcat, which they called Martlet, from land bases since 1940; the first German aircraft to be shot down by a US-built fighter was a Ju 88 destroyed by two F4F Martlets in December 1940. F4Fs were embarked aboard small escort carriers from September 1941 but the Royal Navy was using the Martlets to attack reconnaissance and bomber aircraft out to sea far beyond the range of German fighters. Martlets were successful. Two shot down a four-engined Focke Wulf Fw 200 Condor almost as soon as they were embarked; four more Fw 200s followed. However, when the US Navy pilots flying F4F Wildcats first encountered the Japanese Mitsubishi A6M Zero-Sen fighter during the Battles of the Coral Sea and Midway, they had a rude shock. In terms of manoeuvrability, the Zero could fly rings around the F4F-3 Wildcat. After the combat reports had been analysed US Navy Wildcat pilots were warned:

1. Never attempt to dogfight with a Zero.
2. Never try to out-manoeuvre a Zero at speeds below 300mph unless directly on his tail.
3. Never follow a Zero in a climb at low speed. You will stall just as the Zero has reached his best combat speed and could complete a loop to attack you from the rear.

The only way the slower, less agile, Wildcats could win was in tactics and numbers. One advantage the Wildcat had over the Zero was the four heavy .50in machine-guns; given a clear shot the .50in guns would destroy a Zero in a single short burst. The Zero lacked armour-plating for the pilot and the fuel tanks were not self-sealing. The Zero was later summed up by the Americans as 'a light sports plane with a 1,000hp engine'. That was true but, well flown, as one veteran navy Wildcat pilot said: 'One to one: it was a bad day to fight a Zero. . .'

The early, bitter realization that the Japanese, whom the Americans had dismissed as mere copyists, had produced in the Mitsubishi A6M2 Zero-Sen a fighter that not only equalled but far exceeded the performance of any that the US Navy had in service in 1942 was, to say the least, unforeseen. In fact, the US Navy, even as the F4F Wildcat was entering service, had ordered a replacement in the Chance Vought F4U Corsair fighter. It was decided – presciently as it was to turn out – that as an insurance against that complex project becoming delayed or proving to be unsatisfactory, the Grumman Company should be asked to design a faster version of the F4F Wildcat that was still in production. It was suggested that a more powerful engine – a 1,600hp Wright R-2600 fourteen-cylinder Cyclone radial – might be used in place of the existing 1,200hp Pratt & Whitney R-1830 of the Wildcat.

When the contract for two prototypes, designated XF6F-1, was issued, the Grumman design team, led by Leroy Grumman and William Schwendler, had on their drawing-boards a possible successor to the F4F Wildcat which went much further than a mere engine change. The XF6F-1 emerged as a different aircraft with only a vague resemblance to the earlier Grumman fighter. The new fighter, soon to be given the name 'Hellcat', was a low-wing, single-radial-engined monoplane with clean lines which, while not aesthetically satisfying, possessed a functional aspect that suggested immense strength and fitness of purpose. Just before the prototype had flown, Leon A. 'Jake' Swirbul, the Grumman president, had taken the unusual step for an aircraft manufacturer of flying to Pearl Harbor in order to seek the opinions of US Navy pilots who had flown the Wildcat in combat against the Japanese Zeros during the Battle of the Coral Sea and at Midway, to discuss what was needed from the new Hellcat fighter to counter the Zero. One of the group, Lieutenant Commander John Thach, was considered to be the navy's expert tactician; he had devised the 'Thach weave', which was

Japanese Mitsubishi A6M2 Zero fighters about to take off from one of the carriers, possibly Shokaku, to escort torpedo and dive-bombers attacking the US Pacific Fleet at anchor in Pearl Harbor. The Zeros have long-range tanks between the undercarriage oleos, giving the fighters the phenomenal range of nearly 2,000 miles. In the 1942 Battles of the Coral Sea and Midway, Zero fighters came as a shock to the Americans who had dismissed all Japanese military aircraft as moderate copies of dated Western products.

proving very successful in countering the Zero when flying the slower Wildcat. After the meeting, Swirbul came to the realistic conclusion that, to counter the A6M2 Zero, any new Grumman fighter would have to possess a higher speed and rate of climb than would be forthcoming from the XF6F-1. It was back to New York and back to the drawing-board.

The decision was made to replace the XF6F's Wright Cyclone engine with a Pratt & Whitney R-2800 Double Wasp engine of 2,000hp, the same engine specified for the F4U Corsair. The second Grumman prototype was built with the Pratt & Whitney power plant and was flown, as the XF6F-3, in July 1942, only four weeks after the Pearl Harbor meeting with the navy pilots. Speed was the keynote of the Grumman Company. By October 1942, the first F6F-3 Hellcats were rolling off the production lines. To speed production, a new factory had been required with steel supplies subject to priority permits which were often the subject of interminable negotiations with navy officials' 'flying desks' in Washington. Swirbul went out and bought the closed New York Second Avenue elevated railway and used the scrapped steel to construct the new Plant No. 2 at Bethpage, New York. It is said that the first F6F-3 Hellcat and the roofers reached the end of the production line at the same time!

The first production Hellcat was followed by 12,271 others, 11,000 being delivered within two years; this was an unbelievable rate of aircraft production that no other nation could come close to equalling. The Royal Navy received 1,182 'Lend-Lease' Hellcats, with the first 252 aircraft being given the confusing name Gannet; this name was dropped in favour of Hellcat when all US-built aircraft used the same names in both countries. The Hellcat, a high-performance fighter, had been developed without any dramatic setbacks from prototype to production. The Pratt & Whitney engine offered 2,000hp for take-off and gave the F6F-3 a maximum speed of 376mph at 22,800ft, an excellent rate of climb of 2,260ft per minute with a service ceiling of 37,500ft. The range, a vital attribute for a carrier aircraft flying over the Pacific, was 1,085 miles on internal tanks and 1,620 miles with 125-gallon drop tanks. The armament was six .50in Colt-Browning machine-guns with 400 rounds per gun. The raised cockpit gave the Hellcat pilot a clear view and the sturdy airframe, built to withstand arrested carrier landings, was strong enough to be able to absorb considerable punishment. The folding wings of the Hellcat were of the type called 'skewed axis'. These were devised by 'Roy' Grumman himself using an eraser and two paper clips and enabled Grumman carrier aircraft, beginning with the Wildcat F4F-4, to fold their wings parallel, alongside the fuselage. (Folding wings reduced the Wildcat span from 38ft to 14ft, allowing five fighters with folding wings to be stowed in the space required by two fighters without folding wings.)

In January 1943, the US Navy embarked the first F6F-3 Hellcats aboard USS *Essex*, though the first action was in August that year when US Marine Hellcats from USS *Yorktown* flew cover for a strike against Marcus Island. The F6F Hellcat turned the tables on the Zero and later Japanese fighters, and the 7.7mm gunfire from the Zeros was absorbed by the Hellcat's tough structure. The Hellcat, unlike the earlier Wildcat, could dogfight with the Zero but the agile Japanese fighter could still evade attack by making the tight loop which the heavier F6F could not follow. However, as the high quality of the Japanese carrier pilots who had learned their craft in China waned, due to attrition, the well-trained US pilots, confident in their faster, better-armed Hellcats, became dominant. They soon learned that only a short burst from the six .50 Colt-Brownings usually resulted in an A6M2 Zero, with unprotected fuel tanks, bursting into flames. By the summer of 1943, with Hellcats rapidly replacing Wildcats aboard

US Pacific Fleet carriers, the fighter began to dominate the Pacific air battles, shooting down enemy aircraft on a large scale. With the experience of battle, the Hellcat F6F-3 was supplanted on the production lines, after 4,402 machines had been produced, by the F6F-5. This had a slightly revised wing and engine cowling and also provision for water injection to combat boost the R-2800 engine to 2,200hp in action. Some F6F-5s had the armament revised to four .50in guns and two 20mm cannon. The F6F-5 was about 75mph faster than the A6M5 Zero.

The British Pacific Fleet Hellcats from HMS *Indomitable* provided close escort for bombers on large-scale attacks on Palembang and other targets while preparing to take part in the projected invasion of the Japanese home islands, which never took place following the Japanese surrender. By the end of the war, US Hellcat pilots alone had accounted for 4,947 Japanese aircraft out of the total of 6,470 destroyed by carrier pilots. Shore-based US Marine Hellcats claimed an additional 209. If true (fighter 'kill' claims tended to be optimistic) it would give the Hellcat a ratio of nearly twenty enemy aircraft destroyed to each Hellcat lost in action, which is a remarkable record. Better technology, unsurpassed production expertise and thorough pilot training had enabled the F6F Hellcat to outclass the A6M2 Zero. That fighter had gained an early ascendancy because the Japanese military considered both the fighter and the pilot ultimately to be expendable; the lack of armour and unprotected fuel tanks eventually nullified the margin of performance. This indifference to human life was finally exemplified when hundreds of Zeros and their young pilots were sacrificed in the horrific kamikaze suicide attacks on the Pacific fleets in 1945.

There had been surprisingly few changes made to the Hellcat when all production ceased in November 1945. There was a night-fighter version, the F6F-5N, with air-to-air AN/APS-4 radar in a pod on the starboard wing, and also a radio altimeter to compensate for the poor night vision from the cockpit. There was also a high-altitude photo-reconnaissance Hellcat, the F6F-5P (the Royal Navy's designation was Hellcat FR II). Long focal-length cameras were fitted behind the pilot's cockpit; apart from the camera port, cameras and associated controls, the aircraft was the same airframe as the standard F6F-5s.

Without doubt the F6F Hellcat played a significant role in turning the seemingly inexorable tide of Japanese conquest. On the first day of the Battle of the Philippine Sea in June 1944, Hellcats shot down most of the 300 enemy aircraft destroyed that day and stopped the Japanese attack. It was the Hellcat that overcame the myth of the Zero and showed that the agile fighter could be subjugated in combat. The F4U Corsair, ordered before the Hellcat, did not reach US carriers until April 1944 (the Royal Navy had used them earlier) and the Vought fighter was far more unforgiving that the Grumman. Corsairs supplemented the Hellcats rather than replacing them, though US Marine Corsairs operating F4Us from coral islands did earn a very high reputation and destroyed their full share of enemy aircraft. In some areas the two American fighters became known as the Terrible Twins but the Corsair was a daunting aircraft when operating from a carrier's restricted flight-deck. The Grumman Hellcat in the opinion of most was, quite simply, the best all-round carrier fighter of the war, and remains a truly classic aircraft.

The Fleet Air Arm Museum at Yeovilton in Somerset has a preserved Martlet I (Wildcat) AL 246 and an F6F-5 Hellcat-KE 209, one of a batch of 148 delivered to the FAA from the second Lend-Lease allocation as Hellcat IIs. There are also a number of airworthy Hellcats flying in the United States, some of which come to the UK for the summer shows.

FACT FILE

GRUMMAN F6F-3 HELLCAT

Type
Single-seat naval fighter.

Builder
Grumman Aircraft Engineering Corporation.

Power plant
One Pratt & Whitney R-2800-10 Double Wasp 18-cylinder radial engine of 2,000hp.

Dimensions
Wing-span 42ft 10in
Length 33ft 7in.

Performance
Maximum speed 376mph at 22,800ft
Range on internal tanks 1,085 miles.

Armament
Six Colt-Browning 0.05in machine-guns with 400 rounds per gun.

Service ceiling
36,700ft

Number produced
12,272

CHAPTER THREE

SPECIAL DUTIES

In recognition terms, aircraft can be divided into two basic categories: Lysanders and the others.

Anon

A preserved Westland Lysander shows off its unique shape.

IMAGINE THAT IT IS a winter's night in 1943. On the balcony of the dark control tower of a blacked-out and seemingly deserted airfield, the watch officer is listening for the sound of a single-engined aircraft which is overdue. The night is dark with broken cloud but the stars show clearly, for the universal blackout is enhancing the night sky. Then, faintly at first, comes the unmistakable sound of the single-engined aircraft; the sound grows stronger, the engine note changing as the pilot selects fine pitch for landing. From the control tower a double 'colours-of-the-day' flare soars into the sky. There is an answering flare from the aircraft, now seen dimly against the low cloud, banking towards the runway flare-path which lights up to guide the strange-looking, high-wing monoplane as it makes its landing approach with two powerful landing lights switched on. By the tower an army car is waiting, the ATS (Auxiliary Territorial Service) driver and an RAF officer standing by the door watching, as the aircraft settles gently on the runway and taxis towards the tower. As soon as the aircraft stops, two shadowy figures alight stiffly from the rear cockpit after their three-hour flight. After a brief word with the RAF officer, they walk to the waiting car, which drives away as soon as the two are inside. The aircraft, a black-painted Lysander, taxis to its dispersal. Another Special Duties sortie is completed.

That scenario was commonplace throughout the war years – the delivering and collection of British agents – spies – to and from occupied Europe. The aircraft that flew from airfields in England on Special Duties flights was the unmistakable Westland Lysander, which performed the difficult and specialized cloak-and-dagger role to perfection. It had been designed for the very different function of Army Co-operation, a role it in fact hardly ever played and, although its wartime agent-dropping duties were highly classified, the Lysander was famous for another reason: to fail to identify a Lysander was to gain the wooden spoon in the aircraft recognition stakes.

During the Second World War, recruits to the three armed services were given aircraft recognition lectures; the lecturer invariably began with the quote that heads this chapter. The Westland Lysander was a unique shape and impossible to confuse with any other. It is true that the Germans did cause some confusion by producing the Henschel Hs 126. Both the Hs 126 and the Lysander were high-wing parasol monoplanes (with the wing set above the fusilage) and both were originally produced for the same role: Army Co-opera-

V 9287, a Westland Lysander III, was a genuine 'cloak-and-dagger' aircraft. The long-range fuel tank between the undercarriage and the ladder welded to the fuselage to enable the passengers to exit or board quickly can clearly be seen. A pilot is in the cockpit and the aircraft was probably photographed around 1941 at Westland's factory at Yeovil in Somerset before delivery to one of the two RAF Special Duties squadrons.

tion and tactical reconnaissance. But there the resemblance ended; no one could mistake the rotund, radial-engined fuselage and elongated diamond-shaped wings of the Lysander for the slender lines and swept-back wings of the German machine.

The Lysander was what would now be termed a STOL (short take-off and landing) aircraft. It had been designed to a 1934 Air Ministry Specification A.39/34 calling for an Army Co-operation aircraft to replace the existing Hawker Hector biplanes which were fulfilling that exacting role. Westland, which held the contract to build the Hector, submitted a monoplane proposal by a team led by a young aeronautical engineer, W.E. Petter. The Lysander was Petter's first design and, although the high-parasol-wing concept owed much to earlier Westland aircraft, the Widgeon and Wessex, the Lysander was unconventional in many other respects and was the result of detailed meetings with experienced RAF Army Co-operation pilots as to the precise nature of the duties expected of the new aircraft.

What emerged from the meetings was a request which was the opposite to that which most aircraft designers expect: an aircraft which would fly as *slowly* as possible. This was qualified to mean as slowly as possible when 'spotting' for the artillery or on tactical reconnaissance, with a very low stalling speed to enable the aircraft to fly in and out of restricted airfields. The Westland proposal was accepted by the Air Ministry; the first RAF monoplane with a genuine STOL specification was accepted and two proto-type Lysanders were ordered. The first, K 6127, was test-flown at Yeovil by Westland's chief test pilot, Harald Penrose, in June 1936. (The second prototype, K 6128, was sent to India for tropical trials.) The test-flying of the prototypes was satisfactory and an interim order was placed with Westland for 144 Lysander Mk Is in September 1936.

The Lysander was a large aircraft for a single-engined type. The rather elegant wings had a span of 50ft, the tubby fuselage was 30ft 6in long and the monoplane stood 11ft 6in high, a height made to seem greater due to the parasol wings being mounted at the very apex of the long, fully glazed 'greenhouse' canopy which covered both the pilot and a gunner at the rear. The pilot's field of vision was excellent and befitted the designed role of the Lysander: the pilot had an exceptionally clear view upwards, his head was slightly above the wing spars and, since he was seated ahead of the tapered wing, he had an unobstructed view downwards, forwards and to left and right because the glazing of the canopy extended almost to the floor of the cockpit. The seated height of the pilot gave him an eye-line that was well above the fully cowled 890hp Bristol Mercury XII radial engine. The fixed undercarriage was neatly faired into 'spats' to the wheels. Each wheel cover had a powerful landing light and a fixed .303in Browning machine-gun. Two winglets above the wheels had carriers for up to twelve anti-personnel bombs or stores. The rear cockpit was armed with a single, hand-trained .303in Browning – later, Mk III machines, had a double gun mounted. Curiously, standard Lysanders had no provision for communication between pilot and gunner other than a hole cut into the pilot's armour-plating. When attacked by a fighter, the first – and possibly last – intimation the pilot had would be to hear the rear-gunner firing.

The performance of the Lysander was, in 1936, considered excellent. The top speed was a respectable 237mph at 10,000ft; it had a range on standard tanks of 600 miles and a service ceiling of 26,000ft. The first squadron to replace their 187mph biplane Hawker Hectors with the new Lysanders was No. 16 at Old Sarum, Wiltshire, in the winter of 1938. Unlike the very popular Hector, the Lysander was not a forgiving aircraft. It is true that it could land in a space that no other aircraft of its size and power would contemplate but it could and did trap the unwary. Wing Commander Ken Wallis, better known for his 'James Bond' and other small autogyros, flew Lysanders from Old Sarum during the war. He remembers that:

> Take-off was simple but all the controls were manual. The throttle gate had three knobs: throttle, mixture and the control for the two-position propeller, which was pushed in for fine pitch for take-off. A hand-crank operated the engine cowl gills to regulate the cylinder-head temperatures. The gills were set fully open for take-off. The most essential drill was to wind the trim wheel on the pilot's left forward to a red mark on the scale. This was a vital part of the pre-take-off cockpit checks as it set the tail-plane incidence to zero. When landing, the trim-wheel had to be wound back to set the tail-plane to a negative angle even when making a normal airfield landing. If the pilot was faced with a baulked approach he had to wind the trim forward to the red mark while gently opening the throttle to 'go round again'. If it was left on the landing setting and, instinctively, the throttle was opened fully, the Lysander would uncontrollably rear up, stall and crash – usually with fatal results to the crew.

Ken Wallis survived his tour on Lysanders and confesses that he once looped one!

A Lysander began the war well by shooting down, in November 1939, the first German aircraft, a Heinkel He III bomber, to be shot down in France by the Air Component of the British Expeditionary Force (BEF). Lysanders serving with the BEF during the 1940 retreat to Dunkirk dropped supplies to British troops defending Calais, and Lysanders of No. 4 Squadron were the last RAF unit in action from French bases before the final evacuation from Dunkirk. After Dunkirk, it was clear that the First World War concept of set-piece artillery duels with spotter aircraft signalling the fall of shot by Morse code W/T was not going to be the way the war was to be fought. The German *Blitzkrieg*, unveiled during the invasion of Poland in 1939 and convincingly confirmed with the fall of the Low Countries and France, had shown that the war was going to be one of highly mechanized movement with fluid fronts dominated by air power. Lysanders would not be required for artillery spotting.

By late 1940, in the light of experience, the classic role of Army Co-operation aircraft changed from artillery spotting to high-speed tactical reconnaissance; consequently RAF Lysanders were replaced by the discarded American fighter, the Curtiss P 40 Tomahawk. Lysanders found a new role for which their slow speed suited them admirably: air-sea rescue. A 'Lizzie' had the ability to circle a downed airman and drop a dinghy accurately and continue circling just above the tops of the waves, marking the spot to guide a high-speed

RAF air-sea rescue launch. Other Lysanders were modified for towing training gliders for the newly formed airborne forces and for the dangerous, though essential, task of towing targets for trainee air gunners. The bulk of the 804 Mk III Lysanders were built from the outset for target-towing with the winches and target-handling gear. But the greatest role for the Lysander was yet to come: the Lysander Mk III SAS Special Duties aircraft modified for the hazardous role of dropping agents and collecting them from German-occupied Europe. To land a large and heavy aircraft at night on a field known only to the pilot as a six-figure map reference, which could well be surrounded by trees, demanded a very steep approach and as slow a forward airspeed as possible to end in a short landing-run. Harald Penrose tested a Lysander making such a night landing – on the Westland factory airfield at Yeovil. Here is his account from his autobiography *No Echo in the Sky*:

> *. . . I brought her round for the landing . . . with a rumble of engine I placed her 500 feet above the shadow of the aerodrome boundary. Speed was reduced and engine power increased to predetermined figures, . . . more tail-plane angle was wound on until the Lysander was trimmed in such perfect poise that I could take my hands off the stick . . . down she sank, hanging on the air rushing through the wing slots . . . our stalled, blind descent felt far too fast . . . as I waited, my hand poised to grab the stick, and hoped the undercarriage would withstand the impact . . . as the tail-wheel touched with a bump, I cut the engine, and the Lysander settled on her main wheels. I let her run until she stopped by the bright open doorway of the hangar.*

The Special Operation Executive (SOE) used matt black-painted Mk III Lysanders of Nos. 138 and 161 Special Duties Squadrons, which had long-range fuel tanks fitted between the undercarriage legs to increase the duration to eight hours. The rear guns were removed and a permanent ladder was welded to the port side of the fuselage for the 'Joes' – the courageous male and female SOE agents who were flown into and out of France and other occupied countries. From their bases at Tempsford in Bedfordshire and Stradishall in Suffolk the agent droppers always flew at night when there was a moon, or starlight sufficient for the pilot to navigate by dead reckoning to a certain field deep in rural France. This meant up to three hours flying over totally blacked-out German-occupied country. It was the ultimate in pilot navigation. Lysanders had no autopilots and had to be flown manually all the way; this was exhausting, particularly if it was a turbulent night, as the controls were heavy. Lysanders were noisy and tended to fill the cockpits with exhaust fumes; they were fabric covered and therefore draughty and cold. The single pilot, who had no communication with his passengers, had to fly with extreme accuracy while map-reading and searching for the vital 'fixes' – a bend in the river or some other distinct ground feature by which he could check his position and track. When the estimated time of arrival (ETA) was up, the pilot would circle at low altitude and hope to see the landing strip, which at the sound of the engine, would be marked by just three hand-held battery torches switched on to form an 'L', 150yd long by 50yd wide, to indicate wind direction. As the Lysander circled, a security signal in Morse, a pre-arranged group of letters signifying that all was well, would be flashed by torch and the Lysander would acknowledge with its 'downwards signal lamp' and make its STOL descent to the dimly seen field.

As soon as the aircraft had stopped rolling, the Joes would climb out, their civilian coats billowing in the slipstream of the idling propeller, clutching their cheap suitcases which may or may not have contained a radio transmitter, and perhaps another two agents who had been waiting in the field would embark for the return journey. Packages, Sten guns and ammunition were also carried for the resistance members. The average turnaround was just three minutes before the Lysander pilot opened the throttle and took off into the night sky for the long journey back to the UK. Below, the French resistance men and women and the British agents would have melted into the night, before any patrolling German troops, alerted by aircraft engine noise, had been rushed to the scene.

The Lysander pilots and their unknown Joes faced many dangers: it was not unknown for the landing-site and identifying code to be compromised by treachery and revealed to the Germans. There was also always the danger of night fighters, radar-directed master searchlights and flak. Bad weather could close in; often it was so bad that the Special Duties Lysanders were the only RAF aircraft flying that night. They were then prone to be fired on over home territory by 'friendly' anti-aircraft guns. The navy were so apt to do this that ports like Dover, Portsmouth and Harwich were avoided. All in all, the cloak-and-dagger trips were considered so hazardous that six sorties constituted a full tour. France was not the only destination: one Lysander, with extra tankage, successfully flew a twelve-hour flight to pick up an agent from a field in Czechoslovakia. By D-Day, on sorties to France alone, 300 agents were flown in and 500 picked up to fly back to the UK.

Lysander production at Yeovil ceased in January 1942 after 1,368 had been built; a further 325 Mk IIIs were built in Malton, Canada. Several Lysanders survive. In the RAF Museum there is a MK III Lysander, R 9125, used by No. 225 Squadron in 1940 and later allocated to No. 161 Squadron at Tempsford, one of the Special Duties units. There is no record showing that R 9125 was used as an agent-dropper; it was possibly used for pilot training. The US Air Force Museum in Dayton, Ohio, has a Mk III, one of twenty-four used by the USAF during the war. There are only three known airworthy Lysanders world-wide, all salvaged from a farm in Canada. One is with the Shuttleworth Trust with the serial number V 9441 (its original, Canadian RCAF serial number was 2355). Another, owned privately but flying from Duxford, is coded V 9545, a serial number allocated originally to a Mk IIIA Lysander. The third airworthy Canadian Lysander is based in Belgium.

There was one aircraft that could fly slower than the Lysander – in fact it was possibly the slowest-flying fixed-wing military aircraft ever. This was the German Fiesler Fi 156 Storch. (*Storch* is the German word for stork.) An American marine, Major Al Williams, a military attaché, was invited to fly in a Storch in 1938. This is what he wrote of the experience in his book *Airpower*, published in 1940:

A preserved Fiesler Fi 156 Storch. These aircraft had an amazing capacity for landing and taking off from fields that only helicopter pilots would contemplate using. The photograph illustrates well the full length Handley Page slots which contributed to the STOL (short take-off and landing) performance of the aircraft. Pilots of preserved Storches report that the aircraft is not particularly pleasant to fly. The original Argus engines are now very difficult and expensive to maintain.

It was a funny looking affair with its great windows – all that seemed necessary were a few geraniums to convert it into a conservatory . . . after a ground run of about 50 feet, the [Storch] leapt into the air at an angle that had me lying on my back . . . the air speed indicator showing about 35mph . . .

During the rapid build-up of the nascent *Luftwaffe* in 1935, many were called and many chosen. Fieseler-Flugzeugbau received an order for a two- to three-seat multi-purpose communications aircraft to exploit the then newly perfected high-lift wing designs with full-span slots and flaps to provide a true STOL performance, powered by a 240hp inverted V-8 air-cooled Argus As 10C-3 engine. The aircraft produced was the Fi 156 Storch, which could fly under full control at 32mph indicated; the take-off run on a grass airfield into an 8mph wind was just 154ft. However, the maximum speed at sea level was only 109mph and the cruising speed 90mph. Nevertheless the Storch, the only fixed-wing aircraft to rival the helicopter, was used extensively by the *Luftwaffe* during the Second World War, mainly on communication duties, though reconnaissance units were equipped with the type. Storches were used to rescue shot-down *Luftwaffe* pilots from remote locations, often in enemy territory and under fire. Many Storches were used as air evacuation ambulances; having a large cargo door, and with the rear seats removed, they could carry one stretcher. The slow-flying capabilities of the Storch were utilized for some unusual duties. There is film evidence in the archives of the Imperial War Museum in London, showing a Storch being used to lay German army telephone cables with the aircraft, only a few feet off the ground, paying out the cable from a large drum by the kilometre. Other duties were the proposed dropping of light bombs and French marine depth charges which weighed 300lb, so one could be carried between the undercarriage legs. The German Navy did not pursue the idea though it was tested at the German equivalent of Farnborough, the *Erprobungsstelle* at Rechlin. The Storch was used extensively in the North African desert areas. Both Field Marshal Rommel and General Kesselring used a VIP Storch as personal transports as they roamed the desert inspecting units of the *Afrika Korps*, their Storch being able to land on any level stretch of the desert. (General Kesselring had his Storch emblazoned with his personal insignia as commander of *Luftflotte 2*.)

A number of Storches were captured and impressed into the RAF. One was used by Air Vice Marshal Sir Harry Broadhurst when commanding 83 Group of the 2nd Tactical Air Force at the time of the D-Day invasion. Winston Churchill used that particular Storch, in 'invasion-stripes' markings, when he flew to visit the Allied forces in Normandy. Although the Fi 156 Storch was used on every German front, including Russia, there are two epic Storch flights that no other fixed-wing aircraft, Allied or Axis, could have accomplished.

The first involved the Italian dictator Mussolini. In September 1943, as the Allies fought their way up Italy, the Italian government under Marshal Badoglio surrendered. The Allied armistice terms included the handing over of Mussolini. Pending the inevitable negotiations with the Allies, Badoglio had the Italian ex-dictator placed under house arrest in what amounted to an impregnable fortress, the Albergo-Rifugio, a fashionable peacetime ski-resort hotel that was on a plateau 9,050ft high near the peak of the Gran Sasso d'Italia, the highest mountain in the Apennines. The only access to the hotel was by cable-car.

In view of developments, Hitler ordered that *Il Duce* had to be rescued to head a German-backed puppet government, the object being to keep Italy in the war. He summoned to his HQ at Rastenburge in East Prussia the commander of a special SS unit *SS Hauptsturmführer* Otto Skorzeny and gave him *carte blanche* to locate and rescue the imprisoned Italian dictator. The operation was given the code-name *Eiche* (Oak). It took some time to locate Mussolini and, when found in the mountain hotel, the prospect of release was, to say the least, daunting. However Skorzeny, with the unlimited backing of Hitler, had hand-picked a team of Germany's toughest parachute troops. In all, 120 of them were embarked in twelve DFS (the German research institute for gliding) ten-man gliders which, when released from their tugs, circled towards the mountain. At the lower terminal of the funicular another body of parachute troops overpowered the Italian *carabinieri* guarding the station and forty *Fallschirmjager*, armed to the teeth, rode up the cable-cars towards the hotel, arriving just as the first glider touched down on the hotel parapet. Another seven gliders followed.

Seeing the German parachute troops pouring out, the surprised Italian guards surrendered without a shot being fired and *Il Duce*, unshaven and incongruously clad in a long black overcoat and trilby hat, was hustled by Skorzeny into a Fieseler Storch which had touched down to join the now somewhat crowded, and precipitous forecourt of the mountain resort. If the landing had been spectacular, the take-off of the Storch was to be little short of unbelievable. The only take-off space available was inadequate even for a Storch. Moreover, it was strewn with boulders. To make matters even worse, the take-off would have to be down wind, with the aircraft overloaded, as Skorzeny insisted on cramming his 6ft 2in frame alongside Mussolini in the rear cockpit. The pilot, *Hauptmann* Gerlach, pleaded, in vain, that the high altitude would give less lift to the seriously overloaded Storch which, even at sea level into a stiff breeze with no passengers, would have difficulty in getting airborne in the available space. He was overruled and, after selecting some 40 degrees of flap, with the Argus engine flat out and parachute troops holding the tail, Gerlach signalled them to let go, released the brakes and the Storch slowly ran towards the cliff edge, veering sharply to the left as it hit a rock *en route*, bursting a tyre and damaging the wheel. Then in a shower of stones, it disappeared, dropping from the sight of the German troops, the only indication that it was still flying being the noise of the straining engine. With consummate skill, Gerlach, with the Storch verging on the stall, used the limited airspace of the ravine below the mountain, adjusting the flap-setting to try to find the best lift/drag combination to increase the airspeed and climb out of the valley, the rocky floor of which was now perilously close. He made it to Practica di Mare airfield, landing safely in spite of the burst tyre, where a Heinkel He III was waiting to transport *Il Duce* rather more conventionally to a meeting with Hitler. Skorzeny was decorated by Hitler with an immediate *Ritterkreuz* (Knight's Cross). Gerlach was simply congratulated. The Storch which had made the rescue possible disappeared from history, its fate and identity remaining unknown.

The next story featuring a Fieseler Storch was the flight into the besieged city of Berlin by the German female test pilot *Flugkapitan* Hanna Reitsch. Towards the end of the European war, with Berlin surrounded by Russian troops who were fighting street by street, building by building, into the government centre of the city, Hitler, entombed in the *Führerbunker*, was still ruling his tottering and diminishing empire. He had sent a teleprinter message to *Generaloberst* Ritter von Greim, then commanding *Luftflotte 6* in Russia, ordering him to a conference in the Berlin bunker. There was one small difficulty – that of getting into and, more pertinently, out of the surrounded city. Von Greim had Hanna Reitsch as his personal pilot; this was a little surprising as von Greim was himself a most competent ex-fighter pilot with twenty-eight victories to his name. It was decided that the only feasible way to the *Führerbunker* was to use one of two existing experimental German helicopters, almost certainly Focke-Achgelis FA 233 Drache (*drache* is the German word for kite), which were at Rechlin. Hanna Reitsch was one of the few pilots who had helicopter experience; when the two arrived at Rechlin it was discovered that both the helicopters had been badly damaged in a recent RAF raid and were beyond repair. The only possible alternative aircraft capable of landing on a Berlin street was a Storch; the general was told that there were two at Gatow, the Berlin civil airfield which was still in German hands. The only aircraft serviceable at Rechlin was a single-seat Fw 190 fighter. Von Greim managed to squeeze in behind the seat of the sergeant pilot but Hanna Reitsch, being smaller, had to be wedged into the radio compartment within the fighter's fuselage. The only way in or out was via the access hatch which could only be opened from the outside. Thus laden, the fighter took off for Gatow with other Fw 190s flying cover and landed without incident, though several of the escort were shot down by Russian fighters. There the odd couple discovered that one of the Storches had been damaged by Russian shellfire but the second appeared to be airworthy. Von Greim climbed into the pilot's seat with Hanna Reitsch behind him in the observer's position. They took off, as dusk was falling, for the flight to the city centre.

It was 26 April 1945 and Berlin was ablaze with burning buildings and incessant gunfire as the Russians pounded the capital. When the Storch took off von Greim kept the monoplane very low, flying at treetop height over Russian troops who were camped in the extensive woods of the *Grunewald* on the outskirts of Berlin; Hanna Reitsch was later to recall seeing groups of soldiers sitting around huge camp fires. Machine-gun fire followed the Storch and a fuel tank in one wing was holed; petrol began to stream from the tank but luckily did not catch fire. As they approached the city centre, skimming over the rooftops, von Greim was struck in the right foot by a bullet and slumped unconscious over the controls. Hanna Reitsch leant over him and grabbed the stick. With the Storch only feet from disaster, she continued to fly the stricken aircraft, expecting the wing to catch fire at any moment, towards the Brandenburg Gate. With great skill, she managed to land the aircraft without the use of the rudder and while under fire, on the East-West Axis – a road which, though wide, had tall bronze lamp standards on either side. It was, by any measure, flying of the highest quality by a brave woman.

A German army tank was flagged down, von Greim was lifted aboard, and the couple were driven to the *Führerbunker* where von Greim was attended to by a doctor before seeing Hitler who promoted him to the post of *Oberbefehlshaber der Luftwaffe*, replacing the disgraced *Reichsmarschal* Hermann Göring who had been arrested on Hitler's orders by the SS on a charge of treason. The promotion interview took five minutes: it could have been effected by teleprinter. Four days later von Greim had recovered sufficiently for him to be flown out of Berlin by the indefatigable Hanna Reitsch in a two-seat Arado 96 training aircraft, which was flown in from Rechlin by a young sergeant pilot. What happened to the sergeant is not recorded.

Fiesler production of the Fi 156 Storch had ceased in October 1943 in order to clear the production lines for the Fw 190 fighters. However, production continued in both France by Morane-Saulnier at Puteaux and at Chocen in Czechoslovakia where ex-Fiesler tools and jigs had been sent. By the end of the war, the *Luftwaffe* had placed on charge some 2,900 of these unique STOL aircraft. Many others had been either exported to Sweden and Switzerland or given to allies. After the war, surviving Storches were eagerly sought by the victors. As many as 142 were captured in an airworthy condition; the RAF impressed some sixty, using them for communication duties. One Storch, *Werk Nr.* 475061 and with the RAF serial number VP 546, was landed on the aircraft carrier HMS *Triumph* by the noted naval test pilot, Lieutenant Commander 'Winkle' Brown. Many of the captured aircraft were distributed among the occupied countries; many were scrapped as spares ran out, consequently very few of these wartime aircraft now remain.

FACT FILE

FIESLER FI 56C-2 STORCH

Type
Two-seat air observation post and communication aircraft.

Power plant
Argus 240hp inverted V-8 air-cooled engine.

Dimensions
Wing-span 46ft 9in (the wings could be folded back for the aircraft to be towed by road)
Length: 32ft 6in.

Weight
Normal loading 2,920 lb.

Performance
Maximum speed 109mph
Range at 90mph: 240 miles
Minimum speed 32mph
Service ceiling 15,000ft.

Armament (when fitted)
One 7.92mm MG 15 machine-gun firing from a flexible mounting in the rear cockpit.
Light bombs and other offensive stores could be carried with field modifications.

Number produced (during WWII)
2,900

A wrecked Fiesler Storch standing with wings folded in the Berlin *Tiergarten* is examined by a British soldier in July 1945. This Storch could well have been the one in which Hanna Reitsch made her epic flight with von Greim when the latter was summoned to Hitler's bunker on 26 April 1945. The wide road, the *Charlottenburger-Chausse,* on which she landed ran through the *Tiergarten* is not far from the point where this photograph was taken.

Production of the Storch continued after the war in France as the Criquet (Cricket) and also in Czechoslovakia. The inevitable shortage of German Argus engines resulted in the installation of alternative, small radial engines, typically the French Salmson and the American Jacobs, of around 300hp. Today many of these postwar Storches survive, particularly the later French-built Criquets, though they are expensive to operate in private hands. The US Air Force Museum at Dayton, Ohio, has a genuine Fiesler-built Storch suspended, flaps down, as if about to land. It has desert camouflage and carries the markings SF + YK – that of Rommel's personal aircraft.

The Spitfire is without any question not only a classic but perhaps the most famous fighter aircraft of all time. Yet, although the well-merited exploits of the 'Few' are celebrated each September on Battle of Britain day, there are other, largely unsung, heroes who flew Spitfires, not in the great air battles, but alone on long, dangerous sorties. They were the pilots of the photographic reconnaissance units (PRUs) whose unarmed Spitfires, painted in PR blue, roamed far and wide over Germany and the occupied countries in broad daylight seeking photographic intelligence.

Photographic reconnaissance was one of the first tasks of military aircraft. In 1914 it was a hit-and-miss operation with observers holding a heavy plate camera over the side of slow two-seat observation aircraft. The technique and the cameras improved through the years and two world wars to the point in March 1941 when the first Spitfire IVs were delivered to Benson in Oxfordshire, then the main PRU base.

The development of the RAF's photographic reconnaissance itself is fascinating, though beyond the scope of this book. The arrival of the PR Spitfire in 1940 was due, in essence, to a colourful honorary RAF Wing Commander, Sidney Cotton, who just before the war made clandestine photographic reconnaissance flights in a civil-registered twin-engined Lockheed 12A airliner with, originally, three hidden motorized 35mm Leica cameras shooting through a hole in the fuselage floor. On these ostensible 'charter flights', Cotton had managed to photograph the Italian fleet and large sections of the Siegfried Line. With such excellent results, by the outbreak of the war, Cotton, who was under pressure to use Blenheims (which he rightly considered unsuitable) met the commander of RAF Fighter Command, the redoubtable 'Stuffy' Dowding. Against all odds, Cotton got him to agree to the loan of two Spitfires to be modified at the then PRU base at Heston, West London, to carry RAF F24 cameras for high-altitude photographic reconnaissance.

With enthusiastic assistance from a PR pilot, Flight Lieutenant 'Shorty' Longbottom, the first PR IA Spitfire, N 3071, took off from Seclin near Lille in France on 18 November 1939 for the first sortie by a PR Spitfire. Longbottom had been a major factor in the modification of the IA Spitfire. All the guns, radios and armour-plating had been removed. The plating joins and rivet heads of the fuselage were carefully filled with plaster of Paris and the whole external airframe was hand-polished because the Spitfire's only defence, if intercepted by an enemy fighter, would be speed. The end result was that the PR Spitfire was some 15mph faster than the standard Spitfire Mk I, and capable of operating at over 30,000ft. The wings, with all guns removed, now contained additional fuel tanks bringing the total to 240 gallons, earning the PR Spitfire the nickname Flying Bowser. It had a range of 1,500 miles at 300mph, three times that of a standard Spitfire IA. Armed with the excellent RAF 24 cameras fitted behind the pilot, the Spitfires produced some very good cover. So good was it that the Spitfire was now accepted as the ideal aircraft for the role of PR. With experience gained, the modified Spitfires were developed into a production subtype, the Spitfire PR IV, which entered service with No. 212 Squadron in March 1941.

The arrival of the Spitfire PR IVs coincided with the definitive overall PR cerulean blue colour with only very inconspicuous national markings. The roundels omitted the white section and the serial numbers were very small. The PR IV's fuselage was that of a standard Mk V fighter with the addition of round glazed camera ports, but the type had special wings which were, in all but name, fuel tanks. They held 133 gallons which, with another 85 gallons in the standard Spitfire tanks, gave a total of 218 imperial gallons offering a still-air range of 1,800 miles. There were various camera combinations available, with all the camera exposures controlled by the pilot, though a certain degree of automatic operation was available. Typically, there were two F 24 cameras in streamlined fairings shooting forward under each wing and various combinations of oblique or vertical cameras of differing focal lengths, depending on the nature of the sortie, in the fuselage behind the pilot's seat. The Spitfire IV's were powered by a 1,100hp Rolls-Royce 45 engine. The maximum speed was 372mph with a ceiling of 39,600ft (unpressurized, though a vestigial degree of pilot comfort was afforded by a cockpit heater!). In all, 229 IVs were delivered to RAF PRU squadrons. The type became the mainstay of the PRU during the middle of the war and their pilots produced some outstanding photographs or 'covers'. Two of the low-level photographs, taken from a Spitfire IV were, in the opinion of the late Professor R.V. Jones, the wartime head of RAF Intelligence, 'the two greatest photographs of the war'.

In 1941, R.V. Jones had been very much concerned with the Secret War, the struggle between the scientists of the fighting powers to gain and retain supremacy in the deployment of electronic warfare which, with move and counter-move, was relentlessly pursued by the boffins of either side, principally those of Britain and Germany. Of all the electronic weapons developed during the Second World War, radar was by far the most telling. Radar guided bombers to their targets; radar guided defending fighters, master searchlights and flak to the bombers – it was a never-ending loop. Jones had an intelligence intercept, possible an Enigma decode, which talked of a *Würzburg Gerät*. 'Ferret' Wellington aircraft flying what we would now call Elint (electronic intelligence) sorties discovered pulse transmissions, on a wavelength of 53cm, originating from Brittany. The crews also reported that powerful searchlights were switched on that followed the Wellington 'with good accuracy'. It was clear to Jones that *Würzburg* was a very accurate radar used to direct fighters or searchlights to intruding aircraft. The radar would be difficult to locate because the directional antenna required for 53cm radar would itself be small. The photographic Interpretation Unit at Medmenham, near Marlow in Buckinghamshire, was asked to examine routine cover of the Brittany coast. On a wide-angle photograph taken of the coast at Cap d'Antifer, near the village of Bruneval, there was a château with a path that seemed to lead to the villa but ended in a loop short of the house. Beside the loop there was a dot, so small that Jones ordered several prints to make certain that the dot was not a speck of dust. It was nothing of the kind. Jones came to the conclusion that the dot could be the antenna of a 53cm *Würzburg* radar but the small scale of the photograph made positive identification impossible.

At RAF Benson, only 15 miles from Medmenham, one of the leading photographic reconnaissance pilots, Flight Lieutenant Tony Hill, heard of the difficulty Jones was having and quite unofficially took off in his PR Spitfire, with the oblique camera set to photograph at right angles to the line of flight the mysterious dot on the clifftops at Cap d'Antifer. Flying low past the villa, Hill's camera jammed without recording anything at all. Hill reported, on landing back at Benson, that he had seen the dot object as he flashed past, which he described as: 'Looking like a large electric bowl fire about 10ft across'. The next day, which was 15 December 1941, Tony Hill again took off in his Spitfire and returned with the first of those two 'greatest photographs of the war'. The picture, taken from a Spitfire flying at 350mph at right angles to the subject and at a height of 300ft, showed in perfect detail the German radar looking, as Hill had reported, just like a large electric bowl fire. It was measured by British radar experts who

A still from a wartime film dealing with photographic reconnaissance. Here an RAF interpreter examines a 'cover': aerial photographs taken over enemy territory. Between the years 1939–45, Allied photographic reconnaissance aircraft photographed the whole of Germany twice, revealing – among other German secrets – the V1 flying bombs, the V2 rockets and details of the enemy's defensive radar network.

RIGHT **The suspected existence of an accurate German 53cm radar code-named *Würzburg* was confirmed by this first routine print taken off Cap d'Antifer, Brittany.**

BELOW **A low-level PRU Spitfire sortie flown by Tony Hill** (bottom) **confirmed the *Würzburg* radar beyond doubt, near the village of Bruneval. In March 1942, the 'Bruneval' commando raid captured the secret radar.**

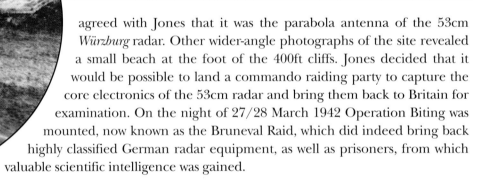

agreed with Jones that it was the parabola antenna of the 53cm *Würzburg* radar. Other wider-angle photographs of the site revealed a small beach at the foot of the 400ft cliffs. Jones decided that it would be possible to land a commando raiding party to capture the core electronics of the 53cm radar and bring them back to Britain for examination. On the night of 27/28 March 1942 Operation Biting was mounted, now known as the Bruneval Raid, which did indeed bring back highly classified German radar equipment, as well as prisoners, from which valuable scientific intelligence was gained.

The second great photograph was also taken by Tony Hill from his Spitfire PR IV. This was also of an enemy radar, this time a long-range device, known as *Würzburg Riese* (giant Würzburg), which had been seen on the Dutch island of Walchern, near Domberg, and reported by a British agent. On 2 May 1942 Tony Hill flew to Walchern and took a remarkable oblique photograph that perfectly framed the radar. It was scaled for the intelligence boffins by a startled *Luftwaffe* operator, frozen by Hill's camera, in the act of climbing a ladder to the radar. From these two pictures, and some very courageous Elint flights and agent reports, R.V. Jones was able to reconstruct the German defensive radar network known as the Kammhuber Line and devise counter-measures including, eventually, the formidable radar counter called Window. This consisted of strips of aluminium foil which completely jammed the German 53cm system.

The Spitfire IV was eventually superseded by other, later PR Spitfires, the last wartime variant being the Spitfire XI which, like all the PR machines, carried no armament. It had a maximum speed of 422mph and a range of 2,000 miles. One of these late PRU Spitfires flies with the RAF Battle of Britain Memorial Flight. A final pressurized, Griffon-engined, PR Spitfire XIX was produced too late for the war, but one of these 454mph Spitfires had the honour to fly the last RAF sortie made by an operational Spitfire. It was made by PS 888 of No. 81 Squadron on 1 April 1954 during the Malayan crisis.

Spitfires were not, of course, the only RAF PR aircraft. Mosquitoes were extensively used, as were other types. The efficiency of the PRUs was such that the whole of Germany was photographed by RAF aircraft, much of it twice, in addition to extensive cover of the occupied countries – a remarkable feat. Several PR Spitfires are preserved. One Spitfire PR XI, PL 965, is owned privately but flies from Duxford at the summer airshow.

OPPOSITE BELOW **Acting on intelligence reports, PRU pilot Tony Hill also took this low-level shot of the 'giant Würzburg' at over 300mph. The radar was on the Dutch island of Walchern and was scaled by the *Luftwaffe* man about to climb the ladder. Sadly, Tony Hill lost his life on another PR sortie shortly after this photograph was taken.**

BELOW **The Griffon-engined Spitfire PR XIX of 1945 was the final photographic reconnaissance Spitfire. The aircraft depicted, PS 915, resplendent in authentic PRU cerulean blue, served in 1946 with No. 541 Squadron on PRU duties and later with a meteorological flight until 1957 when it became a 'Gate Guardian'. In 1984 it was brought in from the cold, restored and now flies with the Battle of Britain Flight as a fitting memorial to the pilots of the wartime Spitfire PRU unit.**

CHAPTER FOUR

ROTATING WINGS

Nature invented the first autogyro in the sycamore seed.
Wing Commander Ken Wallis

THE REMARK ABOVE was made by Wing Commander Ken Wallis during a BBC television documentary 'The Flying Machines of Ken Wallis'. He was in a position to know about autogyros because he had designed, built and flown nineteen, including the celebrated Little Nellie which 007 was seen flying into action in the James Bond film *You Only Live Twice*.

The autogyro is not a helicopter. (It is not even an 'autogiro', the 'i' spelling being a trademark of the Cierva company.) The rotating wing of the autogyro is not powered; it is simply a wind-driven wing and the forward motion of the autogyro is provided by a conventional propeller, either pulling or, as is the case with the Wallis machine, pushing. Although an autogyro can achieve a very short take-off and landing it cannot hover in still air; it must maintain forward motion. The helicopter, which came after considerable development work had been accomplished on the autogyro, has engine-powered rotors. They are, in effect, a variable-pitch propeller turned upwards; they provide all the lift and, when tilted, the forward motion. This tilting is known as cyclic pitch. With the correct power and pitch setting of the rotors, called collective pitch, the helicopter can hover indefinitely, and that is its main virtue. In certain emergency circumstances a helicopter can make a single landing attempt with the rotors 'windmilling' – becoming, in effect, an autogyro – but it is a hazardous action following engine failure and calls for precise and skilled judgement on the part of the pilot.

The idea of an airscrew pulling a man into vertical flight exercised men's minds for 2,000 years. The Chinese certainly had spinning toys based on a rotating helix and Leonardo da Vinci sketched his proposal for an 'Air gyroscope' in about 1500. This was to be hand-powered and would, if built, have been a non-starter, as would the many other schemes put forward by long-forgotten inventors who could not draw as well as Leonardo. Until the internal combustion engine arrived with the twentieth century all attempts to get airborne with rotating wings were doomed to fail. What the inventors failed to recognize when seeing a simple sycamore seed whirl by was that it had the most powerful engine of all: gravity.

From 1907, when the first successful attempt at vertical flight by Paul Cornu, lasting for only twenty seconds, did at least prove it to be possible, progress was slow. Old

'Desert Storm'. A dramatic photograph from the Gulf War as a Royal Navy Westland Mk 3 Lynx of No. 815 Squadron, embarked aboard the frigate HMS *Brilliant*, flies low over a disabled Iraqi T 55 tank with a Mk 4 Sea King of No. 846 Squadron following, apparently engulfed in flames from a blazing Kuwaiti oil well, one of many torched by the retreating Iraqi army.

The Cierva C.6A, the first autogyro to fly in Britain, being demonstrated at Farnborough to the Air Ministry by F.T. Courtney in October 1925. The C.6A had the fuselage and rotary engine of an Avro 504; the normal fixed-wing aircraft controls were retained, the enlarged ailerons being mounted on outriggers. Later, short monoplane wings were fitted inboard of the ailerons.

newsreel pictures show machines either shaking themselves to pieces or, at best (as was the case with the 1922 helicopter of Etienne Oemichen) becoming briefly airborne but with little, if any, directional control or stability. These machines lacked, therefore, any pretensions towards being true helicopters. The many problems of the powered helicopter, mechanical and aerodynamic, were such that it would not become a practical proposition until 1936. By that time the far simpler autogyro was firmly established and in commercial production.

The name synonymous with the autogyro is that of the Spaniard Juan de la Cierva. Cierva was obsessed with the idea of designing an aeroplane that could not stall. In the 1920s many fatal crashes occurring with light aircraft were caused by aeroplanes stalling as they were flying low prior to landing because of inexperienced amateur pilots allowing the airspeed to fall to a dangerously low figure, thus causing the airflow over the wings to cease to generate lift. As the stall was usually followed by an irrecoverable spin at low height, the result was nearly always a fatal crash. Cierva had the bright idea that if the wings were allowed to rotate they could never stall. Instead, they would continue to generate lift by their self-rotation which would be sufficient to allow a soft landing, like the sycamore leaf, even if the aircraft had little or no forward speed. To achieve that goal Cierva had to solve a number of problems. The most difficult had been foreseen by other, earlier, investigators into rotating wings. In simplest terms it is this: the rotating blades of Cierva's autogyro were aerofoils. These were, in effect, thin wings with their 'angle of attack' (the tilt or pitch of the blades relative to the airflow) set to the critical figure which created what Cierva termed 'autorotation' – in other words, once started, they would continue to rotate and generate lift from the air passing through them. However, when the autogyro began to move forward, drawn by the conventional propeller, the air passing over the advancing blades was greater than that over the ones retreating. The advancing blades had their airflow augmented by the airspeed of the autogyro, the retreating blades had minus that figure. The practical result is that a fixed-blade autogyro will roll over because of the asymmetric lift of the rotor disc. The sycamore seed does not topple because it has no forward motion. It is blown by the wind and is always autorotating downwards.

Cierva, an aeronautical engineer supported by the Spanish state, solved the problem of asymmetry with the invention of the fully articulated rotor head. The articulated head perfected on his first successful autogyro, the Cierva C-6 of 1924, allowed each or the four rotor blades to have a drag hinge, which permitted that blade to lag or advance slightly, and a flapping hinge, which allowed each blade to rise a little above the plane of the rotor disc. When the autogyro was flying, the advancing blades dissipated surplus lift by rising and lagging relative to the retreating blades, and thus the lift was equalized around the rotor disc. Centrifugal force prevented too high a 'cone' angle of the blades (there were stops as well, just in case, and dampers were fitted to the hinges to prevent excessive vibration and wear caused by the constant motion of the blades). Cierva's autogyros, when seen in flight, clearly had the rotor disc at a higher angle at the front of the machine than the rear, as the surplus lift was dissipated from the advancing blades by the articulated head, the basic feature of which can still be found on most helicopters today.

The Cierva C-6 of 1924 was a hybrid: it had the engine, propeller, undercarriage and fuselage of an Avro 504-K modified with a four-bladed rotor freely pivoted on a pylon. Short-span monoplane wings with half the span arranged as ailerons were required to augment the conventional fixed-wing aircraft controls of rudder and elevators. The essentially aerodynamic controls were found to be inadequate at the very low landing speeds of the autogyro and the C-6 was apt to topple when taxied in even a moderate crosswind. However, such crashes took place in slow motion and seldom caused serious injury to either pilot or autogyro. The C-6's rotors were free to windmill once airborne, but a system of a drum and a long rope enabled them to be 'spun up' by a number of men running on the ground, rather in the manner of a child's top. Once spinning, the pilot opened the throttle of the Le Rhone rotary and, with the rotors turning at the required 140rpm, took off, the forward airspeed and any wind being sufficient to keep the rotors autorotating and creating lift for flight. A mild breeze being enough for a short take-off, the machine then climbed at a very low forward speed in total safety. Even if the engine failed, the autogyro would descend to earth slowly under full control, the whirling rotors creating enough lift to avoid stalling and to cushion the landing.

In 1928, a Cierva C.8L Mk II, powered by a 200hp Armstrong Siddeley Lynx IVc radial engine, made the first crossing of the Channel by a rotary-wing aircraft. It was piloted by Cierva himself, with a passenger, and took off from Croydon to land in Paris. The C.8L had a level maximum speed of 100mph. The Avro company concluded a licence agreement with Cierva and during the 1930s autogyros became a common sight around major airports (it is thought that Avro made sixty-eight autogyros before the Second World War halted production). The later Avro Type 671, C-30A machines had lost all their 504K ancestry. They had a control column directly attached to the articulated rotor head so that it became a true cyclic-pitch control for direction, climb and descent.

In 1934, the RAF bought ten Cierva C-30A autogyros, from K 4230 to K 4239, which were given the service name of Rota I. Six were on charge to the School of Army Co-

OPPOSITE **Wing Commander Ken Wallis flying his WA-116 autogyro. This small, 60hp machine, G-BLIK, holds no fewer than twelve current (1998) world records for distance and speed in a closed circuit, attaining a maximum speed of 120mph (193.4 kph), a record achieved in 1986 which still stands. The altitude record of 18,517ft (5,644m), set in 1982, has only recently been broken by an American turbocharged autogyro.**

BELOW **A contemporary cut-away of the Cierva C.30A, the definitive autogyro of the 1930s. The drawing clearly shows the 'spin-up' drive to the rotors, though this machine had fixed-pitch blades and so could not make the spectacular jump-start. Nevertheless, the relatively complex developed autogyro head pioneered many features to be found on the powered rotors of the helicopters that followed.**

operation at Old Sarum. The C-30s had a single 140hp Armstrong Siddeley Genet Major radial engine offering a maximum level speed of 100mph; they could climb at 700ft per minute to 8,000ft. The fully articulated head had three metal rotor blades of 37ft diameter. These developed autogyros had the facility of clutching the engine to the rotors to spin up prior to take-off, thus shortening the take-off run. There was a refinement to the technique; an experimental Cierva 'autodynamic' head was fitted to a C-30A, G-ACWF, and demonstrated at Hanworth, Middlesex in 1939. This special head allowed the rotors to spin up at zero pitch, beyond the normal take-off rpm and they then automatically went into positive pitch, the kinetic energy stored in the blades being sufficient for the autogyro to make a spectacular 20ft jump start and take-off without any forward ground run. As soon as it was airborne, the engine had to be de-clutched. Forward motion for all autogyros was still by conventional propeller, though with a marked down-thrust. RAF Rota Is were used during the Second World War by No. 1448 Flight (later No. 529 Squadron) on radar azimuth calibration for which their slow forward speed was ideal. The autogyros would fly to a predetermined height and distance, known to the RAF Chain Home defensive RDF (radar) operators who used the information to verify the radar returns. By 1940 radar calibration duties increased and five civilian Cierva C-30s were impressed into the RAF; they were camouflaged and issued with the service serial numbers AP 506 to AP 510. One of the original ten RAF Rota Is, K 4232, can be seen, beautifully restored, in the RAF Museum.

Although Cierva is the name associated with the pre-war autogyro, other makes were also popular in the late 1930s. The American companies Kellett and Pitcairn, and the British Westland company, today a major helicopter manufacturer, had the prototype CL20 autogyro, with two seats in an enclosed cabin, flight-tested and ready for production when war commitments caused the project to be stopped. It is sadly

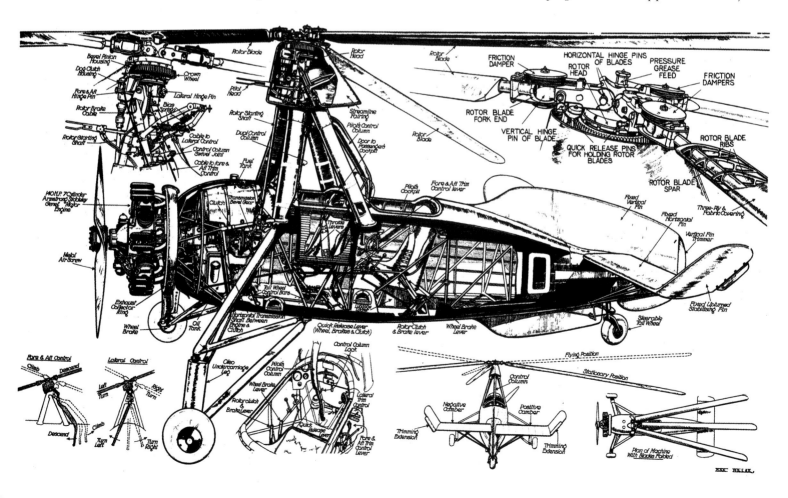

BELOW **An American Pitcairn PA-39, a licence-built Cierva, BW 829, lands on HMS *Massey* during 1941 Fleet Air Arm trials to determine if autogyros could be used at sea. Although autogyros could land and take off from ships, the offensive load they could carry was too limited to be of operational use.**

ironic that Juan de la Cierva, who developed his autogyros primarily for safe flying, should lose his life in a KLM DC-2 airliner which crashed on take-off from Croydon on 9 December 1936.

In many ways the Cierva C-30 autogyros defined the developed autorotating-wing aircraft. The first true practical helicopter, the Focke-Achgelis Fa 61, had been successfully test-flown in Germany by Ewald Rohlfs in June 1936 and other work, principally in Germany, was under way. The imperative of war would advance the development of the helicopter which, for military applications where cost was not a primary consideration, had many advantages over the autogyro. The ability to hover and to land and take off from almost anywhere, including ships at sea, and the far greater load-carrying capabilities made the helicopter, despite its greater complication, a more attractive proposition to the military than the autogyro. Nevertheless, there were a small num-

LEFT **Hanna Reitsch flying the German Focke-Achgelis Fa 61. This is a still from a 1937 film of the German female test pilot's early flights with the world's first practical helicopter. D-EKRA is similar to the Fa 61, which was sensationally flown inside the *Deutschlandhalle* by Hanna Reitsch in 1938. The fuselage of the Fa 61 was adapted from a Focke-Wulf Fw 44 *Stieglitz* biplane, the cut-down propeller being used only to cool the 160hp Siemens-Halske Sh 14A radial engine that powered the twin 23ft rotors.**

A still from a wartime German film showing the launching and flight of Fa 330 *Bachstelze*, relying solely on the 15-knot wind generated by the surfaced U-boat's speed to winch a crew member up to 1,000ft in order to report on possible sightings of enemy shipping. The lightweight machine was carried dismantled in a watertight container on the submarine's deck and assembled by the crew for flight. *Bachstelze* could only operate in distant waters – for example, the Indian Ocean – which were far from land-based Allied aircraft, as the U-boat had to remain surfaced when it towed the autogyro aloft.

ber of military autogyros produced during the war years, perhaps the most intriguing being the Focke-Achgelis Fa 330 *Bachstelze* (*Bachstelze* means water wagtail). This small, skeletal, three-bladed one-man autogyro was a rotor kite, carried dismantled on board long-range type IX U-boats, to be flown from the surfaced submarine in the Indian Ocean when searching for lone ships to attack. An observer could ascend to nearly 1,000ft, enabling him to sight a ship 30 miles or more away, and he had a telephone to the boat to report sightings. The Fa 330 weighed only 180lb and could carry a man aloft in still air with the U-boat making as little as 15 knots. The operational success of the Fa 330 remains questionable but when one was shown at the now famed 1945 Farnborough exhibition of captured German aircraft it excited at least one RAF visitor, Wing Commander Ken Wallis.

Ken Wallis became very keen to design and build a lightweight autogyro that would be capable of free flight, unlike the Fa 330 which was, of course, a man-carrying kite. There had been proposals for such an autogyro; one much admired by Wallis was the Hafner Rotachute designed in 1943 by Raoul Hafner for the British Airborne Forces Experimental Establishment. It was to be towed to a dropping zone carrying one fully armed paratrooper, then released as an autogyro. The Rotachute was test-flown but was never used operationally. In the 1950s, the American Bensen company were offering plans for a modified version of the wartime Hafner Rotachute, the Bensen B-7. In 1959 Wallis built a B-7 but modified it to be powered by a McCulloch piston engine of 72hp, originally designed for target drones. To his delight it flew but exhibited so many design deficiencies that Wallis decided to design and build a lightweight powered autogyro for himself.

At that time Wallis had been invited to deliver a lecture on his wartime flying experiences to an audience at Rolls-Royce. Asked what his fee would be Wallis, in lieu of a cash payment, asked for, and was granted, a half-hour access to their scrap bins! Rolls-Royce aero engines had very high standards and those bins provided a good deal of high-grade steel and parts for the first Wallis autogyro. It was essentially an experimental machine and enabled the designer to gain the experience to develop and patent an improved fully articulated head with conventional aircraft controls for the definitive Wallis autogyro, the WA-116. It flew well, in fact well enough to gain world autogyro records for altitude at 15,220ft and for speed at 111mph, both since broken by the later WA-116 F and WA-121. There are now nineteen Wallis autogyros. All differ because they were designed for specific roles, the most famous being Little Nellie, built in 1962 to become a star in *You Only Live Twice*. Wallis did all the flying for the film, logging forty-six hours on eighty-five sorties for the cameras, most of them over a Japanese volcano with Little Nellie being chased by the bad guys in Bell 47 helicopters. The combat scenes were very authentic – so authentic that the cameraman was seriously injured in a mid-air collision between one of the Bell 47s and the camera helicopter during the filming.

All the Wallis autogyros are flown in the same way. First the engine, a pusher, is started by hand-swinging. The engine, which drives the propeller directly, can also be clutched to spin up the twin rotor blades via an industrial flexible drive and a friction wheel. The take-off drill is simplicity itself: with the engine running, the pilot straps in and starts the rotor by hand. The drive is then carefully clutched in and the throttle opened to spin the rotor to an indicated 275rpm, the figure required for a take-off. When the rotors are up to speed the throttle is opened fully, the brakes are taken off and, as the small machine moves forward, the drive to the rotor is automatically de-clutched, the gathering speed of the autogyro keeping the blades autorotating. A run of about 30yd is sufficient, even in still air, for the machine to become fully airborne.

The Wallis autogyros, the subject of seventeen patents and twelve world records, have been used for a number of specialized purposes. These include military reconnaissance, use by the police in the gruesome task of locating buried bodies, by commercial air photography and latterly being military remotely piloted vehicles (RPVs) – which suits the inherent stability of the Wallis design. They have landed and taken off from ships at sea, including the Royal Navy fishery protection vessel, HMS *Dumbarton Castle*. The engines used by the various subtypes range from the original 72hp McCulloch to the 60hp Franklin 2A-120 engine and the 130hp Rolls-Royce Continental. Wallis autogyros have exceeded 120mph and have climbed to 18,960ft, an

Rotajeep, the ultimate in autogyros. This scratchy still from a now lost film shot in 1942 at the Airborne Forces Experimental Establishment shows the testing of a very large version of the Hafner one-man Rotachute. Rotajeep is seen being towed into the air behind a Whitley bomber on a test flight. It had been proposed that not only Rotajeeps but even Rotatanks should be towed into action by RAF bombers but, no doubt to the relief of the potential driver/pilots, the scheme was abandoned when large Waco Hadrian and Airspeed Horsa cargo-carrying gliders became operational in 1944.

autogyro record set by the WA 121, the smallest Wallis, and only recently (1998) bettered by an American using a fully turbocharged engine. The Wallis autogyros qualify as classic aircraft. They can perform many of the roles of the small helicopter at a tenth of the construction cost and operate at a tenth of the running costs. Ken Wallis, now a flying octogenarian, remains convinced his autogyros have a big future. He still works perfecting and developing his aircraft in his home workshop at Reymerston Hall, Norfolk, possibly the only aeronautical workshop in the world with wainscoting!

The logical development of the autogyro into the helicopter was protracted. The helicopter is more than just a powered autogyro. Helicopters have to have engines powerful enough to generate and sustain all the lift required of the rotors, which act as wings and are the sole source of thrust for flight. The first and most difficult problem to solve is the one defined by Newton's third law of motion: 'For every action there is an equal and opposite reaction.' In simple terms, the helicopter tends to rotate around the rotors. The German designer Achgelis, working with Professor Henrick Focke, solved that difficulty by designing a twin-rotor helicopter with the rotors on outriggers, turning in opposite directions, which cancelled out the unwanted thrust. The Focke-Achgelis Fa 61 of 1936 must be regarded as the first practical helicopter. It created a sensation in February 1938 when, with the name *Deutschland* emblazoned on the fuselage, the celebrated test pilot Hanna Reitsch flew the machine *inside* the packed *Deutschlandhalle* for several nights during the 1938 Berlin motor show. The Fa 61 then set an altitude record at 11,243ft together with a helicopter distance record of 143 miles.

The Germans undoubtedly led the world in the development of the helicopter during the years of the Second World War. They placed the first military helicopter into service, the Flettner Fl 282 *Kolibri* (meaning humming bird), which could carry a pilot and observer. This advanced machine had twin contrarotating intermeshing rotors. The Fl 282 is the only military helicopter which was to see genuine active service during the Second World War with the German *Kriegsmarine* (navy), who used twenty Fl 282s for anti-submarine patrols and armed reconnaissance over the Baltic and North Aegean seas. The *Luftwaffe* had ordered the very large six-seater, twin-rotor Focke-Achgelis Fa 223 Drache (*drache* means kite) but few were produced, though a wartime German film shows an Fa 223 lifting a crashed Me 109 fighter, possibly the first use of a helicopter as a flying crane. It was an Fa 223 in which Hanna Reitsch hoped to fly into Berlin to Hitler's bunker in 1945, as described in Chapter Three. When Allied or, more specifically, American, technical teams evaluated German wartime research in aeronautics they discovered a number of advanced rotating wing proposals and prototypes, including the Doblhoff WNF 342, which proved to be another world first with its tip jet-powered rotors. The Americans lost no time in shipping the best of these machines to the United States together with German designers, aerodynamicists and engineers. (US technical investigation teams tended to take a Nelsonian view of suspected war crimes if the man they wanted had worked on advanced projects.) Many Germans who had been engaged on advanced military helicopter

Without any doubt the most advanced of wartime helicopters was the German Flettner Fl 282 *Kolibri* which first flew in 1940 when test pilots reported excellent handling due to the contra-rotating rotors which overcame the problem of torque. Powered by a single 140hp Siemens-Halske engine, the *Kolibri* had a maximum speed of 90mph. There were two versions of the helicopter, the later one being able to carry an observer in addition to the pilot.

projects were invited to continue their work in the United States, augmenting the postwar lead that the United States gained in helicopters, which it has never lost.

Igor Sikorsky, who emigrated to the United States in 1919, was in the 1930s engaged in the design of the only possible form of long-distance airliners then feasible, the Clipper flying boats. The company for whom he worked was United Aircraft Corporation (UAC). In about 1931 an early interest in helicopters returned and Sikorsky began to experiment in that little-known field. By 1938, possibly as a result of news of the flights of the Focke-Achgelis Fw 61, the UAC board appointed him to the post of engineering manager of the Vought-Sikorsky Division with a remit to develop a practical helicopter. The result, after a great deal of hard, mainly empirical, development work, was the open-framed VS-300, which first flew in free flight in May 1940 with Sikorsky himself at the controls, famously clad in an overcoat and trilby hat. The VS-300 lacked the elegant engineering of the German Flettner or Focke-Achgelis designs but it flew – just. It is often pointed out that Sikorsky invented nothing new with the VS-300; this may be true, but he assembled the best-known techniques to produce his first practical helicopter. The main difference between the VS-300 and the German machines was Sikorsky's use of a single, three-bladed rotor with a collective pitch head and the small anti-torque propeller set at 90 degrees at the rear of the fuselage, a configuration that was to become universal. In May 1941, after no fewer than seventeen major modifications, the VS-300 was demonstrated to the US Army and Navy. An army captain, Franklin Gregory, an experienced autogyro pilot, flew the VS-300. He found it very hard to control, describing the machine as a 'bucking bronco' and difficult but possible to master, given new piloting techniques and intensive development of the helicopter's control systems.

The basic conclusion, following early test-flights by service test pilots of the VS-300, was that it would be relatively easy to fly if the pilot had four hands. Today's fully devel-

The first, tentative and tethered hover of the 1940 prototype Sikorsky VS-300 which, in May 1940, progressed to free flight. Igor Sikorsky himself, though aged fifty-nine at the time and casually attired, did all the early test flying. The skeletal VS-300 went through many forms and was not as advanced as some of the best contemporary German machines but it possessed two very large advantages: it was American and it introduced a most elegant solution to the problem of overcoming rotor torque with the now classic tail rotor.

A Sikorsky float-fitted R-4 Hoverfly lands on board a tanker. The photograph, taken in 1943, depicts Bureau No. 46445, the first R-4 to be accepted by the US Army Air Corps. The machine was assigned to the US Coast Guard, the first of 25 USCG R-4s based at Bennet field, New York. (The US Navy would never have permitted loose cables to be left lying on a helipad.)

oped helicopters have computers to perform some of the duties and make the pilot workload far lighter. In 1941 it was the pilot who had to manage the whole system with just two hands and feet. The main difficulty was simply that the four controls – cyclic pitch, collective pitch, the throttle and the anti-torque controls – though they had separate inputs, all interacted. Alter one and the others had to be adjusted as well. For example, on taking off the pilot had to raise the collective pitch lever, which also had the throttle, in the form of a twist grip, on the end of it. The pilot would open the throttle and the blades would speed up but, with the lever in the lowered position, the helicopter would not rise because the pitch of the rotor blades would be zero; as the collective pitch lever was raised, the pitch of all three rotor blades would collectively increase and generate lift to begin to take the weight of the aircraft. However, since the increased rotor pitch progressively loaded the engine, this would slow the engine down, requiring a larger throttle opening. If the rotor was not to overspeed, the pilot then had to raise the collective pitch still further to keep a balanced load on the engine. By that time the machine would be in the air, requiring some immediate directional control with the 'rudder' pedals, which would alter the pitch of the rear-mounted anti-torque propeller. This, too, would affect the engine loading. So it went on, with every small input affecting another. The pilot had to perform, as one RAF pilot put it, 'like a one-armed paper hanger'. All the early helicopters had the familiar joystick control, which responded to the same inputs as on a fixed-wing aircraft: left-right-up-down. However, the interaction of the controls, the total absence of any inherent stability and the unpredictable control response, together with continuous shaking, vibration and noise, required thorough training and very dedicated pilots.

This was apparent when, early in 1944, the Sikorsky VS-316 became the world's first helicopter to enter continuous production and the only Allied helicopter to see even limited operational service during the war. A hundred Sikorsky VS-316s, designated R-4Bs, were delivered to the USAAF; the US Navy received a number of these which were known as HNS-1s and the RAF received 45 R-4Bs under Lend-Lease as the Hoverfly 1. All were developed versions of the first V-300 Sikorsky design, but still very hard to fly. In RAF service the Hoverfly was used for training at Andover by No. 43 Operational Conversion Unit (OCU). Some Hoverfly 1s replaced Rota autogyros in No. 529 Squadron in August 1944, and others were used by the Fleet Air Arm for pilot training and on utility communication work. It took so long to train the pilots that it is doubtful if any R-4Bs with either the British or US forces saw action before the war had ended in 1945. There is little doubt that when Sikorsky opted for a single main rotor with the anti-torque propeller, he had created a helicopter which was going to prove very difficult to fly. The German twin-rotor Fa 61, for example, was a far more straightforward proposition, because it had a measure of stability. Hanna Reitsch always claimed that she taught herself to fly the Focke-Achgelis in one short flight. This may or may not be the case, but she did fly it inside the Deutschlandhalle; few R-4B pilots would have cared to try that with the Sikorsky machine and fewer still would have cared to have been in the audience!

The Sikorsky R-4B has its place in history because it was the beginning of a line of continuous development that saw the achievement of the fully developed helicopter, with acceptable control response and performance, become commonplace. This is largely because the Allies won the war and the far more advanced work on rotating wing machines in Germany was halted abruptly in 1945. German expertise was, to some extent, exported to the United States or Russia. American postwar helicopter development, encouraged and funded by the military, therefore progressed without disruption. The Sikorsky line that had such a shaky start in 1942 is today one of the major US suppliers of excellent helicopters worldwide. There is a Hoverfly 1 preserved in the RAF Museum at Hendon.

In 1941, as Sikorsky was developing the VS-300, another American, Arthur Young, at work in Buffalo, New York, was designing a small experimental helicopter for the Bell Corporation. The president of the company, Larry Bell, had seen the Fa 61 flying when on a tour of Germany in 1939 and had an ambition to build the world's first civilian certified helicopter. To that end he funded the project privately to the tune of $250,000. The machine was given the model number Bell-30. At the time the Bell company was fully committed to the production of the Bell P-39 Aircobra fighter for the US Army so, Arthur Young's helicopter being a non-government and private venture, he had to work away from the factory in a small workshop converted from a garage adjoining the Bell family home. Appalled by the complexity of the fully articulated head, Young had devised a twin-bladed rotor for the Bell-30. Uniquely, this did not have an articulated head with the traditional drag and flapping hinges. In place of these there was a simple 5ft-long stabilizing bar with streamlined weights at each end. The bar, mounted just below the hub, rotated at 90 degrees to the rotor, which had a universal 'carden' joint in the mast drive. The stabilizing bar was linked to the rotor. As the bar revolved it performed as a gyro-

FACT FILE

SIKORSKY R-4B HOVERFLY 1

Type
Two-seat helicopter with dual control.

Power plant
One fan-cooled radial 180hp Warner Super Scarab R-550-1.

Performance
Maximum speed 82mph.

Dimensions and weights
Rotor diameter 38ft
Length 35ft
Loaded weight 2,530 lb.

Number produced
100

The small Bell-47G Sioux was the workhorse of the US Army from 1955 to 1961. It was used in a wide range of roles of which casualty evacuation was the best known if only because of the popular TV series M*A*S*H. The Bell design was licensed to many countries and remained in continuous production for more than thirty years. Although primarily a military machine, the Bell-47's civilian applications included crop spraying and aerial taxis.

scope, maintaining a given plane irrespective of the angle of the rotor mast and the helicopter itself. As the bar was connected to the rotor hub above the universal joint, the rotors were maintained in a horizontal position relative to the mast. A 'swash' plate, which could be moved up and down the drive mast by the action of the cyclic control, tilted the universally jointed rotor assembly in the direction required. Another swash plate, which did not revolve, controlled the collective pitch. The Bell stabilizing-bar system was patented and was used on all subsequent Bell helicopters.

As the Bell-30 was a private venture, produced unofficially in the midst of war production, the No. 1 was first flown piloted by Arthur Young on 29 December 1942 from the Bell's garden backing on to the garage. After considerable test-flying, No. 1 was wrecked when flown by another pilot in 1943. By then No. 2 was ready. Five Model 30s were built and all but the last one had an open cockpit with side-by-side seating for two. All five had the engine vertically mounted; it was a 160hp six-cylinder horizontally opposed air-cooled Franklin. The cooling air entered from the nose and was ducted by a fan to the engine, and then exhausted from vents in the fuselage sides. The Bell-30 was evolved into the now classic Bell-47G which looks like a goldfish bowl with a skeletal Meccano-like fuselage terminating in anti-torque rotor on the tail. It became familiar to millions as the 'incoming chopper', seen in many episodes of the *M*A*S*H* TV series, with the wounded carried on outrigger stretchers. The US Army's H-13, or Sioux, as the Bell-47G-2s were known in military service, evacuated 25,000 wounded during the Korean War.

Larry Bell realized his ambition for, against competition from Sikorsky, the Bell-47 received the first Civil Aviation Authority (CAA) certificate for a civilian helicopter in March 1946; since that date over 6,000 Bell-47Gs of various subtypes have been built, many under licence in Britain, Italy and Japan. Many are still flying. Although the controls have been refined, this small helicopter changed little in over thirty years of production; except for the final versions it retained that endearing look of the goldfish bowl and Meccano set.

After the Bell 47-G, perhaps the most well-known military helicopter, which dominated the world's television screens during the Vietnam War, was another Bell, the UH-1 Iroquois. This was the official designation, but it is better known from the initial 'UH-

1' as the Huey. The first flight of the UH-1 took place on 20 October 1956; this was, sadly, the same day that Larry Bell died. This Lycoming T53 gas-turbine-engined helicopter was produced in vast numbers; its intended role was as a medical evacuation and general transport aircraft but in Vietnam it was deployed in front-line service, dropping troops in forward positions, evacuating wounded and flying re-supply missions, even on occasion performing as a gunship, a role anticipating the later Bell Cobra attack helicopter. Apart from near nightly TV news appearances on US networks during the Vietnam War, the Huey was also used in feature films about that unpopular conflict, the best-known being *Apocalypse Now*. In actual service, the official load for the UH-1 was six, but one Huey during the conflict took off from a rice paddy with twenty-five US Marines on board plus the crew! During the Vietnam War Bell were producing the Huey at the rate of 150 a month and the last version, the UH-1H, powered by a 1,400shp Lycoming turboprop engine, only ceased production in 1980 after 5,500 had been built. After the Vietnam War was over many surplus US Army Huey's were sold for as little as $100 each to fire, police and air ambulance departments and for use in the world's oilfields to transport rig workers to and from their isolated platforms. The Huey was exported widely; an Argentinean Huey, captured in the Falklands, is on exhibition in the Army Air Corps Museum at Middle Wallop in Hampshire.

Not all Western military helicopters are American. Among the NATO forces there are machines from France and the UK. The most successful, entirely British-made, is the Westland Helicopter's Lynx. Its history began in the mid-1960s after the disparate British helicopter companies, Saunders-Roe, Fairey and Bristol Aviation, had their rotating-wing interests transferred to Westland. At that time there was a naval air staff requirement for a medium helicopter for both the Royal Navy and the RAF; Westland submitted a proposal, WG.1, for a twin-rotor machine along the lines of the present-day Boeing Chinook. After a good deal of argument between the services that project was not proceeded with but a second proposition, GSOR (General Staff Operational

A US Marine Corps 'Huey' in uncharacteristically peaceful surroundings. The Bell Iroquois, or UH-1H, was used in very large numbers during the Vietnam War. They were employed as gunships, for landing troops and marines at the front line and for inevitable casualty evacuation. The Bell twin-bladed rotor with its simple but very precise control system gave hastily trained pilots the confidence to operate in and out of makeshift and restricted jungle strips, often overloaded and often under enemy fire.

Requirement) 3335, was issued for an army helicopter to be in service by 1972. The requirement was for a single-rotor multi-role helicopter capable of carrying seven fully armed troops, or 3,000lb of supplies as a slung load. The service requirements stipulated a speed of 170mph with an operating range of up to 170 miles at full load, with a ferry range of 900 miles. Westland had such a design to hand in the WG.13 which, it was felt, could be upgraded to meet the full service requirements.

From 1967 there was close co-operation between Westland and Aerospatiale, the French helicopter company; there was free collaboration of design, development and production between the two companies. In the event, the Westland design became the Lynx and Aerospatiale produced the Gazelle and Puma helicopters. All three were to serve with NATO forces. (It is of interest that the Lynx was the first British aircraft to be built to metric rather than imperial measurements.) Although the Royal Navy and the British Army would be equipped with the Westland Type WH.13 Lynx multi-role helicopter with a common airframe, as the detailed requirements of each service became clear, the Navy and Army machines diverged considerably in many ways. The WG.13 Lynx prototype, painted bright yellow with the service serial number XW 835, first flew from Yeovil on 21 March 1971 in the hands of Westland test pilot Ron Gellatly. It had the skid undercarriage which identifies – not without exception – an army machine, while the naval ones have a wheeled undercarriage. The Lynx had a new semi-rigid four-bladed rotor which had been extensively tested in a scaled-down form of two Scout helicopters (XP 189 and XP 191). This was to investigate the complex dynamic characteristics of the semi-rigid rotor, which was likely to present unforeseen problems. The Scout programme did result in some important design modification providing, *en passant*, valuable experience in handling qualities and an opportunity to develop techniques for the analysis of vibration and stress for the main programme. Development flying continued with five pre-production prototypes becoming available within a year of the first flight, followed by the prototype army variant and three naval development Lynx. The first definitive army Lynx, XX 153, set up a world helicopter record during its test programme in June 1972 with a speed of 199.9mph. This helicopter created a stir at Farnborough in September that year by being the first helicopter to perform a roll (in public).

It is beyond the scope of this account to detail the intensive work that preceded this very advanced helicopter's introduction to the services. It involved no fewer than 2,000 flight hours. Four Lynx – two XS 170 and 171 with the army and two XZ 227 and 228 with the navy configuration – were tested at the A & AEE, Boscombe Down, for service acceptance trials. Following the successful inter-service trials, the Lynx AH Mk 1 became operational with the British Army of the Rhine (BAOR) at Detmold in West Germany in August 1978. By February 1984 113 army Lynx had been delivered.

The structure of the Lynx can be summarized as a four-bladed semi-rigid 42ft main rotor, the head made from titanium; the 7ft 3in anti-torque rotor is also four-bladed. Unusually, the main rotor can be set to a 6-degree minus pitch; this was at the request of the Royal Navy who needed down-force to keep the helicopter firmly on the restricted helicopter pads aboard Royal Navy Type 21 frigates. The main blades can be folded to save hangar space. Tubular skids are fitted on army aircraft. Pilot and co-pilot have dual controls with side-by-side seating. Maximum accommodation is for pilot and ten fully armed paratroops or twelve lightly armed men. In casualty evacuation role with a crew of two, three stretchers can be accommodated. The details of the weapons and other service equipment of the versatile day or night Lynx remain classified but are known to be under constant review and subject to change dictated by operational requirements, but a brief summary of the weapon options is: AN/ALE-39 counter-measures dispenser with electronic counter-measures (ECM) chaff, the NATO name of the Second World War 'window' radar counter ECM warning systems (these, too, are classified but in general warn the crew when the aircraft is being interrogated by enemy radar), twin 7.62mm machine-gun pods; a 20mm automatic cannon and a tube-launched optically guided weapon (TOW), a guided anti-tank missile. Other missile options include Matra 550 air-to-surface and SNEB 68 and SURA 80mm air-to-ground rockets. Lynx can be fitted with an inertial navigation system, which is accurate to a few feet, with a continuous map display.

The Royal Navy HAS Mk 2 Lynx is a truly multi-role aircraft being capable of air-to-surface vessel (ASV); search and strike, armed with Sea Skua missiles; anti-submarine warfare (ASW), with two homing torpedoes; and search and rescue (SAR) in which role nine survivors can be carried. Other roles are reconnaissance, fire support and communications. The Royal Navy Lynx differs from the army version by having, in addition to folding main rotors, a tail rotor pylon which can also be folded manually to reduce the length from 43ft to 34ft 10in. The HAS Mk 2 has flotation gear and a non-retractable tricycle undercarriage with sprags to lock each wheel. As a further means of keeping the helicopter on board, there is the vital harpoon locking device under the navy Lynx's fuselage, located at the aircraft's turning circle. On landing the 'harpoon' is lowered and engages a grill in the deck; when engaged, the helicopter is firmly secured to the open decks of small ships which can roll to extreme angles in bad weather. Even when safely tethered, with engines and rotors turning, the secured Lynx can still turn through 360 degrees to a take-off direction, allowing the ship to maintain station when flying off the helicopter. After extensive working up, on 27 January 1981 No. 816 Squadron was commissioned at RNAS Yeovilton as the HQ for Lynx ship flights; fifty-one were envisioned with one Lynx on each. The pilots and deck crews were trained to a very high standard in this exacting role; handling a small helicopter in the teeth of a gale on a small ship calls for great dedication and skill, aided by the helicopter's negative down-thrust, wheel-locking capabilities and harpoon, all of which make for an unrivalled shipboard aircraft.

Apart from military development, which is a continuous process, the Westland company decided to attack the world helicopter records in two categories: absolute speed of 229.20mph (368.40kph) and the record speed for helicopters of 3,000-4,000kg, which stood at 211.51mph (340.40kph). Both records were held by American helicopters. The reason for the record attempt was to demonstrate the potential of BERP (British Experimental Rotor Programme) developed jointly by Westland and the Royal Aircraft Establishment at Farnborough which, through rotor aerodynamics and advanced structural techniques, offered a marked increment in handling and performance. In May 1986 the company demonstrator G-LYNX was prepared for the attempt. Two 1,200shp Rolls-Royce Gem 60 engines and the special rotor blades were installed and the airframe cleaned up by removing all fittings considered non-essential – windscreen wipers, antennas and even the crew steps – to reduce drag. The record attempt was fixed for the evening of 11 August 1986 over a measured 15km (9.33 miles) over the Somerset levels. G-LYNX was flown, for the records, by Westland's chief test pilot, Trevor Egginton, with Derek Clews as flight engineer. A new world record was achieved in both categories at 249.10mph (400.87kph), making the Lynx the first helicopter to exceed the 400kph barrier. Despite strenuous efforts in both France and the United States, the records still stand in 1998.

There are some 400 Lynx helicopters operating worldwide; half are with the Royal Navy and British Army. Lynx were involved in the Falklands and Gulf Wars; they are still serving in Northern Ireland and Bosnia. They also serve with no fewer than twelve navies, including the French, German, Dutch and Norwegian. In its current form the Lynx, with a fully integrated mission system, is expected to serve in front-line units until at least 2020.

FACT FILE

WESTLAND
LYNX
HELICOPTER

Type
Lynx HAS Mk 8 shipborne
helicopter; crew of two.

Power plant
Two 1120shp Rolls-Royce
Gem.41-2 turboshaft engines.

Performance
Maximum continuous cruise
of 140 knots (161mph)
Hovering ceiling 10,600ft
Maximum range 368 miles,
extendible to 650 miles with
additional fuel tanks.

Dimensions and weights
Four-bladed 42ft rotor:
Maximum take-off weight
11,300 lb.

Numbers produced
Still in production. Over 400
at end of 1998.

CHAPTER FIVE

PRIVATE PASSIONS

The new light aircraft was intended, above all, for the amateur, for the week-end flyer, and for instruction. Simplicity and safety were of paramount importance . . . a name had to be found . . . It suddenly struck me that the name 'Moth' was just right.
Sir Geoffrey De Havilland, *Sky Fever*

SIR GEOFFREY DE HAVILLAND recalled in his autobiography, *Sky Fever*, how the most successful light aircraft ever built became simply a Moth, or rather Moths, for there were to be many: Cirrus Moth, Gipsy Moth, Puss Moth, Leopard Moth, Fox Moth, Tiger Moth and so on. They were a series of British light aircraft that set the standard for all others. Geoffrey De Havilland had built his first aircraft in 1909; his company designed and built the DH-4, the DH-9A, the Mosquito and the Comet jet airliner, but his most lasting memorial is the DH-60 Moth. The prototype, a Cirrus Moth, G-EBKT, first flew from Stag Lane in north London, then the De Havilland factory airfield, on 22 February 1925, piloted by the then Captain De Havilland himself. No less a person than Sir Samuel Hoare, the Secretary of State for Air, was so impressed by the Moth that he – unbelievably to modern ears – agreed to the Air Ministry subsidizing five selected flying clubs to allow them to buy DH Moths at £650 a time. One Moth that the Lancashire Aero Club received under the scheme, G-EBLV, is, incredibly, still flying, having been preserved for many years by the De Havilland company.

By 1927 twelve flying clubs up and down the country were using subsidized Moths to train aspiring pilots; there were, in addition, some forty Moths in private owners' hands. The RAF ordered six DH-60X, J 8816 to 8821, for the Central Flying School. The Secretary of State for Civil Aviation, Sir Sefton Branker, invoking ministerial droit de seigneur, had one of the RAF machines, J 8818, placed at his disposal with the bogus civil marking G-EDCA, which he piloted himself. These small wooden biplanes were to be the mainstay of private flying in Britain for more than thirty years; they were the chosen machines of record breakers. In 1930, a young Hull typist, Amy Johnson, having learned to fly only the previous year, bought a reconditioned second-hand, long-range Gipsy Moth, G-AAAH, which she had christened *Jason* and took off from Croydon on 5 May to fly solo to Australia, landing at Darwin sixteen days later; it was the first England–Australia solo flight made by a woman and gained her a *Daily Mail* prize of £10,000 and lasting fame. There was even a pop song of the day:

A preserved DH-60G Gipsy Moth. This immaculate biplane seems to invite someone to grasp that wooden propeller, shout 'Contact!', and step back as the Gipsy engine fires. Private pilots of today, flying efficient enclosed monoplanes with full radio and electronic navigational aids can have little conception of what it must have been like to fly solo in an open cockpit Moth, with only a magnetic compass for navigation, over deserts and oceans where engine failure meant almost certain death, yet that is just what the record breakers of the 1930s did.

Amy Johnson stands by a rather battered Cirrus II Moth, probably a London Flying Club school machine at Stag Lane. The fact that Amy is wearing a helmet with Gosport tubes, required to hear the instructor, suggests that she was still a pupil and that the photograph was taken after her first solo, well before her record-breaking flights.

'Wonderful Amy'. Francis Chichester, better known to a later generation as a solo round-the-world yachtsman, flew his DH-60 Gipsy Moth, *Elijah*, also from Croydon to Australia and also in 1930, but he took five weeks. He then flew from New Zealand to Norfolk Island, a mere speck in the Pacific Ocean. This was an epic of dead-reckoning navigation that is still discussed in military navigation classes.

These were only two of a number of long-distance flights by amateur pilots in the heady 1930s when flying was 'the greatest possible fun' for the young who had the means, as there were few restrictions. A new Gipsy Moth cost no more than a good sports car. In the 1930s, thousands of young people flocked to the newly established light aeroplane flying clubs to gain their 'A' licence, which took about thirty hours of tuition at around £2 an hour. Neither sex nor station was a bar; 'wonderful Amy' had proved that, and she had also shown that flying was not the exclusive preserve of super-fit young men or that one needed to be wealthy (though that, then as now, was a help and it has to be said that some clubs did subscribe to the 'right crowd and no crowding' motto of the Brookland's motor-racing circuit, where there was also a fashionable flying club).

The relatively low cost of flying tuition was possible because approved clubs, i.e. those which met certain standards of safety and instruction, continued to be subsidized by the Air Ministry who wished to encourage 'air-mindedness' through private flying. The clubs were able to claim up to £2,000 if they could produce a similar figure from membership dues and fund-raising. In addition, clubs could claim £50 for each member who gained his or her basic 'A' licence. (This largess was not altruistic; the Air Ministry saw the subsidy creating a valuable pool of basically trained pilots and air-crew to be available in the event of war, at a time when the gap between the Moths and the biplane RAF fighters of the day was not nearly as great as the equivalents of today.)

The DH-60 Gipsy Moths used by the clubs for training were built by the hundred at the De Havilland works at Stag Lane; the airfield was also the base of the London Flying Club. The secret of the success of the Gipsy Moth was that it was a simple air-craft with a reliable, though somewhat agricultural, four-cylinder engine of more than adequate power. Another factor was the in-built safety of the design; although Geoffrey De Havilland himself drafted the general arrangement, his senior draughts-man, A.E. Hagg, made a very important suggestion, which was an ingenious differen-tial aileron control designed to reduce the risk of stall/spin accidents in steep turns – these were far from unknown. Hagg's differential control allowed the upwards move-ment of an aileron to be much greater than the downwards movement; this lowered the high, unstalled wing, rather than the existing arrangement that tried to lift the lower and stalled wing, with the increased drag of the full aileron on the stalled wing provoking a spin. Differential ailerons are standard to this day.

The Moth was inexpensive to maintain. The tough wooden airframe was fabric cov-ered and easy to repair while the sturdy biplane wings of the early Moths could be folded back for storage in a suburban garage and the machine could – according to De Havilland publicity – be towed behind the family car. However they arrived on the air-field, Moths were easy and forgiving to fly, with a landing speed of a mere 45mph. The two open cockpits (with a small locker behind them) had dual control and the panel just four instruments: oil pressure, airspeed indicator which read up to 130mph, an altimeter and the engine revolution counter (RPM), usually canted so the 'never exceed' engine speed, about 1,900rpm, was at the twelve o'clock position. Most Moths had a plaque that warned 'No Smoking'; that was in deference to the fuel tank just over the pilot's head in the wing centre section. An aperiodic compass was at the pilot's feet as the sole aid to navigation. A radio was neither fitted nor available. A simple cross level was the only concession to blind flying, which private pilots were warned to avoid at all costs.

Although very much a civil design, the excellence of the Moths was such that the RAF, as noted, became interested in the aircraft as an *ab initio* trainer. RAF Gipsy Moths appeared at the annual Hendon Display in 1930 and 1931 with formation and inverted flying displays performed by instructors of the RAF Central Flying School. Gipsy Moths continued as RAF trainers, but they were replaced by one of the greatest training aircraft of all time, the DH-82A Tiger Moth, which first appeared in RAF service in 1932, and which would train thousands of wartime RAF pilots. Several DH-60 Moths survive, restored to airworthy condition, and the fortunate pilots of these classic biplanes find them as delightful to fly as did those young people in the halcyon days of private aviation.

In the late 1920s, the heyday of the Gipsy Moth, many young people achieved their private pilot's licence. For most that was an end in itself but for the minority who wished to continue to fly, once the euphoria of achievement had faded, the open cockpits of the Gipsy Moth did not appeal if one wished to use the aircraft in all weathers for tour-ing. Young women in particular quickly tired of the novelty of overalls, leather flying jackets and a tight-fitting helmet and goggles ruining their 'Marcel' hair waves and make-up. Even the designer, Geoffrey De Havilland, was to write at the end of a long-dis-tance continental tour in his Gipsy Moth in 1929, 'After the cold and the buffeting we endured on that trip I was more keen than ever to design a light cabin aeroplane which

---

FACT FILE

DH-60G GIPSY MOTH I

Type
Light, two-seat biplane for training and private flying.

Builder
The De Havilland Aircraft Co. Ltd.

Power plant
One 100hp air-cooled De Havilland Gipsy I.

Dimensions
Wing-span 30ft
Length 23ft.

Weight
1,750 lb.

Performance
Maximum speed 98mph
Cruising speed 83mph
Range 290 miles
Service ceiling 18,000ft.

Number produced
1,303

would do away with the draughts and discomforts of open cockpit flying.' He soon had the answer in another Moth; this one was the 1930 DH-80A Puss Moth.

The Puss Moth was an elegant high-wing monoplane powered by a new version of the DH Gipsy engine, the Gipsy II. The original Gipsy was a conventional 'upright' wet-sump engine; this was redesigned to become an inverted dry-sump type. The immediate result was a much lower uncluttered engine cowling, improving the pilot's sight-line ahead and resulting in a very clean fuselage. The comfortable enclosed cabin seated three. The high-wing layout permitted excellent views from the fully glazed cabin; the downward view offered to the pilot, unobstructed by a lower wing, was important in an era when all light aircraft navigation was by compass and map reading, following railways, major roads and rivers, and using towns and villages to keep a check on the aircraft's track. Light aircraft did not have VHF radio or indeed any navigational aids, apart from a magnetic compass, until after the war in 1945.

The prototype DH-80, G-AAHZ, as yet unnamed, was of wooden construction and first flown in September 1929. Geoffrey De Havilland, the test pilot, soon discovered that the monoplane clean lines resulted in a rather high approach speed when compared with the earlier biplane Moth, and the plane had a tendency to 'float' when landing. The problem was solved, not by re-designing the wings to incorporate flaps, but by neatly rotating the long landing gear struts through 90 degrees to act as air brakes. They worked to Geoffrey De Havilland's satisfaction as did the fuel consumption figure of 20 miles to the gallon with three people on board.

G-AATC, the first production Puss Moth, as the type was now named, first flew in March 1930. The production aircraft differed from the prototype in that the fuselage was made of welded tubes covered with fabric. The seating in the well-upholstered cabin was in tandem, with the rear seat staggered sufficiently to accommodate a third seat if required. The same basic instruments found in the earlier Gipsy Moth were fitted. The engine still had to be started by manually swinging the propeller though an impulse magneto made engine starting a little more certain. The 36ft wings could be

Even by the light-aircraft standards of today, the DH Puss Moth remains a most attractive private pilot's aeroplane and the few preserved examples that remain airworthy are much prized. One, G-AEOA, was photographed at Old Warden where it regularly flies as part of the Shuttleworth Collection. G-AEOA leads a charmed life, having been one of many Puss Moths impressed into the RAF in 1941, few of which survived to return to the civil register.

manually folded to save hangar space. The Puss Moth was so clearly in advance of any other light aircraft then available that orders poured in, many from overseas, and the aircraft was widely exported. Altogether, 143 were placed on the British register alone.

Despite the glowing press reports, there was a bad start to the Puss Moth's career as a touring aircraft when G-AAXN, only a month old, was dumped in the English Channel in June 1930. After that damp start the monoplane went on to be owned and flown by some very well-known people. The Prince of Wales owned G-ABBS, which he had painted in the red and blue colours of the Brigade of Guards, and Amy Johnson owned G-AAZV, *Jason II*, given to her by the De Havilland company in grateful recognition of her flight to Australia in *Jason*. A colourful fox-hunting man, Colonel the Master of Sempill, flew his Puss Moth on floats from the Welsh Harp in north London to Copenhagen to attend an air show. Will Hay, the pre-war playwright, comedian and star of *Oh Mr Porter!*, owned G-ABLR. The reliability and speed, and the comfort offered by the enclosed cabin, together with an excellent safety record of the Puss Moths, attracted other than private pilots. The small monoplane became one of the first executive transports with many well-known international concerns owning them, including Dunlop, the Anglo-American Oil Company and Shell. The enclosed comfort of the

The final development of the De Havilland Moth biplanes was the Tiger Moth. Tens of thousands of Second World War British and Commonwealth pilots learned to fly in a 'Tiger'. It was an ideal trainer, being easy and forgiving of the mistakes of trainee pilots but rewarding the skilled hand. Today many Tiger Moths still fly, though not many carry as much graffiti as the one shown.

The DH Puss Moth *Heart's Content*, jointly owned by Amy and Jim Mollison, which made several epic solo flights including crossing the South Atlantic and North Atlantic. An example of the efficiency of this pre-war aircraft (and the price of petrol) is illustrated by the occasion when Jim Mollison flew *Heart's Content* solo from Ireland to New Brunswick in 1932, the total cost in fuel and oil for the 31-hour flight being just £11 1s 3d (£11.07).

FACT FILE

DH-80A
PUSS MOTH

Type
Two/three-seat touring light monoplane aircraft.

Builder
The De Havilland Aircraft Co. Ltd.

Power plant
One 120hp DH Gipsy III or 130hp DH Gipsy Major air-cooled engine.

Dimensions
Wing-span 36ft 9in
Length 25ft.

Weight
2,050 lb

Performance
Maximum speed (Gipsy III) 128mph
Cruising speed 108mph
Range 300 miles
Service ceiling 17,500ft.

Number produced
258

Puss Moth, together with its high performance, also attracted the attention of the record breakers: the record to the Cape (Cape Town) seemed irresistible in those days, possibly because it was largely over land. The greatest of these was by Amy Mollison, *née* Johnson, flying a special, 130hp Gipsy Major-powered Puss Moth, G-ACAB, named *Desert Cloud*, to Cape Town in 10 hours 26 minutes. Her new husband, the well-known pilot 'Jim' Mollison, not to be outdone by his famous wife, made perhaps the greatest solo flight of any light single-engined aircraft after Lindberg when, in February 1933, he flew the Mollisons' jointly owned Puss Moth G-ABXV, *Heart's Content*, from Lympne in Kent to Natal in Brazil, the first flight across the South Atlantic. To achieve the record, the aircraft had a 160-gallon fuel tank in the front cabin giving a range of 3,600 miles. In 1932, Mollison had made the first east-west crossing of the Atlantic flying from the beach at Portmarnock, Dublin, and landing at Pennfield Ridge, New Brunswick, 31 hours 20 minutes later in the Mollisons' other long-range Puss Moth, *Desert Cloud*. All of these epic flights were made without radio or any navigational aid other than a magnetic compass.

The record breakers made the headlines, not always to celebrate their flying achievements; they were the pop stars of their day and their activities were news. Most of the 258 Puss Moths sold were in the hands of private pilots who used them for pleasure. The advanced design of the monoplane was such that when, on the outbreak of war in September 1939, all private flying was stopped, many Puss Moths had been with the owners who had bought them new, nine years previously; they had not been changed because there was nothing markedly better on offer. (The enlarged, though wooden, DH Leopard Moth of 1933 did not have the same appeal and only seventy-one were built.) The RAF, despite the age of the civil Puss Moths, had most of them impressed for communication duties; this was a tribute to the, by then, ten-year-old design of Geoffrey De Havilland.

The RAF had previously ordered twenty-seven DH-80A Puss Moths, delivered in 1930; one, K 1824, is known to have been used by AOC (Air Officer Commanding) Inland Area Home Command. The scores of civilian-owned Puss Moths impressed into the RAF in 1940 included Will Hay's G-ABLR, which became BK 871, and G-ABUX which, as DD 821, served with the USAAF. Few of the many impressed Puss Moths survived the war to return to their original owners; they were lost to enemy action, crashed, damaged beyond economical repair or abandoned, because of the lack of spares on remote overseas airfields at the end of the war. Some did survive and were returned to the civil register. One of these is G-AEOA, impressed in 1941 as ES 921 and now fully restored, with the original Gipsy III engine replaced by a 130hp Gipsy Major. G-AEOA can be seen during the summer shows flying in the collection of the Shuttleworth Trust at Old Warden. Several other Puss Moths have been preserved around the world and are regularly flown by their envied owners.

British light aircraft of the 1930s, by De Havilland, Miles and Percival, were the finest in the world. When the war ended in 1945 this global lead went by default to the United States and to some extent to France. The names that dominated the postwar years were, and remain: Piper, Mooney, Beech and Cessna. All these companies produced great light aircraft, including the Piper Cherokee and the Mooney Ranger. Both the Beechcraft and Piper companies had also built very good light aircraft before the war, including the Piper Cub and the Beech Stagger Wing. After the war the Beechcraft company offered less eccentric designs, the best-known one being the Bonanza. Beechcraft were made in Wichita, Kansas, which is also the home of the greatest light aircraft manufacturer of all: Cessna.

The Cessna Aircraft Company was founded by Clyde V. Cessna, pioneer of American aviation, in 1911. The company has been building aircraft ever since. Without question, the best-known, truly classic light aircraft ever to emerge from the Wichita works is the Cessna 172 Skyhawk. When production of the 172 series ended in 1985, no fewer than 35,643 aircraft had been built, including 2,129 F-172s made in France at Rheims plus 864 military trainer versions of the 172 for the USAAF, the T-41 Mescalero. This is a staggering figure and, by some margin, the greatest number of any single model of light aircraft.

The Cessna 172 is a four-seat, high-wing monoplane, which had its origins in 1948 with the introduction of the Cessna 170, a four-seat high-wing monoplane with a tail-wheel undercarriage. Taildraggers, as they are popularly known, do demand a higher standard of pilot skills, especially when landing in a crosswind. In 1948, when the Cessna 170 was produced, most of the airfields used by light aircraft were grass; aircraft could therefore always land directly into wind, which reduced the difficulty. In addition, many of the people who flew light aircraft in the immediate postwar years were

Very few pre-war biplanes had enclosed cabins and fewer still had a retractable undercarriage; the four-seater Beech-17 had both. It was called the 'Staggerwing', something of a misnomer as many biplanes had upper and lower wings staggered but the Beech reversed the usual layout by staggering the upper pair behind the lower. The object of the design is admirably shown in the photograph of a US registered Beech below, the pilot enjoying an excellent field of view without the restrictions of the upper wing. The original 1935 B-17Ls had a 250hp Jacobs engine, but most 'Staggerwings' flying today are ex-USAAF C-43 Travelers powered by a 450hp Pratt & Whitney Wasp Junior which offered a cruising speed of 200mph.

experienced ex-military pilots. With the growth of twin-engined executive aircraft, paved runways became widespread and with them the necessity of crosswind landings and take-offs. Tail-wheel light-aircraft pilots, especially during the early stages of training, found this difficult, with landings often resulting in ground loops. In 1955, to encourage the increasing numbers of people wanting to learn to fly, Cessna produced their 172 model which was, in effect, a Cessna 170 with a tricycle undercarriage and nose-wheel steering via the rudder pedals. The tricycle undercarriage made the handling on take-off and landing almost child's play, as it could be steered like a car. Indeed, one US reviewer was to call the 172 'a Chevrolet with wings'. It was not quite that, but it was far less intimidating to an inexperienced private pilot than the tail-wheel 170. Surviving Cessna 170s are now much sought after as 'real aircraft', and the Tail Dragger is regarded as a vintage collector's item. (The Bush Company of Udall, Kansas, offered Taildragger conversion of 172s for enthusiasts who could not find a genuine 170!) Cessna 170s remained in parallel production with 172s until 1975, by which time a total of 5,000 170s had been sold. By 1975, Cessna had sold 20,961 tricycle 172 Skyhawks.

An immaculate Cessna 150; the smaller two-seat version of the 172 is a popular flying school *ab initio* trainer, as it is forgiving and economical to fly. Cessna 150s do not have the stylish wheel 'spats' as standard because the aircraft are used mainly for training on grass airfields with many 'circuits and bumps' which in winter tend to clog wheel coverings with mud. The zebra stripes on the propeller are to render it clearly visible in this jet age.

The comprehensive instrumentation of a typical 172 Skyhawk is essential for flying in today's congested and highly controlled airspace. The left-hand command pilot's panel has the 'basic six' instrument flying panel, with the vital airspeed indicator (ASI) upper left, the 'artificial horizon' next and the sensitive barometric altimeter upper right. At the lower left is the 'turn-and-bank' indicator, with the gyro compass to the right. The last of the 'six', lower left, is the vertical-speed indicator calibrated in feet per minute up or down. To the left of the 'six' are the engine temperatures and pressures, fuel gauges and the engine hour meter. Right of the main panel are the two VOR (VHF Omni Range), VHF navigation aids with an ADF (Automatic Direction Finding) dial below. The VHF communication and navigation radio stack is between the two control yokes with the throttle, mixture and carburettor heat knobs below. Some, but usually not all, the instruments are repeated for the right-hand pilot, who is either instructor or co-pilot. An airline 'yoke' control has been a Cessna standard for many years.

With any aeroplane that has been in continuous production for as long as the Cessna 172 there are many variants. The early models had the same 145hp horizontally opposed Continental engine as the 170 and a similar solid cabin – that is, there were windows at the front and sides but not at the rear, the wings joining the fuselage without any rise behind the trailing edge. In fact, at thirty paces the only difference between a 170 and 172 was the undercarriage. In 1960 there were cosmetic changes, the fin and rudder gaining the then fashionable swept-back look. Shortly afterwards the rear fuselage was revised and lowered to allow the wraparound rear windows, which became characteristic of Cessna high-wing light aircraft. The rear window lightened the cabin and allowed the pilot a degree of rear vision; this was useful when visually checking the elevators and trim tab, as part of the pre-take-off litany of 'full, free and correct movement of the controls'. In 1961 the Model No. 172 was supplemented with the official Cessna name of Skyhawk, though in Europe the name was seldom used, the aircraft being known only as Cessna 172.

Although the 172's smaller two-seat relative, the Cessna 150, was perhaps the more popular for *ab initio* training, many flying clubs have 172s for hire and the type is still extensively used for training and touring. It is easy and forgiving to fly, almost to the point of seeming dull; however, as any private pilot will tell you, flying in today's crowded airspace can offer all the excitement needed. Being all-metal aircraft, 172s do not need to be hangared and rows of them can be seen picketed down in lines on most club airfields. They seldom see the inside of a hangar, with engines which have 2,000 hours' time between overhaul (TBO). The engine options include the popular 150hp Lycoming 0-320-E2D as an alternative to the Continental.

When, in 1986, 172 Skyhawk production ceased, the standard aircraft had a very comprehensive instrument and radio fit including a 360-channel VHF voice and VHF omni range (VOR), instrument-landing-system (ILS) radios and automatic direction finding (ADF) – this navigational aid operates from long-wave non-directional beacons (NDBs) and has a display on the panel in the form of a 360-degree dial with the ADF needle pointing to the relative bearing of the beacon. Most 172s in the UK also

have transponders that 'squawk', as it is called, a given number which will appear beside the aircraft's radar return, thus identifying it positively on the air traffic controllers' screens. When flying in controlled airspace – which is most of the time in the UK – the pilot will be asked to 'squawk 1234' or whatever is the required combination. He sets this on the instrument and will then be under constant surveillance. Optional extras include full autopilot and additional radio aids.

The growing complexity and cost of the minimum standards of instruments and radios now required of a light aircraft such as the Cessna 172 would make an old Puss Moth pilot's head reel: artificial horizon or attitude indicator; airspeed indicator; rate of climb instrument calibrated in feet per minute up or down; turn coordinator (the modern version of the old turn-and-slip indicator); and an altimeter with two clock-like hands, the hour hand for the thousands of feet, the minute hand for hundreds of feet. The instrument also has a subscale in millibars for European aircraft (US altimeters use inches of mercury; 1,013mb equals 29.92in Hg). The subscale is used to zero the instrument to one of two standards: QNH and QFE. QNH is remembered as nautical height, the setting which will give a zero altitude reading at sea level on a given day over a defined altimeter setting region (ASR); set to QFE, field elevation, the altimeter will read zero on the local airfield. The edgewise magnetic compass is found above the windshield; a directional gyro can be set to the compass heading but due to gyroscopic precession it should be checked every fifteen minutes or so. There are the engine instruments as well: oil pressure and temperatures, engine RPM and two fuel gauges indicating the contents of the two 18-imperial-gallon wing tanks. There are three engine controls in the form of push-pull knobs: throttle and mixture ranging from full rich to idle cut-off used to stop the engine, and carburettor heat used when throttled back for landing. There is also a key for ignition with four positions: 'off', 'on' with magneto 1, with magneto 2, and 'both' – turn the key beyond the 'both' and the starter engages; 'both' is used in flight for efficiency and reliability. In addition, there is a console with the elevators' trim-wheel and an indicator of the trim position. The Cessna Fowler-type flaps are extended on older Model 172s manually by a large lever between the seats; later models have the flaps operated electrically; in either case they can be set to 10, 20, 30 or 40 degrees and are very effective, reducing the stall to around 45mph on the 30-degree setting. The recommended approach speed is around 60mph, followed by a touchdown at 55mph. If, from the above, you think that the minimum instrument fit of a typical 172 Skyhawk, or any contemporary light aircraft, would seem to equal that of a jet airliner you would be correct. The equipment is of a complexity required for flying in controlled airspace even if you are a hang-glider. The old carefree days of 'kick the tyres and light the fires' are gone for ever.

Flying the 172 is not as difficult as the intimidating cockpit on first sight would suggest. The old joystick has long since been replaced by an airline-type yoke, though the rudder pedals are there on the floor with hydraulic and very effective differential toe-operated disc-brakes which, together with the steerable nose-wheel, make for precise ground handling. In fact the Cessna is very easy to fly; it will practically take itself off and the handling is good without being twitchy. Cessna 172s are excellent for training though that will now (1998) cost about £100 an hour for flying tuition, plus the extensive ground school to master air law, meteorology, navigation, and radio aids and instruments that can bring the cost of the private pilot's licence (PPL) up to £5,000 – no government subsidies these days! If you wish to buy your own, the cost of a good 172 Skyhawk with a low-hours engine and an overhauled instrument and radio fit will be in the region of £40,000.

For all its apparent complexity and cost the Cessna 172 Skyhawk is really only a modern version of the Puss Moth of seventy years ago. They are both classics. Although Cessna ceased production of the 172 Skyhawk II in December 1985, the company had built the similar but more powerful (230hp) Cessna 182 Skylane in parallel with the 172 for some years; production of that was also suspended in December 1985 when the original Cessna company was taken over by General Dynamics but now, in 1998, the 172R Skyhawk and 182R Skyline are back in production, the R suffix standing for restarted. (The price tag on the new 172R Skyhawk is £140,000.) With the numbers of 172s still existing and new 172R and 182Rs available, Cessna monoplanes will still be flying well into the twenty-first century, to delight a generation of private pilots as yet unborn.

FACT FILE

CESSNA 172 SKYHAWK

Type
Four-seat all-metal high-wing monoplane with tricycle undercarriage.

Builder
Cessna Aircraft Co.

Power plant
(typical): Lycoming 0-320, 160hp four-cylinder opposed air-cooled flat four.

Dimensions
Wing-span 35ft 10in
Length 26ft 10in.

Weight
Maximum at take-off (four passengers plus 120lb baggage) 2,300lb.

Performance
Maximum speed 140mph
Cruising speed at 75 per cent power, 135mph
Service ceiling 13,100ft
Landing run (still air): 520ft.

Number produced
20,961 at the end of 1998.

OPPOSITE **Without any doubt the Cessna 172 Skyhawk is the most popular light aircraft of all time. As many as 35,643 have been built and they are now (1998) back in production at the rate of 1,000 units a year. The secrets of the success of this excellent design are many: the high wing offers four comfortable seats, each with a clear unobstructed view of the ground, which passengers enjoy; the tricycle undercarriage makes for easier landings and good ground handling; and the performance with 134mph cruise at an economical fuel consumption with a good range is ideal for touring. Thousands of 172s in Europe and the United States are in constant use with flying clubs as trainers or for hire, and thousands more are in private ownership.**

CHAPTER SIX

TRAVEL AND TRADE

*On 8 December 1934, Imperial Airways announced that their London–Singapore
service was extended to Brisbane, Australia. The flight took twelve days.*
From an Imperial Airways 1934 press release

A PHOTOGRAPH OF CROYDON, then London's major international airport, taken in the 1930s, would reveal three distinct airliners: a Handley Page HP 42 of Imperial Airways, a Douglas DC-2 of KLM, then as now the Royal Dutch airline, and a Junkers Ju 52 of Lufthansa, emblazoned with the Nazi swastika. Each of these very different aircraft represented the national attitudes to air transportation. Imperial Airways, Britain's national carrier, was, as the name suggests, committed to linking the countries of that Empire beyond the seas, carrying mail, diplomatic bags, couriers and other high-ranking officials far and wide. If it took twelve days to fly to Australia, so be it; the only alternative, travelling by ship, could well take six weeks. Speed was, therefore, of little consequence; the paramount remit was reliability and safety. Both were offered in full measure by the majestic, though even then archaic, HP 42s.

The DC-2, on the other hand, was American and designed to span that continent. The imperatives of the US national airlines were different: the entertainment and film industry was located in Los Angles on the west coast; all the money was in New York on the east coast. Trains, with names like the 'Super Chief', plied endlessly between the two; they were excellent trains, with sleeping berths that were essential because even the fastest coast-to-coast train took sixty hours. The Douglas DC-2 could do the trip in nineteen hours. Speed was everything; long range was not required, the flight was entirely over land and federal territory. The DC-2s could land for fuel and comfort stops along the way and still beat the competing trains. The result was a very high-speed airliner of the day which could make the trip as attractive as possible by being as short as possible, luring expense-account passengers away from a comfortable but tedious railway journey.

The last of the Croydon trio, the Junkers Ju 52/3m, was a bomber. It was used as such with the German Condor Legion when the nascent *Luftwaffe* was sent to Spain in aid of Franco and to gain battle experience for the aircrews at the same time. The Ju 52's employment as airliner was part time because the Germans were waiting for the next war to commence, with the Lufthansa pilots

This brilliant 1920s poster was designed to disabuse American businessmen of the firmly held view that flying was all leather and goggles. The Curtiss cabin monoplane offered comfort, and the executive passenger looking at his watch emphasized the time to be saved by flying.

A *Lufthansa* poster, c. 1934, which attempts to convince people that the Junkers Ju 52 is an airliner not a bomber.

DEUTSCHE LUFTHANSA

on military contracts. When the war started in 1939, the Ju 52 was obsolescent as a bomber but performed perfectly by the hundred, ironically dropping parachute troops on the KLM airfields during the invasion of the Low Countries in 1940. After that, the Ju 52/3 became the main supply aircraft of the German forces, 3,000 being built.

The Handley Page HP 42 was designed and built by the same company that had produced the RAF's first four-engined bomber, the V/1500, the 'bloody paralyser' sought by Murray Sueter in 1918 to bomb Berlin and avenge the Gotha raids on London. The eight V/1500s built, as related in Chapter One, soon disappeared from the RAF's inventory with the end of the war but other Handley Page large bomber aircraft followed with suitable colonial names: Hyderabad and Hindi. It was therefore natural that when Imperial Airways wished to replace their geriatric Armstrong Whitworth Argosy airliners they journeyed early in 1928 to Cricklewood in north-west London, to the offices and factory of Handley Page Ltd, to discuss their plans with Frederick Handley Page himself, the hands-on boss of the company that bore his name. No doubt the design of the aircraft Imperial Airways ordered, the HP 42, owed a good deal to the ideas of Sir Frederick, as he was to become.

The Handley Page HP 42 was ordered by Imperial Airways for their growing European services. A wooden mock-up of the passenger cabin was on show at Olympia, London, during the 1929 Aero Show. It created quite a stir, for the large aircraft had been designed to carry thirty-eight passengers, then an unheard-of number; the Armstrong Whitworth Argosy, Imperial Airways' existing airliner, carried only twenty. The prototype HP 42, G-AAGX, majestically rose from the company's airfield at Radlett, Herts., for the first time in November 1930 with Squadron Leader England and Major Cordes hauling on the very large dual control wheels, made necessary by the hundreds of feet of cables running over the dozens of pulleys and trunnions required to move the large control surfaces. Despite the manual effort required, control was reported as satisfactory although the enclosed cockpit, being high up in the extreme nose of the aircraft without the usual engine up front, was felt to require a framework to give the pilot a simple artificial horizon as a datum when landing. This was soon to be discarded.

The prototype HP 42 was formally named *Hannibal*, presumably because in service it was to cross the Alps, and had the cabins arranged to the HP 42E standard, the Eastern model, with twelve passengers in both the forward and rear cabins, the mail and baggage hold intervening. The HP 42Es were to be based in Cairo and were to fly the Cairo-Karachi and Cairo-South Africa routes. In June 1931 *Hannibal* began a series of 'proving' flights to Paris, taking off from Croydon; watchers must have been impressed by the sheer size of the aircraft – it was big. The all-metal biplane wings, which spanned 130ft, were set high on a very modern-looking fuselage and, in place of the usual maze of bracing wires, had a system of 'warren' girders as interplane struts. Among this forest of support were four 555hp Bristol Jupiter XFBM supercharged air-cooled radial engines, each driving a four-bladed propeller through reduction gears. The upper wing had ailerons that were half the span. The wing was also fitted with the, by then, well-known and patented Handley Page slots which automatically opened to delay effectively the stall of the wing.

It was clear that a good deal of thinking had gone into the HP 42 design: the lower wings were canted upwards at the point where they joined the fuselage, to avoid having main spar running athwart the passenger cabin. Another detail was the placing of the cargo space amidships in line with the propellers, the idea being that if a blade broke in flight – by no means unknown – the pieces would strike mailbags, not passengers; this was soon to be proved a prescient precaution. The mid-section also contained two lavatories and a well-fitted kitchen; a corridor ran through the mid-section connecting the two cabins. The sound-insulated cabins were lavishly appointed – surviving photographs and films reveal a standard of decor reminiscent of a Pullman or first-class wagon-lits coach such as might be found on 'Les Grands Express Européens'. There were cut moquette seats, mahogany woodwork panelling, pile carpets, curtained 'picture' windows and decorative lampshades. Externally, too, the fuselage was excitingly modern for the first time; the pilots worked in an enclosed cabin, unlike the old Argosy where they sat in the open, swathed in leather. Now neat blue uniforms with gold-braided caps would be the flight crew's attire. Because the HP 42's corrugated aluminium fuselage was unpressurized, the curtained windows were large, each one affording an unimpeded view downwards. There was a good deal to see, for the HP 42s flew well under 10,000ft and the landscape below passed by very slowly – 100mph was the usual cruising speed. Viewed today on archive film, the HP 42s look as if a Dakota's fuselage had been fitted with the wrong wings and tail but, despite appearances, Imperial Airways had made a very astute decision in buying the Handley Page airliner.

Hannibal was commissioned on 11 June 1931 and began a shake-down service, London to Paris. All went well until 8 August when a propeller blade came adrift and damaged two others. Captain Dismore made a masterly forced landing in a field near Tonbridge, in Kent, thanks to the 50mph approach speed of the big airliner and the pneumatic brakes fitted to the main wheels. The only damage, apart from the propellers, was that overhead telephone wires, which in those days marched along every main road, severely damaged the biplane tail unit. *Hannibal* was repaired and it flew from Croydon to Cairo to join *Hadrian*, G-AAUE, and *Hanno*, G-AAUD, which had already been flown east and had inaugurated the Cairo–South Africa route. *Horsa*, G-AAUC, was the last of the *Hannibal*, or HP 42E class. The first of the 'Western' HP 42W class, *Heracles*, G-AAXC, together with the remaining two, *Horatius*, G-AAXD, and *Hengist*, G-AAXE, formed the European fleet to Paris, Cologne and Zurich. All three had the cabins arranged with eighteen passengers in the forward compartment and twenty in the rear, the luggage and mail space being reduced for the short-haul work from Croydon. *Hannibal* was damaged in a gale in 1932 but repaired and rejoined the fleet; all of the HP 42s then gave excellent service, earning the admiration, affection even, of the many passengers who used them. The reliability and safety record of these majestic and stately giant biplanes had become legendary. By 1935, Imperial Airways was flying a twice-weekly service to Johannesburg and another to Calcutta. A weekly London-Brisbane flight was opened by *Hengist* in December 1934 and there was also a weekly London-Singapore service, the hold crammed with mail: *The Times* and *The Illustrated London News* for the planters up-country in Malaya. On these week-long flights, HP 42s did not operate at night; after tiffin and afternoon tea had been served with china crockery and starched napery, a landing would be made at a palm-fringed outpost of the Empire and the passengers ushered into a cool and comfortable Imperial Airways rest house for a cold bottle, bath, dinner and possibly a rubber or two of bridge with fellow passengers before turning in under a mosquito net, lulled to sleep by the sounds of a tropical night. They would be awaked next morning with a cup of tea, rising, refreshed, in the cool of the dawn for take-off to fly the next leisurely stage: Rangoon to Bangkok, or possibly Kofi Samui on the Isthmus of Kra to Penang.

Captain Dismore, the hero of the HP 42's forced landing, about to enter the flight-deck of 'Heracles' at Croydon. The Civil Air Ensign, granted by King George V in 1931, was always flown when the Imperial Airways airliners were on the ground. The task of raising and lowering the standard was the responsibility of the co-pilot; with certain Imperial Airways captains it was their *only* function.

The right crowd and no crowding. Imperial Airways passengers enjoying a flight in the 1930s. Although this photograph was taken on board an 'Atlanta', the appointments of the HP 42 were just as lavish. No seat-belts, no movies or duty-frees, and no plastic in view. It is to be hoped that the deferential steward opened the young lady's bottled lager with some care in that unpressurized aircraft.

FACT FILE

HANDLEY PAGE HP 42 W AND 42 E

Type
Four-engined passenger 38 or 24-seat airliner.

Power plant
(HP 42W): Four 555hp Bristol Jupiter XFBM air-cooled radial engines.
(HP 42E): Four 490hp Bristol Jupiter XFBM air-cooled radial engines.

Dimensions
Span 130ft
Length 89ft 9in

Performance
(HP 42W): Maximum speed 127mph
Cruising speed 100mph.
(HP 42E): Maximum speed 120mph
Cruising speed 100mph.

Number produced
Only eight were built, and were in service 1931–1940. None have survived.

The 'Western' daily European services from Croydon were less colourful, all flights being more or less direct. The destinations included Croydon to Brussels, Cologne, Prague, Vienna and Budapest, and also Rome and Brindisi, all in comfort with refreshments and light meals served, and in perfect safety. Of course, it was not cheap; the days of the economy class with crowded jet aircraft, overbooking, delays, restricted legroom, plastic cutlery with food to match, served by uniformed young women with warm smiles and cold eyes, was still three decades and a world war away. The era of the HP 42s was the salad days of air transportation and one of growing reliability and safety; one HP 42, *Heracles*, in September 1938, the seventh anniversary of its first flight, had flown no fewer than 1,250,000 miles carrying 95,000 passengers. More importantly, these airliners with their very high standards of safety and comfort, refreshments and courteous service (and profit-making), disabused passengers of the idea that flying was all leather-clad begoggled pilots, wickerwork seats and drumming, noisy and freezing fabric-covered cabins. The HP 42s were slow but they were faster than any alternative ground or sea transport of the day, and they set standards that only first-class passengers can begin to approach in today's crowded market.

The HP 42s throughout the 1930s were a common sight at Croydon and Cairo. In May 1937, *Hengist*, having been converted to Eastern standards, was burned out in a hangar fire in Karachi. *Hengist* was not replaced with a new aircraft but *Hanno* flew home from Cairo to be converted to HP 42W standard to replace the lost *Hengist*. The remainder of the fleet continued in service until 1 September 1939. As the Germans attacked Poland, all the Croydon-based HP 42s were flown to Whitchurch, near Bristol, the pre-arranged wartime base for Imperial Airways, and all commercial services were suspended. By that time Imperial Airways had 21,500 route miles, and had carried, in 1939 alone, nearly 57,000 passengers over nine million miles. The HP 42Ws had, since their commissioning, carried more passengers from London to European cities than all other airliners put together. The Cairo-based machines had also performed with excellent reliability. During a decade of operation and millions of passenger miles, not one person flying in an HP 42 had been killed or injured. This is a unique record for any passenger aircraft.

The home-based fleet continued to fly from Whitchurch and Exeter airfields on government contract, flying supplies to the British Expeditionary Force (BEF) in France. In November 1939, *Horatius* was wrecked when making a forced landing on a Devon golf course in a storm; it was written off after having collided with trees. It was the beginning of the end. There were four HP 42Es abroad in early 1940: *Horsa, Hadrian, Helena* and *Hannibal.* It was decided to fly them home to Whitchurch. *Hannibal* left Delhi on 1 March 1940 with a crew of four and four non-revenue passengers. The aircraft reported by wireless telegraphy after taking off from Jask *en route* for the next stop at Sharjah. But it never arrived. No trace of the aircraft has ever been found; to this day its fate remains a mystery. It was supposed, at the time, that the aircraft must have come down in the Gulf of Oman, though why no radio distress call was sent and why, after an exhaustive air and sea search, no trace was discovered, is unexplained. The tragic fate of *Hannibal* is a question that will probably never now be answered.

The other three HP 42Es made it to Whitchurch but, while carelessly picketed out in the open, *Hanno* and *Heracles* were blown into each other in a gale in March 1940. Then there were three . . . *Horsa, Hadrian* and *Helena* were impressed into the RAF as AS 981, 982 and 983 and flown to No. 271 Squadron at Doncaster in June 1940. Quite what duties these, by now elderly, airliners were to perform was not clear. They did not last long in RAF service. By August 1940 two, *Helena* and *Horsa*, had been written off in forced landings; *Hadrian*, the last surviving HP 42, broke from its pickets in another gale in December 1940 and was swept upside down on to the railway line that bordered the Doncaster airfield. It disintegrated during hurried attempts to clear the line. Then there were none. The last vestige of these magnificent airliners was the salvaged fuselage of *Helena* used by the Fleet Air Arm at Donibristle in Scotland as a squadron office. It did not survive the war.

Bon voyage. 'Heracles' again, about to leave Croydon for Paris. Is the lady on her way to her couturier as a manservant, bowler respectfully held in hand, offers her the packages he has carried? The other passengers hold on to their hats in the slipstream of the four idling Bristol Jupiter engines: a fiftieth of a second from a vanished world.

However bogus the claims to be an airliner pure and simple might have been, there is no denying that the Junkers Ju 52/3m was by any measure a very great aircraft. The one shown is an ex-Spanish air force transport, accurately representative of the wartime *Luftwaffe* workhorse, which flew on every German front from the first day of the European war to the last.

The Junkers 52/3m's claim to classic status would, correctly, be founded in the tri-motor's wartime transport role. That said, it was, when produced in 1932, an up-to-date design with a very long all-metal structure. Its airliner role was essential because of the restrictions placed on German aircraft by the Treaty of Versailles. (It might, in that context, be pointed out that the Dornier Do 17, a bomber used by the *Luftwaffe* in 1940, was also originally presented as an airliner.)

There is a Ju 52 featured in the pre-war German filmed *The Triumph of the Will*, brilliantly directed by Leni Riefenstahl. The Ju 52 was Hitler's personal aircraft and is seen air to air in an unforgettable, beautifully photographed and edited sequence as it flies, descending towards Nuremberg for the great party rally taking place in the city. Lufthansa was the major user of the civil Ju 52; however, other airlines used them too, including British Airways who, in 1937, operated three. One, G-AFAP, was one of the first windowless, dedicated air freighters. The Ju 52/3m in civil airline service offered a very good performance for the day: a maximum speed of 190mph and a cruising speed of 160mph with a ceiling of 19,000ft. As airliners, the Junkers had a three-man crew and seats for seventeen passengers.

There are classic aircraft, there are great classic aircraft and there is the Douglas DC-3 Dakota. To begin at the beginning. On 1 July 1933, on the Douglas company's aerodrome at Clover Field, Santa Monica, California, a gleaming all-metal twin-engined monoplane stood with mechanics fussing around it in preparation for the first flight. The brand new, as yet unflown aircraft, was known simply as the DC-1. The pilot for the first flight of the DC-1 was Carl A. Cover, who was vice-president in charge of Douglas sales. For the flight, Cover was attired in a suit of English tweed with a bright green hat; the only other occupant was Fred Herman, the flight engineer. The throttles of the twin radials were opened and the silver aircraft took off; as the nose was raised, however, the horrified Douglas staff on the ground heard the engines falter and cut out. Cover lowered the nose and they picked up but as soon as the aircraft was put into a climb the engines again spluttered and cut. After a heart-stopping low circuit the DC-1 was force-landed without damage in an adjacent field. The aircraft was recovered and extensive ground running traced the trouble to incorrect settings of the carburettor float chambers. After that inauspicious start, the DC-1, when the flight testing was over, was delivered to the customer who had ordered it: Transcontinental & Western Airlines (TWA). It made a record flight of 13 hours, 4 minutes from Los Angeles to New York in the process.

The story of how this prototype of what was to become the most successful airliner ever built came to be ordered is fascinating. Prior to 1933, most of the domestic US airlines were flying high-wing tri-motors, with fabric-covered wings, which were Fokkers or the Fokker look-alike, the Ford tri-motor. Boeing changed all that for ever on 8 February 1933 by introducing the first modern airliner, the Boeing 247. The 247 was a quantum leap: an all-metal low-monocoque-wing monoplane with a retractable undercarriage and twin Pratt & Whitney 550hp Wasp radial engines in neat cowlings. The Boeing cruised at 155mph with a range of nearly 500 miles and a service ceiling of 18,400ft. Immediately, United Air Lines placed an option on sixty 247s 'from the drawing-board'. United commissioned their first into-revenue service in March 1933 and cut the coast-to-coast time from twenty-seven hours to just under twenty. United had, at a cost of $4,000,000, invested in a winner – they thought – but after the first flush of enthusiasm there were critics: the ten passengers were comfortable enough but the low monoplane wing main spar passed through the cabin, virtually dividing it into two halves. Pilots had noted that when taking off from high altitude airfields in hot weather, the performance at full load with the existing fixed-pitch propellers was marginal. Boeing, to rectify that last complaint, fitted the newly developed Hamilton variable-pitch propellers, uprated the power output of the Wright engines, increased the fuel capacity and cleaned up the airframe to produce the 247D which had a cruising speed of just under 190mph with an increased range of 745 miles. The earlier version was retrospectively converted to the 'D' standard. With its expanding 247 fleet, United Air Lines were undoubtedly the market leaders among US national airlines. One of those badly affected carriers, TWA, wished to order 247s but Boeing's order book was full with the United contract of sixty aircraft and they declined to accept the order. The president of TWA, Jack Frye, next wrote to his friend Donald Douglas, the owner of a small aircraft factory at Santa Monica, with a specification for a new airliner to replace his noisy and slow Fokkers and which would be able to compete with the Boeing 247s of United Airlines. The result was the Douglas DC-1 and the beginning of an historic aircraft.

The sole DC-1 was developed in a remarkably short time into the slightly enlarged DC-2. (The DC-1, rather mysteriously, became involved in the Spanish Civil War, though that is another story.) TWA, delighted by the potential of the prototype, ordered twenty-

The Ford Tri-motor, which bore more than a passing resemblance to the Fokker three-engined airliner, was the mainstay of the domestic airlines in the early 1930s. This Ford of American Airways is typical of the type which was to be rendered obsolete overnight by the second generation of monoplane airliners, the Boeing 247 and the Douglas DC-2. The aircraft in the photograph, NC 9683, was presented to the Smithsonian Institution by the original owners, American Airlines.

eight DC-2s. They could carry fourteen passengers without the encumbrance of a cabin-intruding main spar. The performance was excellent: two 710hp Wright Cyclone radial engines offered a continuous cruise of 170mph with a range of 1,190 miles and variable-pitch propellers were fitted from the beginning of production, ensuring safe take-off in all conditions of altitude and temperature. TWA commissioned their first DC-2 service in July 1934. It was at that time the most advanced passenger aircraft in the world and totally eclipsed the Boeing 247; the machine that had recently made all the previous airliners obsolete was now itself obsolete. Eventually there would be 220 DC-2s worldwide, of which 160 were in commercial service with airlines. One airline, the Dutch-owned KLM, was to make aviation history with one of their DC-2s. On 20 October 1934 the start of an extraordinary air race from Mildenhall airfield in Suffolk to Melbourne, Australia, took place – a distance of 11,333 miles. Many aircraft started, including a KLM Douglas DC-2 with a full crew, three passengers and mail. The press of the day dismissed the entry as a blatant publicity move by KLM. The fancied entrants were the DH-88 Comets that had been built specifically for the race; these twin-engined specials had a maximum speed of 237mph and could cruise at 220mph. The only question was which of the three Comets would win. The answer was to be the G-ACSS *Grosvenor House*, piloted by Charles Scott and Tom Campbell-Black in a time of 2 days, 22 hours and 54 minutes. In second place was the KLM DC-2 with a time of 3 days, 18 hours and 17 minutes; the two Dutch pilots, Parmentier and Moll, said that they could have got there sooner but had to return to Karachi to pick up a missing passenger! Three months later, Imperial Airways announced their twelve-day HP 42 weekly London–Australia service.

Good though the DC-2 was, one US airline, American, was still operating plodding Curtiss Condors; tickets for these were sold on the strength of their being luxury sleepers – you could cross the continent asleep. But most passengers preferred to stay awake on TWA's DC-2s. In those days the aircraft industry in the United States was conducted by the principals on a personal basis: American Airlines president, C.R. Smith, simply

Boeing 247 airliners under construction, c. 1933, at Seattle. Because of full order books, Boeing declined further orders for their new all-Metal monoplane airliner that was sweeping the board. TWA, then Transcontinental & Western Airlines, therefore ordered a new airliner to replace their noisy Fokker Tri-motors from a small Santa Monica manufacturer named Douglas.

telephoned Donald Douglas from his Chicago office and asked him to design a sleeper version of the DC-2. Incredibly, the telephone conversation ended with Douglas agreeing to supply twenty, as yet to be designed, DC-2 sleepers at $110,000 apiece. Delivery was to be as soon as possible. In those days, your word was your bond, even if it was a $2,000,000 deal. The paper contract did not follow until some months after the first delivery. The Douglas Sleeper Transport (DST), was evolved by enlarging the DC-2 fuselage to accommodate sleeping berths for fourteen passengers. The new, enlarged aircraft was sufficiently different to warrant a new designation: it was to be the Douglas DC-3. The prototype rolled off the Santa Monica line just ahead of DC-2 No. 185. The DC-3 prototype, registered X-14988, first flew on 17 December 1935, powered by two 1,000hp Wright Cyclone engines. It created a sensation among the country's airlines. For Donald Douglas had realized, even before the first flight, that the fourteen-berth sleeper could also be a twenty-one seat daytime airliner, a 50 per cent increase over the DC-2 with only a marginal 3 per cent increase in operating costs; moreover, the DC-3 cut the coast-to-coast time to seventeen hours. It was hard, visually, to tell the difference between the DC-2 and the DC-3. But the DC-3 had an increased wing-span, from 85ft to 95ft, and an increased fuselage length, from 62 to 65ft. That first flight of the prototype was thirty-five years to the day that the Wright brothers had proved that powered flight was a practical possibility. The DC-3 test pilot was the same Carl A. Cover who had flown the DC-1. This time all went well. The first DC-3 to enter service with American Airlines on 7 June 1936 was an instant success. Those oft-quoted lines by Ralph Waldo Emerson, 'If you build a better mousetrap the world will beat a path to your door', might well have rung in the ears of Donald Douglas as practically all the major airlines beat a path to his door to order the DC-3. One of the first was United Air Lines who realized that their sixty Boeing 247s were now old hat; they had little alternative with the rival DC-3s knocking an hour off the coast-to-coast time. The company ordered a DC-3 fleet. United were followed by many others. By 1938 DC-3s were carrying 95 per cent of all commercial airline traffic within the United States and were to become the principal aircraft with thirty foreign airlines. By 1939, 90 per cent of the world's airline traffic was flown in DC-3s.

This colour photograph is of the rebuilt and airworthy Boeing 247, which is the only one now flying.

FACT FILE

DOUGLAS C-47 (DAKOTA)

Type
Military transport; crew of three, with twenty-eight troops.

Power plant
Two 1,200hp Pratt & Whitney R-2830-92 Twin Wasps.

Dimensions
Wing-span 95ft
Length 64ft 6in.

Weight
Loaded 25,000 lb, with 31,000 lb as a maximum (often exceeded).

Performance
Maximum speed 230mph
Cruising speed 185mph
Maximum range 2,125 miles
Service ceiling 23,000ft.

Number produced
10,926

The cabin of a DC-3 airliner. Though noisy by the standard of today's jets the DC-3, when introduced in the late 1930s, was considered to offer the highest standard of comfort and reliability. The interior depicted seems a little more de luxe than standard but the space available for seating is more or less what one would be offered on American internal routes just before the war. Compare the DC-3 with the interior of the Ford Tri-motor (below). This aircraft is N414H, preserved and airworthy; the seats, now leather-covered, would originally have been wickerwork. The cramped cabin of the Ford and Fokker airliners explains the appeal of the DC-2 and DC-3s that followed.

With the outbreak of the Second World War, the DC-3 reversed the position of the Ju 52/3m by becoming a military transport – 10,123 of them in all. They were known under many names and designations: C-47, Skytrooper, Skytrain, Dakota, Gooney Bird and so on. C-47s flew on every Allied front (even the *Luftwaffe* operated them, having captured several KLM DC-3 machines in 1940). Although civil DC-3s were impressed, the wartime C-47 differed from the civil airliners by having cargo doors and more powerful engines, which were, usually, two 1,200hp Pratt & Whitney Twin Wasp 1830 series radials. Serving with the USAAF and RAF, C-47s (called Dakota in RAF service) dropped parachute troops at Arnheim, the Rhine crossing, towed Horsa gliders and, in the Far East, dropped supplies to

the Chindits in Burma. C-47s, in twenty-four days of flying, hauled 25,500 troops, 1,500 horses and mules, 42 Jeeps and 48 75mm howitzers, plus smaller arms, over the hazardous mountainous route from Burma to Kweiyang in China. They carried loads far in excess of their design limits and performed ceaselessly as transports, glider tugs, air ambulances and freighters. The Russians paid Douglas the compliment of copying the design as the Li-2. They built 2,700, the only visual difference to the genuine article being that the cargo doors were on the right-hand side instead of the left. When the war ended, thousands of wartime C-47s were sold as surplus to be rebuilt as airliners, in sufficient numbers to last for decades. British European Airways (BEA) had dozens of Dakota 3s and 4s operating from Northolt to most European cities. Perhaps the most noted flying in BEA livery were the Dart Daks, which were used by Rolls-Royce to test their Dart turboprop engines, one of the three so powered being G-AMDB, ex-RAF KJ 829. These experimental aircraft were possibly the fastest of all the DC-3 series and G-AMDB flew on as a Rolls-Royce turboprop engine development test-bed for thirteen years.

Douglas ceased production of the DC-3 in 1945 after 10,926 aircraft had been built. DC-3s performed exceptionally well during the Berlin airlift of 1948–49; the RAF operated their Dakotas until 1958, and by that date there were still more DC-3s flying than all other airliners put together. It was often said that: 'The only thing that will replace the DC-3 is another DC-3.' That, of course, was eventually not the case. However, there are many still (1998) flying with astronomical hours in their logs. There is an ex-Eastern Air Lines DC-3 suspended in the Smithsonian Institution in Washington D.C. which had carried 213,000 passengers over 8,500,000 miles since it first took off in 1937; some DC-3s have far exceeded those figures. There are a number of DC-3s waiting restoration; one, a C-47, lies near the summit of Mount Fujiyama. Another long-term project, at the moment awaiting development, is a C-47 which, in 1947, was inadvertently flown into a Swiss glacier. No one was injured in the accident and the aircraft was little damaged. Heavy snow fell that year and the C-47 was buried to a depth of 50ft. Swiss experts confidently expect it to reappear at the bottom of the glacier, like a permafrosted mammoth, around AD 2648. Even at that date one cannot be certain that it will be the last DC-3 to be restored.

One postwar aircraft that was a Dakota replacement was also the most successful aircraft designed and built by the British. It was the Vickers Viscount, and in the late 1950s it enjoyed sales as dramatic as those of the DC-3s in the 1930s. It began as a proposal, sent in December 1944, to the Brabazon Committee which had been set up to select commercial aircraft for the postwar airlines. After the usual temporizing, the committee approved the Vickers proposal and issued an official requirement for a twenty-four-seat short- to medium-range airliner for European services, to be powered by four turboprop engines. Vickers began design studies and at the end of the war, with official approval, received authorization to build four prototypes. Although twin Mamba engines were briefly considered, four Rolls-Royce Darts were selected after flight trials in Dakota airframes. The prototype, G-AHRF, was first flown in July 1948 from Wisley, in Surrey, by 'Mutt' Summers, who had taken the prototype Spitfire on its first flight; Summers reported that the new turboprop airliner was 'the smoothest and best I have ever flown'.

After intensive trials in Kenya, Canada and Europe, where it was universally enthusiastically received, Vickers were disappointed when BEA, the major British customer, lost interest in favour of the piston-engined Airspeed Ambassador. However, following full certification of airworthiness in July 1950 BEA did place the prototype into limited revenue service

A wartime C-47 of the USAF which had landed, for reasons unexplained, on a jungle strip surrounded by rather casually dressed locals. During the Second World War C-47s operated worldwide from fields that other aircraft could not reach. The small round holes in the windows of all military C-47s (Dakotas) has mystified many: they were there to allow soldier passengers to used their rifles if their 'Goony Bird' was attacked. True!

Although United Airlines were the first to operate the Boeing 247 airliner they soon dumped the Boeing fleet for DC-3s in order to compete with TWA on the lucrative coast-to-coast traffic, as this poster, which depicted the quickest route to the 1939 World's Fair, testifies. Note the railway analogy in the wording of 'The Main Line Fairway'.

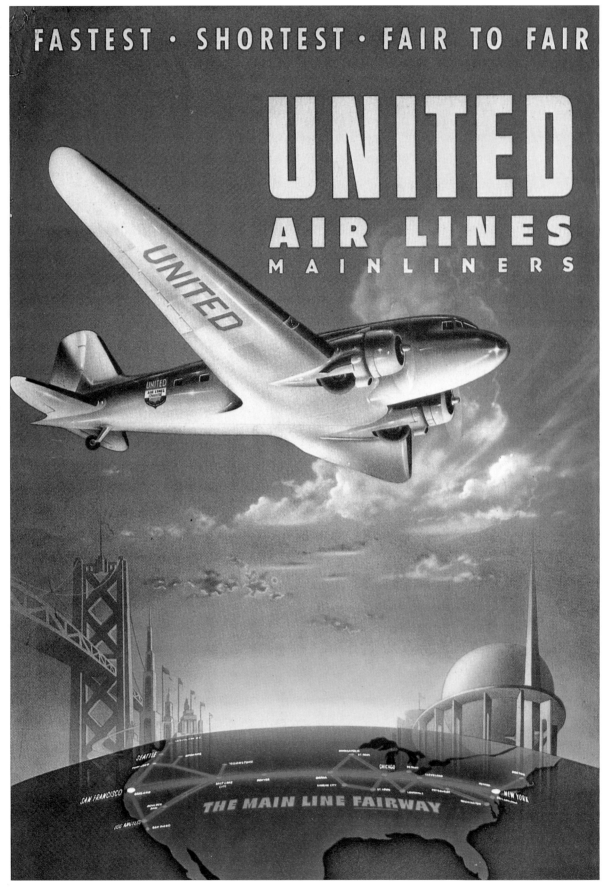

The turboprop Vickers Viscount is far and away the most successful British civil aircraft ever built. It was from the 1950s, a genuine DC-3 replacement, and many airlines ordered and operated the type. It was smooth and, after the piston-engined aircraft, quiet. The picture above shows the well-equipped galley of a BEA Viscount.

on the London-Paris (Le Bourget) route, which it flew in under the hour. The public reaction was very favourable as was that of the BEA pilots. Before the end of 1950, BEA had placed an order for twenty-six slightly enlarged Viscount 701s. The smooth-running engines and the high speed offered, together with economical operation, appealed to airline management; for example, American Capital Airlines ordered sixty Viscounts, and eventually over 300 were sold to around twenty airline operators including some to the Indian and Pakistani air forces. The Viscount has proved to be a most reliable and efficient airliner, which remained in service until the 1980s; some are still flying. There were several subtypes but the typical 700 series Viscount had a pressurized fuselage which maintained sea-level pressure up to 15,000ft. Four Rolls-Royce Dart turboprop engines produced 1,400shp, giving a cruise performance of 323mph. The 700 series was developed into the larger 800 and 810 series which followed, also enjoying considerable international commercial success. The Vickers Viscount was a worthy successor to the DC-3.

It is often forgotten in these days of jet airliners that criss-cross the Atlantic on a daily, almost hourly basis, that no land-based commercial passenger aircraft could fly to and from North America until after the Second World War. Two classics of that era in the late 1940s were American: that most aesthetically satisfying of all airliners, the Lockheed Constellation of 1946 and the Boeing Stratocruiser of 1949. Both have a strong claim to classic status. But, for several reasons, the Boeing has the edge. The Boeing 377 Stratocruiser cost the company very little to develop as it was a civil version of the USAAF's C-97 Stratofreighter which had the wings, tail, engines and undercarriage of the Boeing B-29 bomber. With the B-29s and C-97s all the basic research and development work and accumulated experience had been paid for by the US government. The civil version of the C-97, the Stratocruiser, had the same figure-of-eight pressurized fuselage as the transport aircraft but was fitted out as an deluxe airliner. Various passenger options were available; then, in November 1945, Boeing received an order for 20 B-377 Stratocruisers in a $34.5-million dollar deal with Pan Am. The first of the airline's Stratocruisers, named *Flying*

A portion of the stylish cocktail lounge aboard an SAS Boeing Stratocruiser. BOAC Boeings had a similar layout.

The glory that was Pan Am. *Clipper Flying Cloud* about to touch down at Heathrow in June 1949 to inaugurate their Stratocruiser luxury transatlantic service. The *Clipper* had taken twelve hours on the flight from New York.

Cloud, landed at Heathrow, London, in April 1949. It was first class only and, as the press reports of the time put it: 'The Pan Am Stratocruiser has set new standards of airline luxury.' That was certainly true. There were two decks; the top deck had almost armchair comfort and twenty-eight berths for the night sectors. There was the famous spiral staircase to the lower deck, which had a forward stateroom and a cocktail lounge with seating for fourteen passengers. The level of soundproofing was such that normal conversation was possible (this certainly was not the case in other piston-engined airliners in 1949).

The British Overseas Airways Corporation (BOAC) ordered six Stratocruisers directly and later took over another four that had been ordered by SAS, the Scandinavian airline. Like Pan Am, BOAC ran their Boeings on an all first-class service from London to found their first direct BOAC flight to New York Idlewild. The Stratocruisers were very popular; they flew the Atlantic in around twelve hours from west to east, taking an hour or so longer on the east-west trip due to the prevailing winds; even with a ceiling of 32,000ft they were not totally above the weather. BOAC also operated a Stratocruiser service between New York and the Bahamas and Bermuda. The airliner proved so popular that in 1954 six more were bought from United Airlines. By 1955 BOAC Stratocruisers on the daily London–New York service were all Monarch class, which only carried around thirty passengers. These aircraft were among the last of the great piston-engined airliners; in a way they were latter-day HP 42s with service and passenger comfort the primary concern; but they were at the end of an era of privilege and leisure. The first 707s had flown, and the package holiday and all that followed were soon to arrive. Fittingly, the senior BOAC captain, Captain O.P. Jones, who flew Princess Elizabeth, as she was then, and Prince Philip to Canada in a Stratocruiser in 1951, had been an HP 42 pilot before the war. People who had the good fortune to fly in the giant Boeings with BOAC maintain that there has been nothing to equal them since. This is perhaps true, but by 1956, after they had flown 190,000 hours and covered 60 million miles, they were withdrawn. The jets had arrived. Most of the fifty-five Stratocruisers produced were traded into Boeing against the new 707s. Pan Am did so, then sold the fourteen Stratocruisers remaining to a scrap merchant for a reported $105,000. BOAC did the same. This was a sad end to a great and classic airliner. As a final footnote, a few Boeing Stratocruisers survived to be converted to the grotesque Super Guppies used by NASA to transport rockets to the launch sites.

Airlines, with their cosseted aircraft clean and well maintained and crewed by uniformed men and women flying to strict timetables, are not the only civil aircraft. There were and are others, many neither clean nor particularly well maintained; they are the often single-engined workhorses of the world of aviation at the trade end of the market.

In the 1920s, apart from the men who had flown during the First World War, practically no one else had so much as seen an aircraft close up. Travel by air, as we today know it, was fifty years and more away; it was simply out of reach and unthinkable for all but a few wealthy eccentrics except for the joyriders (barnstormers in the United States). These were a small band of ex-service pilots who would have a Curtiss Jenny in the United States or an Avro 504 in the UK. These pilots would often appear for a summer's day or two flying from any large meadow they could hire from a farmer for a small amount of cash to set up their itinerant business. In the UK it would consist for the most part of an old Morris car and perhaps a tent, when the pilot's wife or a mechanic would take the money and issue tickets for the old Avro waiting to take anyone up for a 'five-bob flip'. Five shillings is only 25p in today's money but in the 1920s it had considerable purchasing power. Still, if the weather was good, sufficient passengers appeared for the fifteen-minute flight, probably the only flight most would ever have. Flying would continue until the light or the flow of passengers ended. One young boy never forgot his five-bob flip, for he was later to write:

I propped my cycle against a fence and breathlessly entered the field. Beneath a limp windsock, beside a battered car and a stack of red Shell petrol cans, stood the Avro in all its spindly elegance. The air was redolent with romance, blended from crushed grass, burned engine oil, and the pear-drop perfume of newly doped wings.

In the years just after the First World War, unemployment was high in Britain and the United States. Ex-military pilots eaked out a living and kept their licences valid in both countries by buying a surplus Avro 504 or Curtiss Jenny and offering the public joyrides. At the time most people had never even seen an aircraft close up so they had many takers for this Avro 504 in 1923. The work was seasonal and dependent on the weather. A few pilots went on to fly with major airlines; most did not.

Three Stearman NS-1s performing as intended as *ab initio* trainers, in this case for the **US Navy**. Many British and Commonwealth pilots learned to fly in these rugged biplanes during the Second World War. Usually the instructor sat in the rear cockpit, though one suspects from the precision of the formation that US Navy instructors flew the aircraft for the photo-call in 1941.

The boy was Harald Penrose, who went on to become the chief test pilot of the Westland Company. His 1919 account of his joyride is remembered in his autobiography *No Echo in the Clouds*. The Avro 502K was one of the few surplus aircraft offered for sale in 1919 that was economic to run as a civil type. The joyrider firms bought over 300 Avros from the Aircraft Disposals Board. Not all the Avros were operated by a single pilot; some quite large companies were formed, flying aircraft from beaches at summer resorts such as Blackpool, Southport, Weston-super-Mare, Margate and many others with firm sand. The Avros, when bought, were ex-RAF trainers with dual control; for joyriding this was removed from the rear seat and a two-seat passenger space provided. The Avro was a gentle aircraft with a rotary engine of around 120hp, typically a Clerget or Bentley. The biplane wings had a span of 36ft. The maximum speed – unlikely to be achieved while joyriding – was only 95mph. The cruise was a mere 75mph. By the mid-1930s Avros had all but disappeared; joyriding became more organized with larger aircraft operating from airfields, the most famous company being Alan Cobham's National Aviation Day displays. Today the Shuttleworth Collection maintains a mint airworthy 1920s' Avro 504 though it is not, alas, available for joyrides.

Another ex-military trainer also used commercially after the Second World War was the American Boeing-Stearman P-17 Kaydet. This quite large biplane was the trainer on which nearly all American and thousands of RAF and Fleet Air Arm pilots gained their wings during the war years. It was the most widely used Allied *ab initio* trainer. After a UK 'grade school', flying DH Tiger Moths, which removed aspiring RAF pilots who were unlikely to hack it, the remainder were sent overseas to complete the wings course, many to flying schools in the Midwest of the United States. The reason was simply that, under wartime restrictions, bad weather and a crowded airspace in the UK, the wide open prairies of the United States offered unbroken training. The Kaydet was built in huge numbers: there were 10,346 machines when production was halted in 1945. It was an ideal trainer, easy to fly but difficult to fly well, showing up piloting errors starkly. For a trainer it had a powerful engine, typically an uncowled 220hp Continental R-670-5 radial driving a fixed-pitch two-bladed metal 8ft 6in McCauley or an 8ft 2in wooden Sensenich propeller. The performance was good; maximum speed was 125mph, with landing at 56mph. The biplane handled delightfully and was fully aerobatic.

After the war, thousands of Stearmans, as the type was universally known, came on to the civil market. Some were used for aerobatic competitions and many were converted to be crop sprayers, then a relatively new and very dangerous way of making a living as a pilot. Crop-dusting called for a rather better performance than the Stearman, when converted with crop-spraying bars and hoppers, had with the standard engine. Many were re-engined at low cost with brand-new war-surplus R-985 Wasp Junior radials of 450hp – twice the original power. Flying at about 5ft above the crops, the pilots needed good control response and good all-round vision because any obstruction over about 6ft was potentially fatal. The Stearman had good control response but not good all-round vision; however, they were cheap and plentiful. One Stearman, registered G-AROY, was seen in the late 1940s in the UK giving demonstrations of crop spraying. Perhaps the best-known, though flawed, demonstration by a Stearman crop sprayer is the famous sequence from the film *North by Northwest* in which Cary Grant is pursued by one. Sadly, that ends with the Stearman crashing into a petrol tanker. Many remain; most of the surviving crop-dusters have been converted back to the original Second World War P-17 state, as they are now collectors' items. They fly, restored to the gleaming blue fuselage and yellow wings with white ARMY or NAVY emblazoned on them, as in their days of glory with sweating young trainee pilots desperately trying to avoid the dreaded 'chop check' which would condemn them to becoming navigators or flight engineers. Most managed to avoid the 'chop'.

Recognizing the double dangers of crop spraying, the natural dangers of low flying and the added hazards of the often toxic chemicals they delivered to the fields, several aircraft manufacturers began to offer dedicated crop-spraying machines. One of the best known and most widely used is the Piper PA-25 Pawnee (the Piper company named most of its light aircraft after native North American tribes). The PA-25 first appeared in 1956, replacing the Stearman and other surplus aircraft in the trade. By 1973, after 4,258 had been delivered, the Pawnee PS-25 D was the definitive crop-duster. The company had recognized the nature of the risks involved by consulting, at the design stage, the Crash Injury Research Unit of Cornell Medical College. The Piper designer had appreciated that the chances of his aircraft ending up as a kit of

A Piper Pawnee crop-spraying. The aircraft is flying at the typically low height required for efficient spraying. The high-mounted cockpit can be clearly seen.

parts, having collided with a wind pump, barn or the old oak tree, or simply flying into the ground on some Midwestern farm, was high. The pilot was given an excellent view from a cockpit placed high on the fuselage of the low-wing monoplane. The wings were cranked to get the spray bars running along the trailing edge as close to the crops as possible. The fuselage was designed to protect the pilot, the cockpit being in effect a strong capsule that was sufficiently substantial to remain undamaged even in a head-on collision. To aid the possibility of the pilot's survival, the metal fuselage was designed to fail progressively; for example, the fuselage longerons were given a slight outward set so that in the slow-speed crashes associated with spraying they would bulge outwards, absorbing kinetic energy, and for that reason all heavy fittings were forward of the cockpit area. The cockpit had a false floor with a 10in gap to absorb energy in a pancake-type crash, and it also had large opening windows on both sides.

The other hazard in crop spraying, which was the contamination of the airframe and cockpit by toxic chemicals, was made less dangerous by positive ventilation of the cockpit with the air intake high enough to avoid the spray fallout. The ventilation air flow also lightly provided positive pressure to the fuselage to keep out chemicals. At the end of the day the entire top section of the fuselage could be removed in a minute or so for cleaning. The Pawnee had a very strong undercarriage with low-pressure 'doughnut' tyres and pneumatic oleos to absorb the rough landings and take-offs from the dirt roads of the farms. The engine was originally a 150hp Lycoming flat four but that was soon uprated to a 235hp Lycoming 0-540 six-cylinder unit. The spray tanks contained 150 US gallons and were interchangeable with hoppers for crop dusting with 1,200lb of dry powder chemicals covering a swath of 60ft. The Piper Pawnee was, and remains, a very strong and purpose-built workhorse now regarded as a classic. One cannot say that if a Pawnee had been used instead of the Stearman it would have caught Cary Grant, but the pilot might well have survived that crash at the end.

A final classic working aircraft, one which was familiar in the 1950s but which has now vanished, was the Bristol Type 170 Freighter. This rather ugly twin-engined aircraft which, in the days before package tours, sent many on their happy way to a continental motoring holiday via Silver City Airways from Lydd in Kent to Le Touquet, is remembered with affection. There must be miles of fading 8mm Kodachrome home movies of the family car being driven up the steep ramp into the ferry's two-car hold; owners were never, perhaps wisely, allowed to drive the car into the aircraft themselves. The car safely tied down and the passengers seated in a small cabin to the rear, the freighter took off on the 25-minute flight, its passengers looking down with glee to the old cross-Channel steamers ploughing through the waves below.

The regular clientele of Silver City car ferries probably did not realize that the Type 170 had an interesting career apart from that Lydd to Le Touquet run. The 170 started as a proposal in 1944 for an RAF transport aircraft to replace the very successful Bristol Bombay, a pre-war design and rather too large for employment in the jungle clearings of Burma and the long pacific war against the Japanese, which was still in prospect in 1944. The aircraft was to be a no-frills design, the main feature being 'clam-shell' doors to allow vehicles to be driven in and out. These doors had first appeared on the German Messerschmitt Gigant gliders and it is unlikely that the Bristol design office did not know of them from that source. Another source influencing the Bristol 170 design was a recommendation from General Orde Wingate of Chindits fame, a man who had learned the hard way about resupplying troops from airstrips hacked out of dense jungle. What was needed was very strong structure able to accept the inevitable overload dictated by operations requirements, ease of field maintenance and few com-

FACT FILE

BRISTOL TYPE 170 Mk I

Type
Freighter and (Wayfarer) passenger aircraft.

Power plant
Twin Bristol 1,675 Hercules air-cooled radial engines.

Dimensions
Wing-span 98ft
Length 68ft 4in.

Performance
Maximum speed 245mph
Continuous cruising speed 163mph
Range on standard tanks 300 miles
Service ceiling 22,000ft.

Number produced
214

plex systems to go wrong. The result was two military prototypes (VK 900 and 903) able to carry a standard British army three-ton truck or Jeep or the equivalent load in supplies. The specification resulted in a fuselage 8ft wide and 32ft long with the floor stressed to accept the imposed load, with a small additional cargo space aft, making a total of 2,360cu ft. They were powered by two 1,150hp Bristol Perseus radial engines.

When the war ended in 1945, the military 170 was redesigned for the civil market and VK 900 became G-AGVP, which was first flown from Filton by Bristol test pilot C.F. Unwins on 2 December 1945. It was an empty shell but valuable data was gained. The second aircraft, VK 903, registered as G-AGVB, was the true prototype 34-seater Wayfarer and the first British postwar civil aircraft when it flew for the first time in August 1946. It was flown by Bristol test pilots in the colours of Channel Airways and made 385 trips to Jersey carrying 10,000 passengers. The next 170 was G-AGVC, built as a Freighter I with the bow doors and the capacity to carry two cars. It made extensive foreign tours in two years, gaining many orders, and full production ensued. It was on 13 July 1948 that the first Silver City Ltd car ferry service was inaugurated. Although remembered for that holiday service, Bristol freighters took part in the Berlin airlift and were sold to eighteen countries and seven air forces as transports. The popularity of the Bristol car ferries was phenomenal: there were other ferry operators but the original Silver City Ltd, when celebrating their tenth anniversary in 1958, announced that they had, over the decade, carried 215,000 cars, 70,000 motor cycles and 750,000 passengers on 125,000 flights. Several new MK 32 Bristol freighters with enlarged capacity sufficient to carry three cars were introduced in 1957, but that was the summit of their popularity. Type 170 production ceased in 1958 after 214 had been delivered to operators worldwide. Eventually, in the UK at least, the rival cross-Channel hovercraft and ro-ro (roll-on, roll-off) ferries, package holidays, plus the finite main-spar life of the type 170, saw the type fade and disappear. By 1963 all in the UK had been withdrawn. However, sixty flew on and some may well still be flying abroad. In Britain none is now airworthy – except on those 8mm movies.

A Jowett Javelin, one of a total of 215,000 cars that the company conveyed, is driven by staff aboard a Silver City Bristol car ferry at Lydd in the 1950s before the days of ro-ro ships and the Channel Tunnel. The popular Bristol freighter could only accommodate a maximum of three cars at a time but the short flight time and quick turn-round resulted in remarkably little delay.

In 1931, the Supermarine S6B seaplane took the world's speed record to 407.5mph, thus becoming the first aircraft to exceed 400mph. Designed by R.J. Mitchell, the S6B is wrongly seen as the prototype for the Spitfire; however, the experience gained by Supermarine and Rolls-Royce in developing the stressed-skin monoplane and the 2,600hp supercharged 'R' engine of the S6B led to the Merlin engine and the Spitfires and Hurricanes of the Battle of Britain.

CHAPTER SEVEN

CUTTING EDGE

ABOVE **The Gloster Whittle E28/39, the first Allied jet, made its maiden flight in May 1941, fifteen months after the German Heinkel He 178. The 900 lb thrust W1 Whittle centrifugal engine of the Gloster, was developed by Rolls-Royce to produce a series of jet engines. The Welland, the Derwent and the 5,000 lb-thrust Nene had, by 1945, created an international lead in jet-engine technology that the UK has never lost.**

OPPOSITE ABOVE **The 1943 Me 163 was the world's first rocket fighter. As a fighter it had serious limitations but the Walter liquid-fuel rocket motor was a brilliant first: it weighed only 366 lb but offered over 3,000 lb of thrust, giving the Me 163 a *vertical* climb at 440mph. The fuel was very unstable but the level speed of 580mph made the Me 163 the world's fastest fighter, and the rocket engine technology had relevance in the postwar space race.**

OPPOSITE BELOW **The Messerschmitt Me 262 was the world's first operational jet fighter. It was over 100mph faster than Allied fighters yet, although first flown in 1942, it did not become operational until 1944 because Hitler insisted that it was built as a bomber. When that order was rescinded it was too late. There is little doubt that if the fighter had been operational in 1943, as it could have been, the *Luftwaffe* might have halted the USAF's daylight bombing. This particular Messerschmidt was one of a number captured and evaluated by the RAF.**

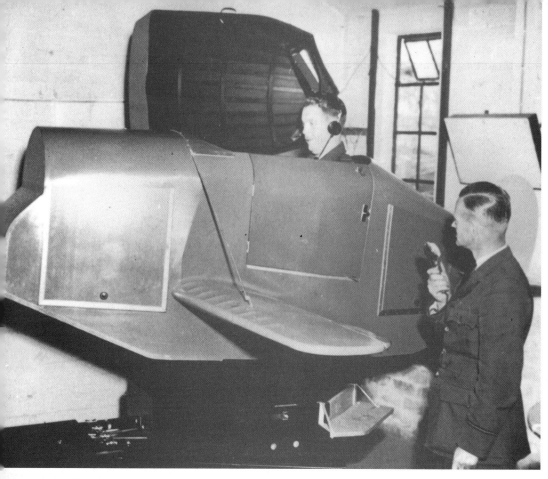

LEFT **The Link trainer was the first practical flight simulator. Designed originally as an arcade amusement device, the trainer was refined by its American inventor, Ed Link, into the wartime AN-T-18 blind-flying trainer which could turn through 360 degrees, climb, dive and bank with the instruments faithfully responding to the pilot's inputs. Over half a million Allied pilots were trained in basic instrument flying skills and radio procedures without risk to themselves or their 'aircraft' in the ubiquitous Link trainers.**

BELOW **The 'Flying Bedstead', or Rolls-Royce 'Thrust-Measuring Rig' of 1954, was the first heavier than air aircraft to fly without either wings or rotors. Two Nene jet engines had their 5,100 lb of thrust directed downwards to provide lift and forward flight. Diverted jets on extended arms controlled the aircraft in roll, pitch and yaw, paving the way for the 'vectored thrust' of the Harrier.**

INSET **The prototype of the Hawker 1127 Kestrel, this aircraft, XP 831, initiated the first hovering trials at Dunsfold in October 1960, with Hawker test pilot Bill Bedford at the controls. Lacking any precedent, the early test flying was with the aircraft tethered. After gaining hard-won experience, Bill Bedford achieved free flight with XP 831 in March 1961; this was the the first successful demonstration of the 'vectored thrust' proposal which became the Harrier.**

MAIN PICTURE **Royal Navy Sea Harriers flying in formation. The Harrier remains the only vertical take off-and landing Western fighter. The unique flying characteristics of the Harrier make it virtually impossible to shoot one down in a conventional 'dog fight'; by 'viffing', that is using the vectored thrust in flight, a technique invented by the US Marines, the aircraft has incredible manoeuvrability. Though slow to gain acceptance, the Harrier is the most original aeronautical concept since the jet engine.**

RIGHT **Although the 'Flying Wing' has, from the 1930s, seemed the ultimate in advanced aircraft, only the American Northrop company produced the YRB-49A in 1950; control problems limited development until recent 'fly-by-wire' computer techniques solved control difficulties for the B-2 'Flying Wing' Stealth bomber.**

BELOW, MAIN PICTURE **In May 1952, the De Havilland Comet inaugurated the world's first jet passenger airline service flying from London to Johannesburg. Tragically, it was to prove a false dawn, unforeseen metal fatigue causing the loss of three Comets and the grounding of the fleet, allowing American jet airliners, principally the Boeing 707, to dominate the world market.**

LEFT **The Boeing 'Dash 80', better known as the 707, took off on its maiden flight in July 1954. The prototype had cost $16 million but it was to prove a bargain at the price, for 707s became the world's major airliners of the 1960s.**

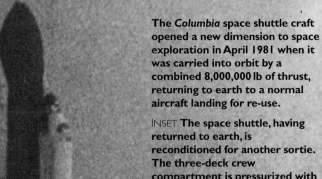

The *Columbia* space shuttle craft opened a new dimension to space exploration in April 1981 when it was carried into orbit by a combined 8,000,000 lb of thrust, returning to earth to a normal aircraft landing for re-use.

INSET **The space shuttle, having returned to earth, is reconditioned for another sortie. The three-deck crew compartment is pressurized with airlocks, allowing access to the 60ft cargo hold which has an opening roof to allow the payload of a satellite to be launched or recovered. By 1986, twenty-five successful missions had been flown when the *Challenger* disaster, through no fault of the shuttle, occurred. Since 1986 many perfect launches and recoveries have been made.**

G-BOAF is the twentieth and last Concorde constructed. It had been hoped that many more would have been sold but the problem of the sonic boom restricted route availability, and objections from environmentalists in America discouraged sales. Although only Air France and British Airways operate Concorde, it remains the first and only supersonic passenger transport in the world, and the seven operated by BA are expected to remain in service well into the twenty-first century.

RIGHT **The V-22 Osprey can take off, land and hover as a helicopter and can tilt the twin 'proprotors' through 45 degrees to fly as a conventional turboprop aircraft with a maximum cruising speed of 390mph. The Osprey is the outcome of many years' development work by Bell/Boeing and was designed to meet a US Joint Services requirement. For ship board service, the 38ft rotors can be folded in line with the wings, which are folded along the fuselage.**

BELOW RIGHT **The Osprey, which completed trials in 1989, including shipboard evaluation aboard the carrier USS *Wasp*, has been ordered for the US Navy, Marines, Army and Air Force – a total of 1,213 aircraft at a cost of $16 million each. Although designed as a military project, the versatility of the Osprey enables it to operate from existing helipads in city centres, plus a wide range of civilian applications normally undertaken by helicopters.**

The shape of things to come? The **F-117A** was so secret that this and other photographs of the Stealth fighter were banned until 1988. The unique shape, together with composite materials, reduce the aircraft's radar 'signature' to the minimum.

'The last major event in atmospheric flight' is how Dick Rutan described his historic 1986 non-stop 24,986-mile circumnavigation of the globe in *Voyager*. Dick Rutan and co-pilot Jeanna Yeager took off on 14 December, returning 9 days, 3 minutes, and 44 seconds later, with just 37 of the original fuel load of 1,208 US gallons left in the twin-engined 110ft wing-span aircraft. *Voyager* was designed by the pilot's brother, Burt Rutan, and used a paper-based honeycomb structure.

Selected Bibliography

C. H. Barnes, *Bristol Aircraft Since 1910* (Putnam, London, 1964)

Martin Bowman, *The USAF at War* (Patrick Stevens, Yeovil, 1995)

Admiral of the Fleet, Viscount Cunningham of Hind Hope, *A Sailor's Odyssey* (Hutchinson, London, 1951)

Sir Geoffrey De Havilland, *Sky Fever* (Hamish Hamilton, London, 1961)

A. Galland, K. Ries and R. Ahnert, *The Luftwaffe at War 1939–1945* (Ian Allan, London, 1972)

Charles Gibbs-Smith, *The Aeroplane: An Historical Survey* (HMSO, London, 1960)

Carroll V. Gliens and Wendell F. Moseley, *Grand Old Lady: The Story of the DC3* (Pennington Press, Cleveland, Ohio, 1959)

William Green, *Warplanes of the Third Reich*, 3rd impression (Macdonald and Jane's, London, 1976)

Leonard R. Gribble, *Heroes of the Fighting RAF* (Harrap, London, 1941)

James Hay Stevens, *The Shape of the Aeroplane* (Hutchinson, London, 1953)

Terence Horsley, *Find, Fix and Strike* (Eyre & Spottswoode, London, 1943)

A. J. Jackson, *British Civil Aircraft 1919–1959*, vols 1 and 2 (Putnam, London, 1958)

Brian Johnson, *Fly Navy* (William Morrow and Co., Inc, New York, 1981)

Brian Johnson, *The Secret War* (BBC Books, London, 1978)

Brian Johnson and H. L. Cozens, *Bombers* (Thames-Methuen, London, 1982)

A. H. Lukins, *The Book of Westland Aircraft* (Harborough Publishing, Leicester, 1945)

Robert C. Mikesh, 'Japan's World War II Balloon Attack on North America', in *Smithsonian Annals of Flight*, No. 9 (Smithsonian Institution Press, Washington, 1973)

John Nesbitt-Durford, *Open Cockpit* (Speed & Sports Publications, London, 1970)

Harald Penrose, *No Echo in the Sky* (Cassell, London, 1958)

Janusz Piekalkiewicz, *The Air War 1939–1945* (Blandford Press, Poole, Dorset, 1986)

L. J. K. Setright, *The Power to Fly* (George Allen & Unwin, London, 1971)

John Taylor, *Flight*, 3rd edn (Hulton, London, 1959)

John Taylor, *A History of Aerial Warfare* (Hamlyn, London, 1974)

Owen Thetford, *Aircraft of the Royal Air Force 1918–1958* (Putnam, London, 1958)

S. E. Veal, *Tomorrow's Airliners, Airways and Airports* (Pilot Press, London, 1945)

A. Williams, *Airpower* (Coward McCann, New York, 1940)

Index